D0933177

The Source®
Intervention in
Autism Spectrum
Disorders

Second Edition

Phyllis Kupperman

8700 Shoal Creek Boulevard
Austin, Texas 78757-6897
800/897-3202   Fax 800/397-7633
www.proedinc.com

© 2017, 2008 by PRO-ED, Inc.
8700 Shoal Creek Boulevard
Austin, Texas 78757-6897
800/897-3202   Fax 800/397-7633
www.proedinc.com

All rights reserved. No part of the material protected by this copyright notice may be reproduced or used in any form or by any means, electronic or mechanical, including photocopying, recording, or by any information storage and retrieval system, without prior written permission of the copyright owner.

Limited Photocopy License

PRO-ED grants to individual purchasers of this material nonassignable permission to reproduce the Evidence-Based Practice page, and Chapter 2 Appendix, Chapter 3 Appendix, Chapter 4 Appendix. This license is limited to you, the individual purchaser, for use with your students or clients.

This license does not grant the right to reproduce these materials for resale, redistribution, or any other purposes (including but not limited to books, pamphlets, articles, video- or audiotapes, and handouts or slides for lectures or workshops).

Permission to reproduce these materials for these and other purposes must be obtained in writing from the Permissions Department of PRO-ED, Inc.

Library of Congress Cataloging-in-Publication Data

Names: Kupperman, Phyllis, author.
Title: The source intervention in autism spectrum disorders / Phyllis Kupperman.
Other titles: Source for intervention in autism spectrum disorders
Description: Austin, Texas : PRO-ED, Inc., [2017] | Revision of: Source for intervention in autism spectrum disorders. ©2008. | Includes bibliographical references.
Identifiers: LCCN 2016031138 (print) | LCCN 2016045640 (ebook) | ISBN 9781416410621 (pbk.) | ISBN 9781416410638
Subjects: LCSH: Autistic children—Rehabilitation. | Autism in children.
Classification: LCC RJ506.A9 K86 2017 (print) | LCC RJ506.A9 (ebook) | DDC 618.92/85882—dc23
LC record available at https://lccn.loc.gov/2016031138

Art Director: Jason Crosier
Designer: Tom de Lorenzo

Printed in the United States of America

1 2 3 4 5 6 7 8 9 10   26 25 24 23 22 21 20 19 18 17

Disorder	Ages
Autism spectrum disorder (ASD)	All ages

Evidence-Based Practice

Clarifying terminology, improving description of the core features of ASD and other dimensions that interact with them and providing more valid and reliable ways to quantify them, for both research and clinical purposes, will move forward both practice and science (Lord & Jones, 2012).

Treatment should address core features of ASD, including impairments in social communication and joint attention, social reciprocity, language and related cognitive skills, and behavior and emotional regulation (ASHA, 2006a).

- Intervention programs should begin as soon as ASD is suspected. Children who participate in intensive intervention beginning by age 3 have a significantly better outcome than those beginning after age 5. Intervention beginning before age 3 appears to have an even greater impact (National Research Council [NRC], 2001).

- Individuals with ASD should actively engage in intensive instructional programming for a minimum of 5 hours per day, 5 days a week, in home, school, or community settings (NRC, 2001).

- Goals and objectives should be targeted in systematically planned, developmentally appropriate learning activities with low student/teacher ratios (NRC, 2001).

- There should be mechanisms for ongoing assessment and program evaluation with corresponding adjustments in programming (NRC, 2001).

- Teaching in natural learning environments appears to be the most effective intervention approach because the behaviors involved are more likely to translate into a better quality of life and increase social acceptance (ASHA, 2006a).

- All of the comprehensive intervention programs with the best treatment outcomes included a strong family component and parent training (NRC, 2001).

- Treatment for individuals with ASD should emphasize access to not only academic but also curricular, extracurricular, and vocational activities (ASHA, 2006a).

  © 2017 by PRO-ED, Inc.

- Legislation mandates that all children, including children with ASD, be taught to read in ways that are consistent with reading research and target the five components of evidence-based reading instruction: phonemic awareness, phonics, reading fluency, vocabulary, and comprehension strategies. Results have indicated that children with ASD can benefit from reading instruction consistent with reading research (Whalon, Al Otaiba, & Delano, 2009).

- When used as part of a multiple-strategy method, there is evidence that reading comprehension is improved by comprehension monitoring, cooperative learning, use of graphic and semantic organizers, question answering, question generation, story structure, and summarization (National Reading Panel, 2000).

- The multiple developmental and behavioral problems associated with ASD necessitate multidisciplinary care, coordination of services, and advocacy for individuals and their families. Early, sustained intervention and the use of multiple treatment modalities are indicated (Volkmar et al., 2014).

- It is necessary to study communication disorders in human and animal models to inform behavioral interventions as well as future research on diagnosis, interventions, treatments, and/or causes of ASD (Llaneza, DeLuke, Batista, et al., 2010).

About the Author

Phyllis Kupperman, MA, CCC-SLP, founded the Center for Speech and Language Disorders (CSLD), a not-for-profit agency with locations in Lombard and Chicago, Illinois, in 1979.

In 1964, Phyllis received her master's degree in speech and language pathology from the University of Illinois at Urbana–Champaign. She has been a faculty member at colleges and universities as well as in public and private schools. She has conducted evaluations and family training and developed family-centered therapy programs for children with ASD and hyperlexia throughout the United States and in several other countries. At CSLD, Phyllis has worked with many individuals from early childhood through adulthood. Through this work, she has gained a unique understanding of how to develop communication and learning at various ages and levels of functioning.

Phyllis has presented workshops and seminars to numerous professional organizations, school districts, and universities; at state and national conferences for the Autism Society of America; and at national and regional conferences for the American Speech-Language-Hearing Association and Speech-Language and Audiology Canada. Topics have included autism spectrum disorders, hyperlexia, social communication, language disorders, reading, and reading comprehension. Phyllis has published articles in journals and newsletters and has produced multimedia products for distribution through CSLD. In addition to this book, she is the author of *The Source for Social Competency* and *The Reading Comprehension Kit for Hyperlexia and Autism, Level 2*, originally published by LinguiSystems.

Dedication

To the children and families of CSLD and to the memory of my brother Joe. They have inspired my life's work.

Acknowledgments

The second edition of this book benefited greatly from the expertise of Beth Donnelly and Lakshmi Bollini at PRO-ED. Thanks are also due to Carolyn LoGiudice, Barb Truman, and Kelly Larson for their contributions to the original manuscript. Many colleagues have shared their ideas, enthusiasm, and expertise over the years: Mary Ziegler, Christina Rees, Kathy Kirkwood, Karen Supel, Anne Barclay, and Lynn Scheuer Kozak. Helen Rehn's listening ears and help with applied linguistics are much appreciated. I am especially grateful to the families and the children who taught me so much. Their stories fill this book.

I would not be who I am without my husband, David. His patience, his devotion, and his technical assistance have kept me going. Sons Jeff and Justin, daughters-in-law Susanna and Danielle, and grandchildren Max, Ollie, Bryce, and Layla provide laughter and life lessons. Thank you to the friends and family, far and near, who gather around in celebration and in sorrow in the circle of life.

Contents

Introduction to the Second Edition

So much has changed since 2008, when this book was first written. Technology has improved the lives of many children with autism spectrum disorders (ASD): Smartphones and iPads can now be used as augmentative and alternative communication (AAC) devices. Siri can provide information and answers to questions instantly. Video security cameras can monitor the activities in many homes 24/7. Parents can choose from hundreds of educational apps that 2-year-olds can operate with one finger. Families can easily connect in Facebook groups. With many more tools for studying genetics and scanning the brain, researchers can now accomplish whole genome sequencing in a matter of days. A big change came in 2013 with the publication of the *Diagnostic and Statistical Manual of Mental Disorders–Fifth Edition (DSM-5)*, when the diagnostic criteria for ASD were revised. This second edition of *The Source® Intervention in Autism Spectrum Disorders* explains these changes and adds up-to-date developments in research and intervention. It also provides practical tactics and templates for evaluation that can be put into immediate use.

Not everything has changed, however. The children and their families still have the same challenges that require tried-and-true intervention strategies. Although we are learning more and more about ASD, we don't know how and why it occurs. It is still difficult to obtain appropriate services in many areas of the country, and adult services are woefully lacking. Public awareness is increasing, but obtaining public support and insurance coverage is problematic.

It is hoped that this second edition will inspire clinicians, parents, and students to embrace what is new while building on prior knowledge and strategies as we help those with ASD reach their full potential.

Phyllis

Introduction to the First Edition

When graduate students come to the Center for Speech and Language Disorders (CSLD) for their practicum experiences, they are usually amazed as they meet the children, adolescents, and adults with ASD. The students often are surprised to see how different individuals with ASD are from one another. Each individual has a set of strengths and weaknesses and a unique personality. The expression of symptoms varies widely. As the students get to know them, they recognize the core symptoms and the learning style common to those with ASD. They observe their difficulties with language, academics, and social functioning. They understand the role of families in working with their children with ASD and the impact these children have on family members.

This book serves four purposes:

- to introduce students, professionals, and parents to the complexities of ASD;
- to describe the common learning style of individuals with ASD;
- to discuss strategies developed to improve academics, language, and social skills; and
- to suggest tactics for intervention and teaching.

You will read about issues that arise throughout the lifespan of an individual with ASD. You will meet many children, teens, and adults through the stories and illustrative examples. I hope that through these stories, you will gain insight into the inner workings of their minds and hearts. I hope that you will see them not just as cases, but as people deserving of our best efforts.

Chapter 1 describes and defines ASD. Information about diagnosis, comorbid and related conditions, and issues of scientific study of ASD are presented.

Chapter 2 discusses the particular learning style of those with ASD as it affects language development; academic achievement in reading, writing, and math; visual motor challenges; social learning; and the development of theory of mind.

Chapter 3 deals with assessing the child, family, school, and community in order to identify goals, objectives, and treatment strategies.

Chapter 4 presents general and specific tactics for language intervention, academics, and social skill development. A chart in the Chapter 4 Appendix allows you to easily locate tactics and to find related suggestions for intervention.

Chapter 5 addresses priorities and concerns that families have about those with ASD from early childhood through young adulthood.

As you read this book, think of a child, adolescent, or adult with ASD. Think of how the descriptions and suggestions fit that particular person. When you see the plethora of news releases, breakthroughs, treatments, and research reported so often in the media, analyze them carefully in light of what you learn about ASD and about your particular individual.

I am lucky to have been a part of the treatment programs for hundreds of individuals with ASD and their families and to be able to follow their progress over decades. They have taught me a great deal about communication, cognition, and social interactions. They have shown me the power of human resilience. They have helped me see the beauty of tiny details. They have taught me how to teach them and to experience joy in small successes. I am grateful to be able to share these insights with you.

Phyllis

Note: I am grateful to the families of children and adults with ASD for allowing me to use their stories. The stories are all true, but some of the names have been changed to protect the identity of the individuals.

Chapter 1
Who Are the Children?

Marlon was a cranky infant. He didn't like to be cuddled and didn't respond to his parents' voices or faces. His parents thought Marlon might be deaf, but he would wake at the least little sound. He never learned to talk and would spend hours looking at the dust in rays of sunlight streaming in the window.

Eugene was a bouncy, happy youngster who met all of his early milestones. He even had a few words when he was a year old. Between 18 months and 2 years of age, he lost those words. Though Eugene was affectionate with his parents, he seemed to lose interest in other people. At playgroup he wouldn't join other children, but he would walk around the periphery of the room touching the walls.

Brianna was an active, busy child, but she insisted on doing things her own way. She would only wear her brother's clothes, insisting that she was a boy. She had frequent tantrums when her routine was changed. Though she could talk, her language was mostly about what she wanted or didn't want. Brianna couldn't really carry on a conversation, but she loved other children.

Josh was a bright, quiet boy who learned to read and write when he was 3. He was very sensitive to negative feedback and insisted on being first at everything. Josh developed strong interests in NASCAR and certain DVDs and devised creative games with complicated rules that everyone had to follow.

Katherine was homeschooled for much of her elementary and high school careers. Although she received As in honors English and creative writing classes at school, she just couldn't handle the pressures of school all day. Katherine was hopeless in math, but she was a talented poet and writer. She enjoyed trips with her parents, but she had no friends her age. Katherine was working on broadening her horizons by taking some college classes outside of her usual interests. Although she earned good grades, her interactions with other students remained polite and superficial.

All of these young people have been diagnosed with autism spectrum disorder (ASD), a neurological disorder that affects the way the brain functions. The symptoms of this disorder vary across individuals and are present in different degrees of severity, hence the descriptor *spectrum*. ASD is a complex developmental disability that usually becomes evident by age 3, though some symptoms may be noticed earlier or later. It is a lifelong disability, but improvement and reduction in symptoms can occur with treatment and further development.

Certain characteristics are common in children with ASD; however, not every child with ASD presents with all the characteristics. ASD affects a child's behavior, social functioning, ability to communicate effectively, academic performance, and understanding of and response to the environment.

Background Information/History

Leo Kanner and Hans Asperger, who did groundbreaking work in the field of autism spectrum disorder, were both born in Austria–Hungary. After receiving a medical degree from the University of Berlin in 1921, Kanner emigrated to the United States in 1924 and later became head of the pediatric clinic of Johns Hopkins Hospital in Baltimore. Kanner used the term *early infantile autism* in 1943 to describe children who displayed odd behaviors and who withdrew from personal contact. Soon after, professionals in other U.S. clinics found similar cases. Asperger remained in Vienna and spent his career at the University Pediatric Clinic, which evolved from a hospital setting to an educational and therapeutic center. In 1944, his second dissertation describing *autistic psychopathology* was accepted, but was not translated from German until much later. Asperger was primarily interested in more verbal and more functional children, but he recognized the various presentations of children with autism. Both Asperger and Kanner were interested in identifying and recognizing autism as a major developmental disorder, rather than just a rare, interesting childhood affliction. It was a coincidence that both adopted the term *autism* (first used by Eugen Bleuler in 1916 to describe a schizophrenic's withdrawal from the world) (Frith, 1991). They could not have known how the term would be used today, nor could they have predicted the huge number of children diagnosed with autism and related disorders.

Researchers have dedicated years to finding a cause and/or developing and validating effective treatments. I have known children who were taken from their homes and put into therapeutic schools because some mistakenly believed that "lack of maternal warmth" caused autism. Desperate parents have tried treatments of all kinds, seeking medications, breakthroughs, or cures reported by the media.

Much has changed since Kanner's and Asperger's day. We now understand that autism spectrum disorder is a neurological disorder, and we can use sophisticated brain-scanning devices to observe subtle differences in brain function. The diagnosis of autism spectrum disorder, however, is still based on observable behaviors. There is no medical or genetic test. The autism spectrum is still a puzzle waiting to be solved.

Changes in Guidelines for Diagnosis

Studying and diagnosing autism has been difficult because its definition has changed over the years. Medical professionals rely on the *Diagnostic and Statistical Manual of Mental Disorders* (*DSM*), which outlines the symptoms and gives guidelines for making a diagnosis of autism. Each revision of the *DSM* reflects current thinking based on available research. The *DSM-IV* (1994) described separate disorders under the umbrella of pervasive developmental disorder. There were separate criteria for diagnosing autistic disorder, Asperger's disorder, and pervasive developmental disorder not otherwise specified (PDD-NOS). The *DSM-5* (2013), the latest major revision, brings all of these under the heading of autism spectrum disorder (ASD), specifying three levels of severity.

There is no definitive medical diagnostic tool that can diagnose autism spectrum disorder. Although some gene mutations or variants have been associated with ASD, even identical twins are not always concordant for ASD (Veenstra-VanDerWeele & Cook, 2003). Further complicating the diagnostic process are the many comorbid conditions common in those with ASD. Diagnosticians need to specify whether or not an individual presents with an accompanying intellectual or language impairment. They need to note any accompanying medical or genetic conditions (e.g., premature birth, Fragile X, epilepsy). They need to note any associated neurodevelopmental, mental, or behavioral disorder (e.g., anxiety, depression, sensory issues, self-injurious behavior). Professionals diagnosing ASD must rely on clinical observation, standard evaluations, and reports of parents and teachers.

DSM-5 diagnostic criteria for autism spectrum disorder are reproduced in Table 1.1.

You will note that there is no longer a separate criterion for language and communication deficits. Rather, deficits in nonverbal communication and verbal language are included within the domain of social communication/social interaction. Repetitive aspects of language (e.g., stereotypic

Table 1.1
DSM-5 Diagnostic Criteria for Autism Spectrum Disorder 299.0 (F84.0)

A. Persistent deficits in social communication and social interaction across multiple contexts, as manifested by the following, currently or by history (examples are illustrative, not exhaustive, see text):

  1. Deficits in social–emotional reciprocity, ranging, for example, from abnormal social approach and failure of normal back and forth conversation; to reduced sharing of interests, emotions, or affect; to failure to initiate or respond to social interactions.

  2. Deficits in nonverbal communicative behaviors used for social interaction, ranging, for example, from poorly integrated verbal and nonverbal communication; to abnormalities in eye contact and body language or deficits in understanding and use of gestures; to a total lack of facial expressions and nonverbal communication.

  3. Deficits in developing, maintaining and understanding relationships, ranging, for example, from difficulties adjusting behavior to suit various social contexts; to difficulties in sharing imaginative play or in making friends; to absence of interest in peers.

  Specify current severity:

  Severity is based on social communication impairments and restricted repetitive behavior. (see Table 1.2)

B. Restricted, repetitive patterns of behavior, interests, or activities, as manifested by at least two of the following, currently or by history (examples are illustrative not exhaustive; see text):

  1. Stereotyped or repetitive motor movements, use of objects, or speech (e.g., simple motor stereotypies, lining up of toys or flipping objects, echolalia, idiosyncratic phrases).

  2. Insistence on sameness, inflexible adherence to routines, or ritualized patterns of verbal or nonverbal behavior (e.g., extreme distress at small changes, difficulties with transitions, rigid thinking patterns, greeting rituals, need to take same route or eat same food every day.)

  3. Highly restricted, fixated interests that are abnormal in intensity or focus (e.g., strong attachment to or preoccupation with unusual objects, excessively circumscribed or perseverative interest).

  4. Hyper- or hyposensitivity to sensory input or unusual interests in sensory aspects of the environment (e.g., apparent indifference to pain/temperature, adverse response to specific sounds or textures, excessive smelling or touching of objects, visual fascination with lights or movement).

  Specify current severity:

  Severity is based on social communication impairments and restricted repetitive behavior. (see Table 1.2)

C. Symptoms must be present in the early development period (but may not become fully manifest until social demands exceed limited capacities, or may be masked by learned strategies in later life).

D. Symptoms cause clinically significant impairment in social, occupational, or other important areas of current functioning.

E. These disturbances are not better explained by intellectual disability (intellectual developmental disorder) or global developmental delay. Intellectual disability and autism spectrum disorder frequently co-occur; to make comorbid diagnoses of autism spectrum disorder and intellectual disability, social communication should be below that expected for general developmental level.

  Note: Individuals with a well-established *DSM-IV* diagnosis of autistic disorder, Asperger's disorder, or pervasive developmental disorder not otherwise specified should be given the diagnosis of autism spectrum disorder. Individuals who have marked deficits in social communication, but whose symptoms do not otherwise meet criteria for autism spectrum disorder, should be evaluated for social (pragmatic) communication disorder.

  Specify if:

  With or without accompanying intellectual impairment

  With or without accompanying language impairment

  Associated with a known medical or genetic condition or environmental factor

  Associated with another neurodevelopmental, mental, or behavioral disorder

  With catatonia

Reprinted with permission from the *Diagnostic and Statistical Manual of Mental Disorders—Fifth Edition.* Copyright 2013 by the American Psychiatric Association.

speech, echolalia, verbal rituals, repeated questions) are included within the domain of restricted and repetitive behaviors (Lord & Jones, 2012). Severity levels (see Table 1.2) are then applied separately for the two domains of social communication and restricted, repetitive behaviors.

Even though many individuals with ASD have overall language delays or intellectual impairments; neurodevelopmental, mental, or behavioral disorders; and/or medical or genetic conditions, those disorders can also exist outside of ASD. The *DSM-5* instructs the diagnostician to signify whether those conditions are associated with ASD in the individual, but they are not core diagnostic criteria of ASD.

There is an extensive discussion in the *DSM-5* about the variability of the diagnostic features over the course of an individual's development. Some restricted or repetitive behaviors diminish as the individual gets older, through the course of development, and/or through treatment interventions. The demands on social communication and social interaction become more nuanced with age. Presenting symptoms may be affected by severity, developmental level, and chronological age. Symptoms may be masked by intervention, learned compensatory behaviors, the particular environment, and the presence of supports. The umbrella of autism spectrum disorder allows for variability in presentation in an individual without changing the diagnosis.

Social (Pragmatic) Communication Disorder

There are some individuals who present with difficulties in verbal and nonverbal social communication but have not manifested the restricted/repetitive patterns of behavior, interests, or activities

Table 1.2
DSM-5 Severity Levels for Autism Spectrum Disorder

Severity level	Social communication	Restricted, repetitive behaviors
Level 3 "Requiring very substantial support"	Severe deficits in verbal and nonverbal social communication skills cause severe impairments in functioning, very limited initiation of social interactions, and minimal response to social overtures from others. For example, a person with few words of intelligible speech who rarely initiates interaction and, when he or she does, makes unusual approaches to meet needs only and responds to only very direct social approaches.	Inflexibility of behavior, extreme difficulty coping with change, or other restricted/ repetitive behaviors markedly interfere with functioning in all spheres. Great distress/difficulty changing focus or action.
Level 2 "Requiring substantial support"	Marked deficits in verbal and nonverbal social communication skills; social impairments apparent even with supports in place; limited initiation of social interactions; and reduced or abnormal responses to social overtures from others. For example, a person who speaks simple sentences, whose interaction is limited to narrow special interests, and who has markedly odd nonverbal communication.	Inflexibility of behavior, difficulty coping with change, or other restricted/repetitive behaviors appear frequently enough to be obvious to the casual observer and interfere with functioning in a variety of contexts. Distress and/or difficulty changing focus or action.
Level 1 "Requiring support"	Without supports in place, deficits in social communication cause noticeable impairments. Difficulty initiating social interactions, and clear examples of atypical or unsuccessful responses to social overtures of others. May appear to have decreased interest in social interactions. For example, a person who is able to speak in full sentences and engages in communication but whose to-and-fro conversation with others fails, and whose attempts to make friends are odd and typically unsuccessful.	Inflexibility of behavior causes significant interference with functioning in one or more contexts. Difficulty switching between activities. Problems of organization and planning hamper independence.

Reprinted with permission from the *Diagnostic and Statistical Manual of Mental Disorders–Fifth Edition.* Copyright 2013 by the American Psychiatric Association.

characteristic of ASD. The *DSM-5* created the new diagnosis of social (pragmatic) communication disorder to describe these individuals. *DSM-5* criteria are reproduced in Table 1.3.

In the discussion of the development and course of social (pragmatic) communication disorder, it is noted that this diagnosis depends on adequate speech and language development, usually achieved by age 4 or 5, and therefore it is rarely diagnosed before that age. It is also noted that milder forms of the disorder may not become apparent until early adolescence, when the requirements for successful social communication become increasingly complex and nuanced. Data about the reliability, validity, or prevalence of this disorder are sparse (Lord & Jones, 2012); however, this diagnosis is related to semantic–pragmatic disorder, identified primarily in England since 1983 (Rapin & Allen, 1983). (See the discussion of semantic–pragmatic disorder later in this chapter.)

What Happened to Asperger's Disorder?

Asperger's disorder, often called Asperger syndrome (AS), first appeared in the *DSM-IV* in 1994 as a diagnosis distinct from autistic disorder, under the umbrella of pervasive developmental disorders. Since then there have been confusion and controversy as to whether Asperger's disorder can be reliably differentiated from high-functioning autism or PDD-NOS (Happé, 2011; Lord et al., 2012; Lord & Jones, 2012; Sharma, Woolfson, & Hunter, 2012). In a study involving 12 university-based autism providers, it was found that even though test scores were similar across sites, clinical diagnoses using *DSM-IV* subtypes were not consistent (Lord et al., 2011). *DSM-5* no longer differentiates Asperger's disorder, bringing those who would have been diagnosed with Asperger's in *DSM-IV* under the general umbrella of ASD.

Many in the "Aspie" community are not happy since they wished to be viewed as distinct from those diagnosed with autistic disorder by virtue of their special skills and higher abilities. Baron-Cohen (2009) and others were concerned about the disenfranchisement of individuals with

Table 1.3
DSM-5 Diagnostic Criteria for Social (Pragmatic) Communication Disorder
315.39 (F80.89)

A. Persistent difficulties in the social use of verbal and nonverbal communication as manifested by all of the following:

  1. Deficits in using communication for social purposes, such as greeting and sharing information, in a manner that is appropriate for the social context.

  2. Impairment of the ability to change communication to match context or the needs of the listener, such as speaking differently in a classroom than on the playground, talking differently to a child than an adult, and avoiding use of overly formal language.

  3. Difficulties following rules for conversation and storytelling, such as taking turns in conversation, rephrasing when misunderstood and knowing how to use verbal and nonverbal signals to regulate interaction.

  4. Difficulties understanding what is not explicitly stated (e.g., making inferences) and nonliteral or ambiguous meanings of language (e.g., idioms, humor, metaphors, multiple meanings that depend on the context for interpretation).

B. The deficits result in functional limitations in effective communication, social participation, social relationships, academic achievement, or occupational performance individually or in combination.

C. The onset of the symptoms is in the early developmental period (but deficits may not become fully manifest until social communication demands exceed limited capacities).

D. The symptoms are not attributable to another medical or neurological condition or to low abilities in the domains of word structure and grammar, and are not better explained by autism spectrum disorder, intellectual disability (intellectual developmental disorder), global developmental delay, or another mental disorder.

Reprinted with permission from the *Diagnostic and Statistical Manual of Mental Disorders—Fifth Edition*. Copyright 2013 by the American Psychiatric Association.

Asperger's. On the contrary, the goal for the new criteria is to increase equity across the existing subcategories in terms of treatments covered by third-party payers (Lord & Jones, 2012). *DSM-5* notes that "individuals with a well-established *DSM-IV* diagnosis of autistic disorder, Asperger's disorder or pervasive developmental disorder not otherwise specified should be given the diagnosis of autism spectrum disorder" (*DSM-5*, 2013). On the other hand, Lord and Jones (2012) pointed out that there is no reason that advocacy organizations cannot continue to use the term *Asperger syndrome* and that people could benefit from joining groups that define themselves in terms of previous definitions.

Assessment for ASD

In October, 2007, and reconfirmed in a statement by its president, Dr. Sandra Hassink, on August 3, 2015, the American Academy of Pediatrics adopted a universal autism screening procedure. The screening is conducted at 18 months and again at 24 months at well-baby checkups, along with regular developmental surveillance, regardless of whether there are warning signs. Because early intervention results in better outcomes, pediatricians are urged to refer for treatment of symptoms even before a formal diagnosis of autism is confirmed. Warning signs that prompt further evaluation include the following:

- Lack of response to child's own name by 12 months
- Failure to look at what a parent is pointing to by 12 months (joint attention)
- Social smiling later than 4 months
- Failure or reduced ability to make eye contact
- Lack of babbling, pointing, or other gestures by 12 months
- No single words by 16 months
- No two-word phrases by 24 months
- Regression or loss of language or social skills at any age

There has been controversy, however, as to whether *all* children should be screened at 18 and 24 months. In February 2016, the U.S. Preventive Services Task Force (USPSTF) published this recommendation in the *Journal of the American Medical Association* (JAMA): "The USPSTF concludes that the current evidence is insufficient to assess the balance of benefits and harms of screening for ASD in young children for whom no concerns of ASD have been raised by their parents or a clinician" (Siu & USPSTF, 2016, p. 691). Their conclusions are based on an exhaustive review of the evidence, the results of which were inconclusive (McPheeters et al., 2015). It should be noted that this recommendation should not be considered to be for or against screening. In light of insufficient evidence, doctors should use their clinical judgment to decide whether it is appropriate to screen children in their care for whom no concerns about ASD have been raised.

Accurate identification of ASD is important for planning clinical treatment, designing educational strategies, and conducting research. If we catalog particular behaviors, assess levels of functioning, and determine severity of symptoms, we can choose appropriate treatment and educational programs. These assessment tools differentiate ASD from other developmental disorders and determine where on the spectrum a particular child falls.

Assessment Tools

The assessment tools listed in Table 1.4 are specific to identifying ASD symptoms. With the exception of the *Autism Diagnostic Observation Schedule, Second Edition* (ADOS-2; Lord, Rutter, et al., 2012), the assessment tools are all rating scales. Lists of symptoms are rated as to presence, absence, severity, and/or frequency of occurrence. Parents, teachers, and caregivers may complete the scales independently or in an interview format. Although rating scales can be useful in identifying distinguishing behaviors, the reliability and biases of the informant and the environment of the observation should be taken into consideration. The assessment tools in Table 1.4 have been revised to correspond to *DSM-5* guidelines.

DSM-5 requires diagnosticians, in addition to identifying ASD symptoms, to specify accompanying or associated conditions. Evaluation of language, intellectual abilities, behavior, medical conditions, and other areas of functioning can specify whether associated conditions are present. Standard evaluation measures used by speech and language pathologists, psychologists, neuropsychologists, medical professionals, and educators should accompany the diagnosis of ASD. Interpretation of the standard scores should be carefully scrutinized, however. Standardized tests base their norms on the performance of typically developing individuals. Individuals with ASD often develop in a different sequence. They may lag behind in some areas and at the same time exceed expectations in others. They may not be able to answer questions as expected at age 3, but they may be able to read at that young age. They may not be able to follow verbal directions but will learn quickly through demonstrations. Their performance on various subtests on measures

Table 1.4
Assessments for Symptoms of Autism Spectrum Disorders

Title	Ages	Purpose
Autism Diagnostic Observation Schedule—Second Edition (ADOS-2; Lord, Rutter, et al., 2012)	12 months to adult	Semistructured observation tool that allows you to accurately assess and diagnose autism spectrum disorders across age, developmental level, and language skills. Used extensively for research and clinical diagnostic purposes, along with the *Autism Diagnostic Interview—Revised* (ADI-R).
Modified Checklist for Autism in Toddlers—Revised (M-CHAT-R; Robins & Fein, 2013)	18 to 24 months	This screening tool for early identification of ASD symptoms is available on the Autism Speaks Web site (www.autismspeaks.org). There is also an M-CHAT-R follow-up interview available on the Web site.
Gilliam Autism Rating Scale—Third Edition (GARS-3; Gilliam, 2014)	3 to 22 years	Items and subscales reflect *DSM-5* diagnostic criteria for ASD, yielding standard scores, percentile ranks, severity level, and probability of autism.
Social Responsiveness Scale—Second Edition (SRS-2; Constantino, 2012)	2.5 years to adulthood	Identifies the presence and severity of social impairment within the autism spectrum and differentiates the social impairment from that which occurs in other disorders. Yields total score; scores for 5 treatment subscales; scores for 2 *DSM-5* compatible subscales.
Checklist for Autism Spectrum Disorder (CASD; Mayes, 2012)	1 to 17 years	Consistent with *DSM-5* recommendation that autism is a single-spectrum disorder. Consists of a list of 30 symptoms scored as present (currently or by history) or absent in a semistructured interview, information from teacher or child care provider, direct observation and other available records.
Autism Spectrum Rating Scales (ASRS; Goldstein & Naglieri, 2009)	2 to 18 years	This multi-informant rating scale helps identify ASD symptoms and behaviors. Has updates to help assess *DSM-5* symptom criteria.

of intellectual abilities may vary widely. Results of genetic and medical tests may be ambiguous. These issues underline the complex and individual nature of ASD. Thorough assessment, however, will point the way to effective intervention.

Prevalence of ASD

In recent years, estimates of the prevalence of autism spectrum disorder in children and adults in the United States and other countries have increased with each new study. These studies used *DSM-IV* criteria that included autism, Asperger's disorder, and pervasive developmental disorder. In 2014, the U.S. Centers for Disease Control and Prevention (CDC) published a study that reviewed the school and medical records of 8-year-olds (CDC, 2014) in various monitoring sites. It estimated the prevalence of ASD to be 1 in 68 American children. In a survey of parents of children from ages 3 to 17 conducted by the National Center for Health Statistics (NCHS), the reported prevalence of ASD was 1 in 45 (Zablotsky et al., 2015). A South Korean study that directly screened schoolchildren for autism spectrum disorder (ASD) revealed a prevalence of 1 in 38 children. Two thirds of the affected children were in mainstream classrooms, previously undiagnosed, and receiving no services (Kim et al., 2011).

In *DSM-5*, it is noted that "it remains unclear whether higher rates reflect an expansion of the diagnostic criteria of *DSM-IV* to include subthreshold cases, increased awareness, differences in study methodology, or a true increase in the frequency of autism spectrum disorder" (p. 55).

Thirty years ago, most professionals had little training in autism, particularly in its milder form. Now there are hundreds of conferences and training sessions dealing with ASD diagnosis and remediation each year. School districts provide training to their regular education teachers as well as their special education staff because there is a high probability that there will be a child with ASD in their classroom. If there are developmental concerns, children are now referred to early intervention programs for evaluation and treatment. If ASD is suspected by the team, the child is referred for a medical diagnosis.

Comorbid and Related Conditions

Many children diagnosed with ASD have symptoms of other disorders too. These are known as *comorbid disorders*. These disorders can occur in children without ASD, but when two or more disorders occur together, the effect is compounded and the challenges are greater. There is debate in the literature as to whether some conditions or behaviors, such as obsessions or oppositional behaviors, are core symptoms of ASD or are separate comorbid diagnoses (Matson & Nebel-Schwalm, 2007). The following discussion reflects *DSM-5* criteria.

Sensory Integration Dysfunction

Some children with ASD can't tolerate loud noises, don't like to be touched, and/or are bothered by the flickering of fluorescent lights. They may be hypersensitive or hyposensitive to information coming in from the senses and may have difficulty with self-regulation. These symptoms as well as the repetitive behaviors common in children with ASD may arise from sensory integration dysfunction.

Sensory integration dysfunction refers to difficulty in neurologically processing the information from the five senses (touch, sight, smell, taste, hearing) as well as from movement and body position. Occupational therapists (OTs) diagnose and treat this condition according to guidelines based on the seminal work of Jean Ayres, Lorna Jean King, and others (King, 1987; Mauer, 1999). Speech–language pathologists (SLPs) have borrowed many good strategies from OTs through the years, such as special seats, weighted vests, swinging in a sheet, and doing "heavy work." It is controversial as to whether children who present with sensory processing difficulties have a distinct disorder of the sensory-neural pathways in the brain, or whether the sensory problems are characteristic of other conditions, such as autism spectrum disorder, attention-deficit disorder, childhood anxiety disorder, or developmental coordination disorder. After finding no universally accepted framework for diagnosis in the literature, in 2012 the American Academy of Pediatrics (AAP) issued a policy statement that pediatricians should not use sensory processing disorder as a diagnosis, but rather should consider evaluation for the conditions of which sensory disorders are characteristic. Because the evidence for the efficacy of sensory integration therapy is limited and inconclusive, the AAP recommended that pediatricians teach parents how to evaluate the effectiveness of sensory integration therapy for their particular child.

> Cindy wouldn't engage in joint attention to anything I presented, but when the OT and I put her on her tummy on a swing, she began to look up in anticipation of the next push. Her floppy body became completely engaged and soon she pulled us over to the swing in her very first communication.

Attention-Deficit/Hyperactivity Disorder

Children with ASD may be distractible, impulsive, and/or overly active. While some focus on tiny details or line up things for hours, they may have difficulty shifting their attention to new or different stimuli. All of these are symptoms of attention-deficit/hyperactivity disorder (ADHD). Both diagnoses, ASD and ADHD, can be given if a child meets criteria for both disorders.

Attention-deficit/hyperactivity disorder is defined as a persistent pattern of inattention and/or hyperactivity-impulsivity that interferes with functioning or development. An individual may present with symptoms that are predominantly inattentive, predominantly hyperactive and impulsive, or combined (*DSM-5*, 2013). Behavioral and pharmacological treatments are available for this common disorder, but treatment is much more complicated when it occurs together with ASD.

> Jimmy's attention deficit was the inattentive type. His mind would wander, and he often did not tune in to auditory stimuli. His mother complained that he didn't answer when she called his name unless she physically got his attention. We thought that he heard but was too distracted to answer, so we developed a key phrase: "If someone speaks to you, you must answer." When we cued him by saying, "If someone speaks to you, you must _____," it seemed to break Jimmy out of his reverie and he would finish the sentence.

Motor Dyspraxia and Childhood Apraxia of Speech (Verbal Dyspraxia)

Some children with ASD have great difficulty learning to talk even though their cognitive abilities are sufficient to support speech and language development. Some develop verbal abilities but their speech is difficult to understand. We have also seen a number of children who can spell and type on the computer but lack sufficient motor planning abilities to write. The reduced ability to translate signals from the brain into the complex muscle coordination needed for speech or fine motor skills is known as *dyspraxia*.

Verbal and motor dyspraxia are highly comorbid with ASD. It is important to monitor all children diagnosed with apraxia for signs of autism and all children diagnosed with autism for signs of apraxia (Tierney et al., 2015). Researchers are studying the underlying genetic and neural mechanisms to determine whether these disorders have similar origins. While there are no pharmacological treatments, there are many programs that help treat dyspraxia. A number of children with dyspraxia learn to talk and write, albeit with some difficulty, as they get older.

> We have learned to never give up on trying to help individuals learn to talk or write. Alex was an early reader and could type very fast with two fingers, but he did not have the motor planning abilities to wave appropriately or to write. Alex didn't write until he was 10. We learned to break each action into basic movements and write instructions for him. For example, to get him to wave, we wrote, "Hold your arm out in front of you and move it from side to side." It isn't a great wave, but it is better than hand flapping. His mother and I also figured out ways to get Alex to form his letters. Again, each letter had an instruction. For A it was "line up, line down, line across" and for M it was "up, down, up, down." His letters and numbers are large and somewhat idiosyncratic, but his writing is usually legible, and his writing speed has increased.

Obsessive–Compulsive Disorder

Many individuals with ASD develop rigid rituals. They also get fixated on particular topics or have difficulty getting scripts, videos, or ideas out of their heads. The intensity of their obsessions and compulsions may increase or diminish over time and may also relate to anxiety levels. In *DSM-5*, *obsessive–compulsive and related disorders* (OCD) are characterized by obsessions with unwanted recurrent and persistent thoughts, urges, or images, and by compulsions to perform repetitive behaviors in response to obsessions or to rigid rules. Restricted, repetitive patterns of behaviors, interests, or activities are key diagnostic criteria of autism spectrum disorder, and OCD is diagnosed as a separate disorder only when it is not better explained by another mental disorder (such as ASD). Though related, these disorders are not considered comorbid.

When the obsessions and compulsions are severe enough to interfere with daily functioning or with learning, they can be treated pharmacologically. While medications provide some benefit to children and adults with ASD by reducing restricted, repetitive symptoms, the medication does not cure ASD. Some individuals learn to deal with their symptoms with cognitive–behavioral techniques. Others embrace their compulsions and become highly skilled experts in narrow fields of interest.

> Michael was obsessed with Bob Ross oil painting techniques for many years. He watched the videos over and over and bought the books. He recreated so many Bob Ross paintings that he began to sell them at art fairs. Michael developed wonderful artistic skills and sometimes was persuaded to create "original" works by moving a Bob Ross tree or by using different colors than the model.

Depression

Individuals with ASD, particularly as they enter adolescence, are at risk for depression (Ghaziuddin, Ghaziuddin, & Greden, 2002; Ghaziuddin & Greden, 1998). *Depression* is characterized by severe and persistent feelings of sadness and hopelessness that interfere with daily functioning. Sleeplessness or too much sleep, loss of appetite, and lethargy may also be present. It is important for parents and professionals to look for symptoms of depression, since treating depression may significantly improve the individual's ability to function at school, at home, or at work. It is especially hard to diagnose depression in teens with ASD because, like their neurotypical peers, they also experience the emotional ups and downs, the altered sleeping habits, and the push for independence that occur with hormonal changes common in puberty. It is sometimes difficult to differentiate the cause of the symptoms. The social isolation experienced by teens with ASD may also contribute to depression. Sterling, Dawson, Estes, and Greenson (2008) and Hedley and Young (2006) found that adults with ASD with better social and cognitive skills are more likely to report symptoms of depression. Those individuals are more likely to be able to perceive differences between themselves and others.

Depression is a neurological disorder that has been studied extensively. Medications that affect neurotransmitters have been developed for the general population. As with all medications, the effectiveness in those with ASD varies, and careful evaluation by a psychiatrist is needed. In those with high-functioning ASD, various psychological therapies may also help. The therapist should understand the learning and thinking style common in individuals with ASD for the most effective therapy.

While the neurological relationship between ASD and depression is not completely understood, it is now being recognized in young children (Hazel, 2002). *Bipolar disorder*, also known as *manic depression*, is characterized by mood swings over a period of days, weeks, or months in adults. In children, it may be expressed as rapid mood swings over a few minutes or hours (Carlson, Jensen, & Nottelmann, 1998; Geller & Luby, 1997). While the genetic links of either disorder have not been established, we have seen families in which one child was diagnosed with ASD and a sibling was diagnosed with childhood bipolar disorder. We also know that both ASD and depression run in families with varying degrees of severity (Ghaziuddin & Greden, 1998).

> Adam, an intelligent, creative young man with ASD, had a very difficult time during his high school years. He had difficulty staying awake and did not respond to treatment for depression. Adam earned his high school diploma by completing online courses at home. Finally, when he was in his twenties, the symptoms of depression abated somewhat, and he was able to complete college coursework and earn a degree. With strong support from his family and therapists, Adam was able to weather the worst times and emerge with his wry sense of humor intact.

Seizure Disorder (Epilepsy)

EEG abnormalities and seizure disorders are observed in 20% to 30% of individuals with ASD, becoming more prevalent in adolescents and adults. The high rates of epilepsy suggest a role for neurobiologic factors in autism (Olsson, Steffenburg, & Gillberg, 1988; Tuchman & Rapin, 1997; Volkmar et al., 2014). Seizures can range from staring spells or muscle twitches to more global seizures. Not all seizures look alike; teachers and parents should be alert to symptoms and seek a neurological evaluation if they suspect possible seizures. Some young children may show abnormalities on their EEGs, whether or not they experience clinical seizures. Others may have their first seizure as they enter puberty.

The concordance of epilepsy and autism is well documented, but there is a lack of clinical trials to support specific treatments for seizures in those with ASD. Medication for epilepsy may be effective, but careful monitoring by a neurologist is necessary to adjust types of medication and dosages as needed. Only a few antiepileptic drugs (AEDs) have undergone carefully controlled trials in ASD, but these trials examined outcomes other than seizures. Limited evidence supports non-AED treatments (Frye et al., 2013). Frye et al. (2011), in an online survey, found that for children with ASD and clinical seizures, parents perceived on average that AED treatments reduced seizures but worsened other clinical factors (e.g., sleep, communication, behavior, attention, mood). We still don't understand the underlying medical etiology of seizures in those with ASD. We should be aware of the high concordance of epilepsy and ASD and look for signs in our clients, but treatment for epilepsy does not necessarily improve ASD symptoms.

Other Related Disorders

Some disorders related to ASD describe a single aspect of the spectrum of symptoms.

- *Semantic–pragmatic disorder* describes difficulty in processing, comprehending, and using language. The disorder has been identified primarily in England since 1983 (Rapin & Allen, 1983). While it is often acknowledged that there is a relationship between semantic–pragmatic disorder and ASD (Rapin & Allen, 1983), the term is used when other symptoms of ASD are mild or absent. Children with semantic–pragmatic disorder may have trouble with social communication, but some attribute their difficulty to their language problems rather than to their social perceptions (Coulter, 1998). Others disagree with this conclusion. Rapin (1996) wrote that semantic–pragmatic disorder is rarely encountered outside the context of ASD. *DSM-5* addressed this issue by creating the criteria described earlier in this chapter for social (pragmatic) communication disorder, distinguishing it from ASD by the absence of restricted and repetitive behaviors.

- *Specific language impairment* (*SLI*), as used in the United States, refers to a language problem in the context of normal intelligence and otherwise normal presentation, including social/emotional profiles. Some children with SLI have difficulty using language for social communication, but their deficits are characterized by grammatical errors and poor working memory. Reading and learning are often affected as well; however, the SLI diagnosis is generally differentiated from the ASD population (Bishop, 2003).

  Clinically, when you are determining a diagnosis for a particular child, it is sometimes hard to establish whether the problem is primarily in language comprehension and use, and also whether symptoms fall within the range of ASD. In a study at Massachusetts General Hospital using magnetic resonance imaging (MRI), De Fossé et al. (2004) found that boys diagnosed with autism and boys diagnosed with SLI had similar structural differences in parts of the brain associated with language. This brain area was different from that of typical language learners. It seems that boys with autism and boys with SLI have the same kind of differences in language-learning "wiring."

- *Hyperlexia* is precocious reading identified within the context of another developmental disorder, most often ASD. Some children can decode words and sentences when they are 2 years old. Others have memorized a long list of sight words. While typically developing children may read early, hyperlexia is not diagnosed unless there is another presenting problem. Some researchers have defined *hyperlexia* as "reading without understanding" (Healy, 1982), but we have not found that to be the case in our clinical experience. Children with hyperlexia may decode much better than they can comprehend, but these children comprehend what they read about as well as they comprehend oral language. It is important to identify hyperlexia as a comorbid condition along with ASD because it can be a powerful tool to develop language and social skills. Children with hyperlexia respond to lists of activities to help them transition and follow directions. They learn what to say by reading written scripts. Oral language is fleeting, but written language is concrete and can be referred to as often as needed.

  > Some children with hyperlexia are obsessive about reading and focus on letters and words everywhere. When I showed Fareed a picture of a compass on a vocabulary test, he looked at the direction letters and responded "NEWS." Another boy, who was 3 years old, spilled a big box of crayons on the floor. When we looked down, he had arranged the crayons to spell PONDEROSA STEAK HOUSE.

- *Nonverbal learning disability* (NLD) describes children who have a significant discrepancy between their higher verbal IQ scores and their lower performance scores. According to

Rourke (1989), these children evidence problems in psychomotor coordination; visual–spatial organization; nonverbal problem solving; tactile perception; adapting to new situations; pragmatics; and social perception, judgment, and interaction.

> Bobby and his siblings were playing in the family room. Though they all knew better, they began tossing popcorn at each other. When their dad heard the noise, he came running in. Bobby's brother and sister quickly stopped as soon as they heard Dad's footsteps, but Bobby was caught with his hand in the popcorn bowl. He didn't notice his dad in the room and he didn't understand why his siblings had suddenly stopped.

Children with NLD may have strengths in verbal memory, vocabulary, and decoding. Their difficulties in social skills overlap with those seen in higher functioning individuals with ASD. Techniques for helping to interpret nonverbal communication, such as tone of voice or body language, are useful for both groups (Duke, Nowicki, & Martin, 1996).

- *Multisystem developmental disorder* is a term used by Greenspan and Wieder (1997a) to describe sensory and motor processing disorders in young children that affect communication and social skills development. The treatment developed by Greenspan and Wieder (1997a), known as *DIR/Floortime*, is used with many children diagnosed with ASD. This developmental, individualized, relationship-based play therapy involves families and clinicians and follows Greenspan's theories of neurodevelopment. The book *Engaging Autism: Using the Floortime Approach to Help Children Relate, Communicate, and Think* (Greenspan & Wieder, 2006) describes their ideas and methods.

Research in ASD

ASD has been exceedingly hard to study scientifically. Historically, the number of subjects in a study has been small and the reported results have been difficult to replicate. The changing diagnostic criteria of autism spectrum disorders and the range in expression and severity of symptoms complicate making comparisons of data. Recent innovations in technology have provided tantalizing neurological and genetic research, but they also have illuminated the complexity of the problem.

Genetic Differences

According to *DSM-5*, individuals who meet criteria for ASD and who have a known genetic condition, such as Fragile X or Rett syndrome, should be diagnosed with ASD. The separate genetic conditions are designated as associated features of ASD. This allows for adding new genetic and biological findings that may be discovered that would shed light on the etiology of ASD (Lord & Jones, 2013).

Developments over the past several years give us reason for optimism for better understanding the etiology of ASD. Clinical evidence shows that ASD tends to run in families (Veenstra-VanDerWeele & Cook, 2003). Mapping of the human genome and improvements in the technology of studying human genetics have presented huge opportunities. Despite the high likelihood of inheritance, no single genetic origin has been identified. It is likely that many genes and regions on chromosomes are involved. Different variants on the same gene may also be involved and may cause different expression of ASD symptoms. Published studies have found some suspects (International Molecular Genetic Study of Autism Consortium, 1998–2008), but the results have not been consistently replicated. Organizations such as the Autism Genetic Resource Exchange (AGRE) have been established to provide a collaborative gene bank and sharing of information among researchers.

Studies of genetically identical twins have reported that if one twin has autism, the other has an approximately 60% to 70% chance of also having autism (using *DSM-IV* criteria). The probability of the other twin having the broader definition of ASD is over 90%, but the expression and severity of symptoms may differ. Recurrence risk for autism in siblings may be as high as 18.7% when broad spectrum is considered (Ozonoff et al., 2011), yet genetic causes are only partially understood because of clinical and genomic heterogeneity (Jiang et al., 2013). These statistics support that the inheritance of ASD is multifactorial or complex and that there may be other factors that affect the severity and presence or absence of specific symptoms (Veenstra-VanDerWeele & Cook, 2003). Yuen et al. (2015) emphasized the heterogeneous genetic nature of ASD in their study of families with two affected children. Using whole genome sequencing, they found that some (69.4%) of the affected siblings carried *different* ASD-relevant mutations. These siblings with discordant mutations tended to demonstrate more clinical variability than those who shared a risk variant.

Epigenetics is the study of mechanisms that control gene activity without changing the underlying DNA that makes up our genes. In essence, epigenetic molecules control when and where genes turn on and off to coordinate the body's development and function. Precise epigenetic control is particularly crucial during brain development. Methylation is a type of epigenetic change in which methyl groups are added to DNA and switch the underlying gene on or off. Studies have shown differences in DNA methylation in identical twins who are discordant for autism (Wong et al., 2013). These epigenetic marks can be influenced by any number of environmental exposures, such as everyday behaviors, infections, diet, and stress.

A growing body of research has found epigenetic changes in the cells that make sperm and eggs. Sperm-making cells may be particularly vulnerable to such environmental exposures, and some believe that this explains why autism rates are significantly higher among the children of older dads. Feinberg et al. (2015) analyzed the epigenetic markers on DNA in the sperm from 44 dads who already had one child with ASD. When their wives became pregnant again, DNA and epigenetic analysis was performed on their sperm samples. One year after birth, the second child was assessed for early signs of ASD. The researchers then looked at the likelihood that the child's autism symptoms corresponded to an epigenetic change at a particular site in a father's sperm DNA. Their data suggested that epigenetic differences in paternal sperm may contribute to autism risk in offspring. When the researchers looked at which genes were near the "high risk" sites, they found that many were in or near genes crucial to brain development. They then looked at postmortem brain tissue of individuals with autism and found several epigenetic changes in the cerebellum, which has been previously associated with autistic symptoms.

Willsey et al. (2013) found that nine autism-linked genes all contributed to abnormalities in one type of brain cell called cortical projection neurons. These cell changes occurred in the deep layers of the prefrontal cortex involved in complex decision making and social behavior.

The rate of progress in discovering genes and gene mutations has been increasing rapidly in recent years. Genetic research illuminates the variance in the presentation of ASD symptoms. These studies are important because if we can identify how genes change the brain during development, it opens the way for possible medical diagnosis of ASD. As we find out more about how genes affect the brain, we can tailor intervention to specific deficits. Right now we can understand that there are no one-size-fits-all treatment strategies for those with ASD.

Brain Structure Differences

Brain tissue studies and MRI scans have examined brain structure differences in people with ASD. Researchers have found slight differences in the size and location of the language areas in children with ASD, as well as differences in the sizes of cells in particular structures within the brain (Herbert et al., 2002; Herbert et al., 2004). Rapid growth in head circumference during the first year of life is documented and has spawned theories about differences in how neurons connect in the brains of those with ASD (Courchesne, Carper, & Akshoomoff, 2003; Just, Cherkassky, Keller, & Minshew, 2004). The development of the functional MRI (fMRI) has provided a safe way of detecting brain activity by looking at tiny metabolic changes resulting from increased blood flow during particular tasks. The brain changes as we learn, and researchers can actually see those changes on fMRI scans. It is now possible to detect changes in neural function after providing treatment.

Studies have documented differences in the brain activity of individuals with ASD when presented with visual stimuli (such as faces) as compared with that of typical controls (Dapretto et al., 2006). An fMRI study showed that it is possible to normalize activity in the part of the brain that is active in social judgment merely by directing individuals with ASD to attend to particular social cues (Wang, Lee, Sigman, & Dapretto, 2007).

Recent advances in scanning technology have allowed researchers to view how the brain is "wired." High-definition fiber tracking (HDFT) diffusion weighted imaging that uses fMRI technology looks at connectivity within the living brain and traces the extent and direction of white matter tracts by measuring water diffusion differences in brain tissue. You can see beautiful images of the connections of neurons in the brain online at the Human Connectome Project (www.humanconnectomeproject.org/gallery/). Researchers there are developing a database of brain images of healthy people engaged in various activities. You can also see a YouTube video (*CMU Researchers Scan Temple Grandin's Brain to Study Autism*) of the brain connectivity of Temple Grandin, a well-known author and autism spokesperson.

Diffusion tensor imaging (DTI) was further refined using tract-based spatial statistics (TBSS). DTI technology illustrates differences in white matter connections in those with ASD. Cheng et al. (2010) reported that in subjects with ASD, the frontal lobe exhibits an abnormal white matter microstructure, supporting the frontal disconnectivity theory of autism. Further refinement of the DTI resolution allowed Verstynen et al. (2011) to map white matter connections and determine their direction.

Scanning devices are illuminating the connections and structure of the brain so that we can see differences in those with ASD. We can see how learning changes the brain. We can see that there are differences in the developmental trajectory. We can see that "neurons that fire together, wire together." We can see that structured behavioral programs AND daily experiences have an impact on the developing brain. While we know that the brains of children with ASD are "wired" differently, we don't know how or why. We need to know how the structural and connective differences relate to emotions, intelligence, and behavior. There is reason to hope that the confluence of advances in genetics and imaging will yield possible treatments.

Environmental and Metabolic Influences

Other research has focused on the influence of environmental factors, toxins, and metabolic or hormonal function on the developing brain (Gilberg & Coleman, 2000; Mills et al., 2007; Roberts & Hartford, 2002). Epidemiological studies conducted around the world have not found correlates to the increase in ASD diagnoses (Lauritsen, Pedersen, & Mortensen, 2004; Schechter & Grether, 2008; Tebreugge, Nandini, & Ritchie, 2004). In a study of 95,727 privately insured children with older siblings with and without ASD, the receipt of the measles, mumps, and rubella (MMR) vaccine was not found to be associated with increased risk for ASD, even among children already at higher risk for ASD (Jain et al., 2015).

The Need to Evaluate Research Findings

Several years ago, my colleagues and I studied several journal articles describing basic neurological research in the field of ASD to see whether these studies might influence how we thought about

ASD and how we structured our intervention. We were looking for better understanding of the neural organization of children with ASD. Instead we learned how difficult it is to construct a scientific study and how difficult it is to draw conclusions from that study. The number of subjects in the studies was often very small, and the differences cited were minuscule. Even though conclusions had been reported in the media, the journal articles were much more cautious and indicated the need for more confirming data and further research.

When parents and professionals hear media reports about advances in research or new treatments for those with ASD, they should analyze the information as scientifically as possible. Here are some suggestions that may help in evaluating the research.

1. First, find the original article. Then ask yourself the following questions:

   - Is the article in a peer-reviewed journal?

     While peer review is not always a guarantee of validity, it is a good start. Also, look at the next few issues of the journal for any rebuttals or comments on the research.

   - What are the characteristics of the subjects in the study?

     Procedures for evaluating subjects for inclusion in the study should be outlined. The sample of subjects should be a reasonable size. Since many studies are done with small numbers of subjects, the authors should explain the limitations of the conclusions as they relate to the general population. While single-subject studies have yielded some valuable information, one cannot generalize conclusions until the study has been replicated.

   - Is there a control group?

   - Have the results been replicated?

   - Have other researchers followed up on the particular line of research?

     Because there is a lot of interest in finding a cure for ASD, the field is particularly susceptible to the "cure du jour." It is important to remember that some treatments may be of benefit to some individuals and not to others.

2. Correlation does not prove cause. Just because two things happen at the same time does not mean that they are related or that one caused the other. Children with ASD may show developmental improvements that some may attribute to treatment.

3. Is there another way to explain the results? Are there other variables that could have influenced the results? For example, a trial of medication may coincide with the onset of a new educational program, making it difficult to determine which one may have caused any resulting improvement.

4. Do the results mesh with current knowledge? Science is not static. Old theories are replaced with new ones in light of new information.

   For many years, people believed that children with ASD were mentally handicapped and couldn't learn. Many did poorly on standardized intelligence tests that put a premium on verbal directions and verbal reasoning or were presented in a manner that was difficult for children with autism. Later studies call into question the reported high prevalence of mental retardation in autism (Edelson, 2006; Koegel, Koegel, & Smith, 1997).

   Parents find it hard to wait for research to be validated. They are eager to try treatments that have any chance of success, even if efficacy studies have not been done. It is important to treat such treatment trials as scientifically as possible.

- Take baseline data. If you are trying to reduce or increase a particular behavior, count the number of occurrences per hour or per day prior to treatment.

- Maintain routines by keeping daily schedules the same, with the exception of the treatment trial. Try to control the variables, so that it is likely that improvement can be attributed to the treatment rather than to other factors in the child's life.

- Gather data during the treatment trial by counting the number of occurrences per hour or per day.

- Based on the data, continue or discontinue the trial after a reasonable time period.

The future of research in ASD is promising. The National Institutes of Health have awarded grants to establish Autism Centers of Excellence in the United States. These centers contribute their data to the National Database for Autism Research so that information can be shared with researchers throughout the world. This coordination of efforts among researchers in many disciplines should significantly increase the chances of solving some of the mysteries of ASD.

Chapter 2

Learning Styles in Children With ASD

In children with ASD, neural organization affects the manner and sequence of learning in the areas of language, academics, and social communication. Typical children differ from one another in personality, and we all have strengths and weaknesses coded in our DNA that are influenced by environment and education. Within a range, however, most humans follow similar developmental sequences, and teaching methods are therefore geared toward the "typical" learner. While it is clear that most children with ASD can develop and learn, their sequence of development and learning styles may vary. They often need to be directly taught language, concepts, and interactions that other children pick up naturally.

Language Learning

> It was one of those lightbulb moments. I had been working with children with autism for a number of years, but I never understood why my therapy was (or was not) effective or how the children learned language. In 1982, Barry Prizant published an article in *Topics in Language Disorders*, "Gestalt Language and Gestalt Processing in Autism," that immediately resonated with my observations. It would not be an exaggeration to say that each of my therapy sessions with children with ASD, to this day, is guided by the concepts put forth in that article.

Gestalt vs. Analytic Processing

What did Prizant say that was so illuminating? He looked at the linguistic research of Peters (1977) and others and saw that typical children acquire and use language via two modalities: analytic and gestalt. In the analytic mode, the basic unit is the word (or morpheme). As children mature, they combine words to create phrases and sentences. In the gestalt mode, the basic unit may be a word, multiword phrase, or sentence that is understood and spoken by the child as a whole unit, or a gestalt.

When a child processes words analytically, she is able to combine them flexibly in a number of ways. Note the following examples of analytic processing:

"Bye-bye."

"Go bye-bye."

"Daddy go bye-bye."

"Go bye-bye Daddy."

"Daddy go."

"Bye-bye Daddy."

Many children learn whole phrases well before they are able to use the individual words to create novel utterances. Take, for instance, the following example of gestalt processing:

"See you later, alligator." "After a while, crocodile."

It's as if "seeyoulateralligator" is all one word that carries linguistic meaning.

Although typical language learners use both modalities to comprehend and use language, they predominantly use the analytic mode. They are able to discern basic grammatical units in a language at a very early age. Typical language learners can express their thoughts by combining word units into phrases using early grammatical structures between 2 and $2\frac{1}{2}$ years of age.

Children with autism learn language predominantly through gestalt processing (Prizant, 1982). They learn whole phrases, repeat scripts, echo what they hear, and have trouble understanding a phrase if it's changed even slightly. They have difficulty breaking down word (morpheme) units and recombining the words or phrases to express new thoughts. Some phrases may sound quite sophisticated and may even be used appropriately in conversation, but even highly verbal children with ASD may have difficulty expressing their thoughts using original sentences.

Many young boys with ASD will quote Thomas the Tank Engine stories verbatim when they handle the toy trains, saying, "Toby is a tram engine. He is short and sturdy. He has cowcatchers and side plates and doesn't look like a steam engine at all" (from *Toby the Tram Engine*, a book in the Railway Series by W. V. Awdry).

> Another example of difficulty using original sentences was shown when Liam fell and hurt his knee. He cried and said, "It's okay. Mommy will help you. You'll feel better soon." Without changing the pronoun references, he repeated what his mother had said to him on a previous occasion.

Research (DeFossé et al., 2004) supports Prizant's ideas about gestalt processing and the atypical neurological "wiring" for language in children with ASD. There is a subset of children who began to talk in a typical way early in their second year of life but then lost those early words between the approximate ages of 18 months to 2 years. They also stopped responding to verbal language and developed other symptoms of ASD. Many of them began to learn language again, but they evidenced the patterned language, echolalia, and difficulties with pragmatic language characteristic of gestalt processing.

Recent studies illuminate underlying brain structure and function relating to language-learning differences in children with ASD. Using MRI and diffuse tensor imaging (DTI), Joseph et al. (2014) studied children with ASD ages 4 to 7 and found atypical asymmetry in language-related white matter structures as well as an atypical pattern of brain–language relationships compared to a matched control group of typically developing children. This suggests that children with ASD meet language milestones and acquire normal language via a neurodevelopmental trajectory different from that of typically developing children. Verly et al. (2014) studied differences in the development of language, social interaction, and communicative skills in children with ASD. In an fMRI study of verbal children with ASD with language impairment, they found preserved connectivity between the classic intrahemispheric language centers, Wernicke's and Broca's areas. However, they also found decreased connectivity in other areas of the brain that underlie the abnormal language functions in children with ASD.

Pruning Periods

Using sophisticated techniques, researchers since the 1990s have discovered that typical brain cells experience periods of growth in numbers and periods of pruning (Gogtay et al., 2004; Miller, 2007). An infant's brain may have approximately 2,500 synapses per neuron. By the second year of life, the number of synapses increases to as many as 15,000 synapses, twice as many as the adult brain. In synaptic pruning, the weaker synapses are eliminated as the brain responds to genetic coding and experience (Gopnik, Meltzoff, & Kuhl, 1999). Pruning is part of *neural plasticity* (Huttonlocher, 2002), which is the brain's ability to change and build itself in response to normal developmental processes, experience, learning, and injury. Pruning is designed to streamline the brain and prepare for the next period of growth. These pruning periods occur at predictable times in a child's development, and one such pruning period begins at 18 months to 2 years of age. It may be postulated that the brains of children with ASD develop in a way that affects the language learning circuitry. A study using fMRI demonstrated that the language areas in the brains of boys with ASD were indeed different from those of typical boys (DeFossé et al., 2004).

In typical development, several genes control a constant and concurrent process of forming and eliminating (pruning) synapses in the brain. Microglia are cells that infiltrate the developing brain, providing a surveillance and scavenging function and having a role in synaptic pruning (Paolicelli, 2011). Zhan et al. (2014) created a reduction of microglia in mice, causing a deficit in synaptic pruning. They showed an association between weak synaptic pruning and decreased functional brain connectivity, deficits in social interaction, and increased repetitive behavior in the mice. Tang et al. (2014) found evidence of insufficient pruning (autophagy) of spines forming synapses on the dendrites in neurons in the temporal lobes of postmortem brains of individuals with ASD. Using genetically engineered mice, researchers were able to correct autistic-like social behaviors and enable spine (synapse) pruning without affecting spine (synapse) formation by introducing a drug. David Sulzer, who was instrumental in developing this study, has pointed out that "while people usually think of learning as requiring the formation of new synapses, the removal of inappropriate synapses may be just as important" ("Children with Autism Have Extra Synapses in Brain," 2014, para. 11).

As the brain develops, synapses undergo periods when more and more synapses are created, followed by periods when more and more synapses are pruned. Although this takes place throughout infancy, childhood, and adolescence, different regions of the brain are pruned at different points in development. Generally, the brain regions in which pruning is taking place are associated with the greatest changes in cognitive functioning at that time (Steinberg, 2011). At the same time, myelination of nerve fibers increases in waves in various parts of the brain, beginning in the prenatal period and continuing into adulthood.

Another pruning period in the typical brain occurs approximately at puberty. It has been thought that early language-learning circuits that allow us to analyze words and formulate simple grammatical structures are eliminated at this time, but this idea has been called into question recently (Steinhauer, White, & Drury, 2009). It appears that the stage of pruning in adolescence streamlines the brain to allow it to build new circuits to better understand abstraction and to reason logically as adults (Miller, 2007).

The Second-Language-Learning Analogy

While it appears that many children with ASD are not "wired" in the typical way for learning language by mere exposure, many learn to talk and communicate in a different way. Similar to adolescents and adults who need specific lessons in grammatical structures, vocabulary, and pronunciation to learn a new language (Perani et al., 1998), children with ASD need specific instruction to learn to communicate (Prizant, 1983). Children on the autism spectrum learn best when language is simple in structure, highly repetitive, and consistent in form and content in particular situations.

Perhaps children with ASD are using secondary-language-learning circuits spared during the pruning process. Some fMRI studies have localized distinct cortical areas associated with native and second language functions (Kim, Hirsch, Relkin, DeLaz Paz, & Lee, 1996; Kim, Relkin, Lee, & Hirsch, 1997; Ruschemeyer, Fiebach, Kempe, & Friederici, 2005). Other studies have shown that while similar language areas are used for first and second language learning, older learners of a second language also recruit additional cortical areas to support more effortful language processing (Stowe & Sabourin, 2005). It would be interesting to determine whether the second language areas coincide with language areas used by those with ASD.

> When my older son lived in Japan, we went to visit him. He took us out to the countryside, where very few people spoke English. There I felt what it must be like for children with ASD. I heard people talking in streams of sounds that were indistinguishable as separate words, often punctuated at the end with the syllable "hai." When my son tried to teach me some common phrases, I could remember them for several hours or a day, but the next day I couldn't recall them without a prompt. By the end of my 10-day immersion experience, I was dismayed at how little I had learned.

Not only must children with ASD be specifically taught vocabulary, grammar, and language concepts, but they must also be taught how to communicate with others using the language they have learned. Language use and content (pragmatics and semantics) involves so much more than saying grammatically correct sentences. Prosody (tone, rhythm, stress), body language, context, and interpretation of intent must also be carefully taught.

Auditory vs. Visual Processing

Several studies (Napolitano & Sloutsky, 2004; Robinson & Sloutsky, 2004; Sloutsky & Napolitano, 2003; Vouloumanos & Werker, 2007) found that typical children have an innate bias toward attending to auditory stimuli as opposed to visual stimuli during the critical language-learning years. In contrast, many children with ASD attend more to visual input than to auditory input. In fact, one of the early red flags in diagnosing an autism spectrum disorder is the child's inability to shift attention to a parent calling his or her name while the child is playing with a toy.

Although many children with ASD cannot process spoken language very well, some have an uncanny ability to attend to visual detail and some may recognize letters and even read at a very early age. Temple Grandin, a well-known, highly successful adult with ASD, described her well-developed visual abilities in her book *Thinking in Pictures* (1995).

Children with ASD seem to lack (or have lost) the neurological circuitry that is basic to the universal language abilities of typical children. Typical children can be immersed in a language-rich environment and pick up the language around them. Children with ASD learn language via gestalt processing. Language must be specifically taught. Their language-learning style affects both language comprehension and language expression.

Language Comprehension

Language comprehension is not a single construct. Rather, it comprises a complex combination of simultaneous verbal and nonverbal processes that are impacted by memory, background schemas, and social interpretations. Children with ASD typically have difficulty with the aspects of language comprehension discussed in this section.

LANGUAGE PROCESSING

Children with ASD process language as patterns and have trouble analyzing language as word units. The patterns may have specific words and/or a particular intonation. The children may note that a certain phrase is uttered in a particular time and place and they may not respond if the phrase is changed in any way. They become confused if the phrase is used in a different context or even spoken by a different person. Children with ASD like predictable verbal patterns. They play parts of a DVD over and over to hear it the exact same way. Sometimes they associate a phrase with a certain visual, inadvertent gesture, or action.

> For a time, I developed a habit of saying, "You know what?" to mark a transition when I was working with the children. I must have said it many times at the end of sessions with Roger. I'd say, "You know what? It's time to go." One day, in the middle of the session, I said, "You know what?" Roger immediately jumped up and headed for the door.

> I recently evaluated a 2-year-old girl whose mother suspected ASD. Her mother told me that she could fill in the words to the spider song, so I began to sing, "The eensy weensy spider went up the . . . ," but the girl didn't respond. I asked her mother to try it, and when she sang, "The itsy bitsy spider . . ." her daughter gleefully joined in. She didn't respond to me because I didn't use the words she was used to hearing.

LITERAL INTERPRETATION

Comprehension is further compromised by a very literal interpretation of language. Idioms, metaphors, and other figures of speech are particularly confusing to children with ASD. Language is complex, including language we use with very young children.

> When James said he "had a ball" at the party, Jennie wanted him to give her the ball.

> When Anna's aunt called her "sweetie pie," Anna protested that she was not a pie, she was a girl.

> When Arthur's dad held out his hand and asked Arthur to "give me five," Arthur gave him the plastic numeral 5 from his magnetic board.

PARALANGUAGE

Prosody, facial expression, gestures, and context cues help listeners interpret shades of meaning. This is known as *paralanguage* or *paralinguistic information*. People can stop talking, but their body language is always present. The messages sent by these nonverbal signals are fluid and constantly changing. At a very young age, a typical child learns when his parents are annoyed by their stances and facial expressions. Children with ASD often miss these cues because they have difficulty looking and listening at the same time. Reduced eye-gaze is a common contributor to poor paralinguistic interpretation.

> Darnell, a third-grade boy with ASD, was having a hard time with kids who were teasing him. Since he couldn't tell who was really being mean and who was just joking, he overreacted and got upset several times a day. We helped him understand that sometimes people say one thing but mean the opposite. We helped him recognize the tone of voice and facial expression that signal sarcasm or irony. One day Darnell boasted that he had seen a spider that was bigger than his hand. Another boy replied doubtfully, "Oh, sure you did!" Darnell looked at him with a gleam in his eye and said, "Aha. Irony."

PROCESSING SPEED

When someone doesn't understand, a natural response is to try to explain. Explanations use a lot of words and make the communication even more confusing for individuals with ASD. Instead, what may be needed is more time to process what is said to them. Studies have demonstrated reduced processing speed in those with ASD. Schmitz, Daly, and Murphy (2007) found that reduced frontal lobe parenchymal volume (i.e., fewer neurons and glial cells) and decreased white matter density in individuals with ASD correlated with slower response to target stimuli on a computerized reaction time task. Gepner and Feron (2009) presented evidence that slower processing speed seen in those with ASD may have resulted from Multisystem Brain Disconnectivity–Dissynchrony (MBD), defined as an increase or decrease in functional connectivity and neuronal synchronization within/between multiple neurofunctional territories and pathways. They wondered if the world was changing too fast for a miswired brain.

Hedvall et al. (2013) studied a group of preschool children with ASD. They were evaluated on cognitive tests and on the *Vineland Adaptive Behavior Scales*. They concluded that preschool children with ASD had uneven cognitive profiles with low verbal skills, and, relatively, even lower processing speed quotients (PSQs). Except for the category of socialization, adaptive functioning was predicted to a considerable degree by PSQ. These results support clinical observations that it helps to speak slowly and allow time for the individual to respond. Processing speed is reduced further when children with ASD are anxious or emotional. At those times, they may not be able to comprehend questions, much less formulate answers.

> Simon was working on following multistep directions, but it didn't seem as though he could remember more than two steps. When we presented the steps more slowly, with pauses in between, we found that he could remember as many as five steps. The problem wasn't with his memory, it was with his ability to process quickly.

QUESTION FORMS

Children with ASD usually have difficulty understanding question forms. What makes the task even more difficult is that we can ask the same question in a variety of ways:

> *Why are you crying?*
> *How come you are crying?*
> *What is making you cry?*

Responses to these questions are often abstract, making it difficult for those with ASD. As gestalt language learners, they scan language for recognizable words or patterns. They may miss words that carry no concrete meaning, which are often at the beginning of the sentence. It doesn't help that many question words start with *wh*. It is interesting to see how often children with ASD give good answers that don't relate to the questions. They may have the information but are unsure what is being asked. Beverly Vicker and Rita Naremore published the *WH Question Comprehension Test* (2002) through the Indiana Resource Center for Autism. It surveys a variety of question forms and graphically illustrates the confusion experienced by children with ASD.

> When Amy was asked, "When do you get presents?" she answered, "Santa brings them."
>
> When Roman was asked, "Where do you eat?" he responded, "Chicken nuggets."
>
> I often compare the difficulty with question forms to my experience in France with my high school French class. In French, many question words begin with *qu*. When someone would ask me a question, I'd try to listen for words and phrases I knew and made a guess as to how to respond. When my answer provoked laughter, I knew that I did not understand the question. I know that I learned French predominantly via gestalt processing. I can certainly empathize with my young friends with ASD.

PRONOUNS

Understanding pronouns and referents is also difficult for gestalt learners of language. Consider the following example:

> Mary was carrying a book to John's house.
> When she got there, she gave it to him.

In order to understand the second sentence, you need to know that *she* refers to Mary, *there* refers to John's house, *it* refers to the book, and *him* refers to John.

It is even more confusing when the referents change within a single conversational exchange.

> When you come to my house, please bring the book to me.
>
> Okay. When I come to your house, I'll bring it to you.

Typical language learners sort out pronoun referents at a young age. Children with ASD need specific instruction and practice to make sense of pronoun use. Comprehension increases with the ability to associate pronouns with their referents (O'Connor & Klein, 2004). This process (called *anaphora*) will be discussed in relation to reading comprehension in Chapter 4.

VOCABULARY

Some verbal children with ASD are quite good at understanding specific vocabulary, particularly nouns. They can learn new words after only a few exposures (fast mapping), especially when they are interested in the topic. They often link words to the specific contexts in which they first learned them. They may not, however, understand the words when they are used in different contexts or when they have alternate meanings.

> Alex loves to peruse the dictionary. He can give definitions of many words, and he may even paraphrase definitions rather than recite them verbatim. For example, he knows the definitions of words like *malign*, *torrent*, *luminescent*, and *scepter*. He can use the words appropriately in sentences when asked, and he remembers them for months and years. He does not, however, use these words in conversation and may not understand them when he hears them in another context.
>
> Evan was confused when I said that his favorite program would not "run" on my computer and when I said that the water was "running." How could they run when they don't have feet?

Language Expression

Parents of children who are later diagnosed with ASD often first become concerned when they notice that their children are not talking. While some do not talk at all or are delayed in language expression, many children with ASD try to express themselves in a different way.

ECHOLALIA

Even though echolalia is considered a stereotyped, repetitive behavior in *DSM-5*, it may also perform a communicative function. Gestalt processing in children with ASD affects expressive language as it does language comprehension. *Echolalia* (repeating words and phrases verbatim immediately or at a later time) and *scripting* (using scripts or past phrases to try to communicate) were once thought to be nonproductive verbal tics to be eliminated. Prizant and Rydell (1984), Krashen and Scarcella (1978), Sterponi and Shankey (2014), and others have helped us understand that echolalia and scripts are often children's best efforts to take turns in conversations. They want to say something, so they repeat what they have just heard (immediate echolalia).

An interchange may sound like this:

> "Which ball?"
>
> "Ball."
>
> "Yellow ball?"
>
> "Yellow ball."
>
> "Yellow ball or orange ball?"
>
> "Orange ball."

They may not be able to formulate their own sentences, but they can plug in a previously heard phrase (delayed echolalia or scripts).

Just before winter break, one of my students stood at the door, placed a finger at the side of his nose and intoned, "Merry Christmas to all and to all a good night."

LANGUAGE FORMULATION

In his 1987 book, *Psycholinguistics: A New Approach*, McNeill talked about how we think in both images and words (inner speech). Typical language learners "unpack" their thoughts into words in a continuous manner, rarely planning what they are going to say. Gestalt processors have difficulty "unpacking" their thoughts because they need to search for the phrase that best fits the situation. They also have to find phrases to describe an image they may "see" in their heads.

> Austin went through a phase of trying to find words for his images. The results were delightful. His family called them "Austinisms."
>
> a flying closet = an elevator
>
> indoor heaven = a funeral home
>
> a floating hotel = the *Titanic* ("Actually," he would say with a smile, "it was a sinking hotel.")
>
> a bottom sneeze = (You figure it out!)

While the range of success in language expression varies across the spectrum, we have seen a number of individuals fluently express themselves using gestalts and patterns. They break the patterns into smaller pieces until they discern the word or morpheme segments. Some have even become writers and poets.

This poem comes from Kate Duvall's book *That's All* (2004):

Daisy

Underneath
Her faded yellow
Sunbonnet
And musty-colored
Perfume
Lies
The sunshine
Of
A new
Millennium

SCRIPTS

We all use scripted language to some degree in our everyday conversation. We use scripted greetings when meeting new people ("It's nice to meet you"), when leaving a party ("Thanks for inviting me"), or when apologizing ("I'm sorry. Please forgive me"). We teach children with ASD social scripts and scripts for playing games ("It's your turn"). Some children with ASD use scripts memorized from books or DVDs to narrate pretend-play.

Some individuals with ASD have learned to combine scripts and patterns with novel phrases so that unfamiliar listeners do not recognize the difference.

> Jonathon, an adult with ASD, has a college degree in music and knows many facts about composers. If someone mentions going to a Beethoven concert, Jonathon may reply, "Did you know that Beethoven died of liver disease?" Jonathan has learned not to offer too much information at once and to allow the listener to comment or ask a question. It is only after you have heard him use the exact same words in another conversation that you realize Jonathon is scripting.

REPETITIVE PHRASES

We all have had catchy tunes stuck in our heads. Individuals with ASD can become obsessed with particular phrases and scripts. These repetitive patterns are generally not communicative in nature and actually interfere with the ability to respond. It is important to distinguish obsessive repetitions from the more functional use of echolalia and scripts.

> Jimmy has been stuck on the topic of wood and types of furniture for months. He can inhibit his obsession for short periods of time, especially if he knows that he can talk about it at the end of the time period. He is quite adept at unobtrusively turning the conversation toward his topic, and I have fallen for it more than once. He might say to me, "Phyllis, what TV shows did you watch in the 50s? Did you watch *Leave it to Beaver*? Did you watch *Father Knows Best*? Was the furniture dark wood or light wood? I just want to know."

Sometimes these obsessions can be bothersome.

> When Mike's class studied China, the teacher brought in the movie *Mulan*. She thought that Mike would like it because he had talked about *Mulan* quite a bit at the beginning of the year. Instead, as the time for the movie approached, Mike became increasingly agitated and finally had a full-blown meltdown. He did not stay in class for the movie. When he finally calmed down, he said, "No more *Mulan* in my brain. No more *Mulan* in my brain." He did not want to get it stuck there again.

FOCUSED INTERESTS

There is a difference between focused interests and obsessions, though the line between them is sometimes fuzzy. Many times highly focused interests can be used to gain new information. Many children with ASD have good memories for learned information and sometimes gain encyclopedic knowledge about particular topics. Some topics are quite obscure, but in the age of the Internet, there are usually Web sites devoted to even the most arcane subjects.

> Nate has always been fascinated by plumbing equipment. His greatest reward is visiting a new men's room at a shopping center or a museum. If you don't think there are others who share this interest, check out www.toilets.com to learn more. They even publish a toilet calendar with pictures of urinals around the world. Nate has learned to limit his time perusing the Web site, but through his interest, he has become quite adept at surfing the Internet.

Focused interest can also stimulate productive conversations.

> Nineteen-year-old Austin loves the movie *Cars*. When he learned that Pixar's John Lasseter traveled the old Route 66 in preparation for the movie, Austin surfed the Web for pictures of the old road and found out that parts of it were closed and several bridges were out. He found various locations on a map and traced the route across America. His focused interest provides Austin with things to talk about.

RECIPROCAL COMMUNICATION

Children with ASD often have difficulty developing reciprocal communication. At the very basic level, we often need to teach a child with ASD to respond to her name when it is called. The child may actually hear her name but may not realize she has to respond in some way. Typical children will respond to their names by turning their heads and making eye contact, but this nonverbal communication is not natural for children with ASD and often needs specific instruction.

> Blake would not respond when his mother called him. Usually it was because he did not want to stop playing his computer game. This became quite frustrating. When we gave

Blake the script, "Just a minute, Mom," it acknowledged his mother and gave him time to come to a stopping point. Because Blake is a child with ASD, this exchange was usually repeated several times before Blake could actually leave the computer.

Reciprocal conversations are particularly difficult for those who have learned language via gestalt processing. We can teach children what to say in a variety of situations, but it is impossible to predict how a conversation partner will actually respond. The task for the child with ASD is to understand what was said, interpret the speaker's intent, and retrieve a relevant response from a repertoire of learned phrases. It is truly daunting, when you think about it.

Michael has been working on having adult conversations, but he has difficulty discerning the main idea of the conversation. He wants to take a turn in the conversation and actually likes talking to people, so he steers the conversation back to topics that he knows. Michael likes to help out at our family holiday party, and one year when Santa was a bit late, he said, "Santa is late. That reminds me of when Toby the Tram Engine was late getting to the station. . . ."

Academic Learning

Academic learning in children and adolescents with ASD is certainly affected by their language-learning differences. Each area (reading, writing, and math) presents its own special challenges as well. This section addresses common problems seen as children with ASD try to achieve academic goals.

Reading Research Results

In one of the few studies conducted about reading and children with ASD, Frith and Snowling (1983) outlined the difficulties they observed. The illustrative examples come from my clinical experience.

GOOD WORD RECOGNITION/POOR COMPREHENSION

According to Frith and Snowling (1983), most of us can read (decode) much more than we can understand. Many children with ASD seem to disconnect the decoding process from comprehension. They may read along, sometimes with good expression, but they don't automatically make the associations necessary for understanding what they have read. Even when reading picture books, the children may not realize that the words and pictures go together.

Jack was reading a Henry and Mudge book. The text described a man walking with his collie. The picture on the page showed a man and his dog. Jack could not figure out that a collie was a kind of dog.

LIMITED OR DELAYED UNDERSTANDING OF SYNTAX AND SEMANTICS

Frith and Snowling (1983) recognized the connection between reading comprehension and language comprehension. Children with ASD have a lot of difficulties with syntax and semantics. They may find tense markers and temporal words to be particularly confusing.

Jacob read the sentence "Before the boys went to the petting zoo, they bought food for the animals." He insisted that the boys went to the zoo first and then bought food. When he read "The boys bought food for the animals before they went to the petting zoo," he understood what happened first. He responded to the sequence of the words, ignoring the word *before*.

DIFFICULTY INTEGRATING INFORMATION

Children with ASD often learn bits of information but have difficulty integrating these bits to form a whole concept. It is hard for them to create a mental picture from a verbal or written description. They have often been described as thinkers who can name each variety of tree, but have little concept of the forest.

> When Travis's second-grade class was reading *Sarah, Plain and Tall*, Travis became agitated. To him, Sarah was the girl who lived across the street, and she was not at all like the Sarah in the book. His vision was of a particular Sarah, and it got in the way of creating a new Sarah.

DIFFICULTY IN REFERENCING

Frith and Snowling (1983) found that referencing is a key element in reading comprehension. Just as it affects language comprehension, understanding pronoun referents is important in reading comprehension. Many readers with ASD skip over or misread pronouns, even though they may be competent decoders. Their attention is focused on the nouns and verbs in the passages. They have difficulty scanning a paragraph to find the answer to a comprehension question, particularly if the question paraphrases the words in the paragraph.

> There is a passage in a Henry and Mudge book that describes how Henry feels now that he can walk to school with Mudge (a dog). I asked Marcus how having a pet could give a boy courage. Marcus, a very bright second-grade boy with ASD, could not find the answer because the words *pet* and *courage* did not appear in the text.

POOR ACCESS TO PRIOR KNOWLEDGE

Neurological research is shedding some light on how information is stored in the brain and how short-term memories transfer into long-term memory. Frith and Snowling (1983) observed that individuals with ASD have poor access to certain kinds of prior knowledge, which has been substantiated (Koshino et al., 2005; Minshew, Goldstein, & Siegel, 1997). It is also true that many people with ASD have amazing memories for events and facts (Beversdorf et al., 2000); however, they may not know which of these facts are relevant to what they are currently reading.

> Austin is working on tuning in to the greater world by reading about current events on the Internet. When we read an article about wildfires in California and tried to talk about how people were affected by the fires, Austin spied a picture of Governor Arnold Schwarzenegger inspecting the damage. Austin then switched the topic to Terminator movies. "We like Arnold," he said. "He's an actor. He made the first Terminator movie in 1984."

Clinical Observations of Reading Difficulties

As we explore our SLP role for developing literacy in children with communication disorders, it is important to catalog observations and filter those observations through a lens that considers each child's learning style. In the case of children with ASD, if we break the reading process into its component parts, we can begin to assess each child's reading strengths and weaknesses. If we look at the results of an extensive literature review published in 2000 by the National Reading Panel (NRP), we can determine factors that influence successful comprehension in typical readers. We can then focus our lens and apply the findings to children with ASD. Although there are some references to "disabled readers" in the NRP report, there are only a few studies specific to children with ASD.

Clinical experience has shown that many aspects of the reading process present challenges to children with ASD.

PHONEMIC AWARENESS

Developing phonemic awareness is a listening skill. Children are taught how to identify and manipulate sounds in syllables and words. NRP (2000) reported that in typical children, phonemic awareness training was significant in developing reading and spelling skills. They also found that phonemic awareness training did not improve the spelling abilities of "disabled" readers. Many of the children we have seen with ASD are confused by the concepts of rhyming and syllables. Some children with hyperlexia, who have visual representations of words in their minds, are confused that two words with very different spellings can still rhyme (e.g., *enough* and *stuff*).

> Concrete thinking can interfere with rhyming tasks. When I gave Micah the sentence "I saw a mouse run into the _____," he refused to say "house" because he never saw a mouse in a house, and he did not ever want a mouse to be inside a house. No way!

Gestalt learners have difficulty picking out word units, and even more trouble counting the number of phonemes in a word. The presence of mild or significant verbal apraxia (trouble sequencing and producing speech sounds in words and sentences) adds another layer of difficulty. While children with verbal apraxia may hear sounds others say, they may not be able to repeat them.

PHONETIC DECODING

Phonics instruction emphasizes sound–letter correspondence and how letters are linked to form words. NRP (2000) found that systematic phonics instruction produced significant improvement in reading and spelling in all children studied, including those with reading disabilities. The report cautions, however, that while these skills are necessary for learning to read, integration with phonemic awareness, fluency, and reading comprehension is vital.

> Children with ASD like rules. Unfortunately, English spelling has many exceptions to rules. Orrin said that he read a book about a "k-ni-get." It took us a while to figure out that he meant a knight.

> Mike went through a period when he would only read words phonetically. Each time he read a word, he painstakingly sounded out each letter. It didn't matter that he had just read the word *big* in the previous sentence and that he knew what the word was. He followed the rules of phonics for each letter; to him, following the rules was more important than the reading task itself.

JOINT ATTENTION

Joint attention is important in many aspects of reading and reading comprehension. The diagrams, charts, or photographs in textbooks may be distracting to the child with ASD. It may be hard to ignore the supplemental information while trying to decode and comprehend the text. Within the text, there may be references to illustrations, and it may be difficult for a child with ASD to shift attention back and forth from the text to the illustration.

> Sometimes the page itself may offer distractions. If I had a dollar for each time a child looked at the page number at the bottom of the page, I would be a wealthy woman. One child was very upset because only the odd-numbered pages were marked in the book she was reading. We had to go back and number all the even pages before she could go on.

> Ben's reading is much improved these days because he spends a lot of time on the Internet. He gets annoyed by all the pop-up ads, however, because he has trouble ignoring them.

READING FLUENCY

Reading fluency is the ability to read aloud with accuracy, speed, and expression. It is one of the elements necessary for good reading comprehension. Rehearsal in silent reading and reading aloud is thought to increase fluency. NRP (2000) seemed to show that guided oral reading in the classroom was beneficial, but there was insufficient evidence that independent silent reading alone was effective in improving reading fluency. Having children with ASD read aloud whenever possible is enlightening. Many readers with ASD read in a monotone or with a stereotypic intonation pattern, but others can read with great expression. Excellent readers, such as those with hyperlexia, often skip words or lines as they are reading. They may misread words and don't seem bothered if the resulting sentence doesn't make sense.

> Four-year-old Clifford, a boy with ASD, amazed his family and teachers by reading the Preamble to the U.S. Constitution with perfect expression. Holding a big book, he intoned, "We, the people of the United States, in order to form a more perfect onion. . . ." He continued, unaware of his mistake.

MAIN IDEA VS. DETAIL

One of the major challenges for those with ASD is to understand the big picture as more than just a summary of details. Many people with ASD are great at remembering details they have read, but they have a hard time summarizing the plot or seeing how the information fits together. It is as though they are painting by number. Each little colored shape is filled in, but they don't step back to see how the little shapes create a beautiful landscape.

> Darryl, an adult with ASD, is a trivia expert. Recently, as we were watching a video together, a character quoted a poem: "Tiger, tiger burning bright. In the forests of the night." Darryl knew the poem was written by William Blake, and he continued reciting, "What immortal hand or eye. Could frame thy fearful symmetry?" Although he knew the poem, he had no idea what it was about and didn't think it was at all necessary to understand it.

> Austin and I were reading about Orville and Wilbur Wright. I thought it would be a good topic because Austin loves flying. After reading a section about the Wright brothers' childhood and how they liked to invent things, I asked Austin what he remembered about the chapter we had just read. Austin thought for a moment and said, "Their father was a minister."

VISUALIZATION

Most of us think in words and in images and can switch back and forth. When you think of the Eiffel Tower, a particular image of the tower most likely comes to mind. If you think of your shopping list, you probably see a list of words, but you can also picture images of bread, milk, or cheese. Many of those with ASD have difficulty creating an image from the words they read. If they read a description such as, "It was a dark and stormy night when a tall man in a long cloak knocked on the iron gates of the gray, looming castle," it is unlikely that they will be able to picture it as an ominous scene. Likewise, many people with ASD think primarily in pictures, and they have difficulty translating what they see into words.

FACT VS. FICTION

Many adults with ASD tell us that they much prefer reading factual, informational material to reading fiction. They find facts to be less ambiguous. Facts can be learned as lists. They have interesting vocabulary and labels. There is a discernable organization and sequence. Facts are supposed to be accurate and true. (It is difficult to explain to a person with ASD that something learned as fact may no longer be true.) Fiction, on the other hand, is not true at all. It deals with ambiguities like feelings. Elements like time sequences and locations may be mixed up. Fiction is very confusing to a concrete thinker. Fictional writing assumes that the reader has a basic prior knowledge. Most people with ASD lack a typical knowledge base.

Most children's literature is fiction. There are animals who wear clothes and talk. They live in places that don't exist on any map. Magical things happen. Children frolic with wild beasts. The line between fantasy and reality is blurred. Is it any wonder that children with ASD have difficulty listening to stories at kindergarten circle time?

> Orren loved the *Wheels on the Bus* book because it had wheels that actually turned, doors that opened and shut, and wipers that really moved. He did not like the page where the babies opened their mouths to cry. It looked too much like his little brother, and he didn't like it when his brother cried. Whenever we got close to that page, Orren ran to the other side of the room until that part of the book was over.

SCHEMAS

One of the ways we make sense of our experiences in the world is by building schemas, or frameworks. These schemas serve to organize what we know and serve as templates for attaching new information to what we already know. Schemas can be built in a number of ways, such as through direct experiences, videos, movies, radio, television, oral explanations/teaching, and reading. For children with ASD, building schemas may be tricky. For example, if you take a child to the zoo, you may assume that the child is building schemas about animals he sees. The child with ASD may be having a different experience. The zoo may have lots of fences with vertical bars. There is noise and many people squeezed into one space. There are unfamiliar smells and lots of walking. What schema is that child building? If someone reads *Goodnight Gorilla* to him, what does this child know about zoos?

> Zoe loved the planets and anything to do with outer space. She could name the planets in order and knew which ones had rings. She knew the names of many constellations and could identify them on a star map by their shapes. She knew the Dippers. She knew Orion was three stars in a row and Cassiopeia was shaped like a W. In contrast, when her father pointed out Venus in the night sky, Zoe could not believe that the tiny bright star was Venus. That was not the Venus in her book or in her astronomy video. Her confusion made me think about how we build schemas for things we can never experience: Oral and/or written language is key in the formation of these important templates.

INTEREST AND MOTIVATION

Committees of educators have decided what children should learn in school. Teachers work very hard to make their lessons interesting and to motivate children to learn about assigned topics. Unfortunately, many children with ASD are not motivated to learn school material as they prefer more obscure topics. Even the promise of a wonderful culminating activity may not be enough to keep them interested.

> I have had this conversation with Austin a number of times. I say, "Let's do this. It will be fun." He replies, "You always want me to have fun. Why do I have to have fun?"

Math

Math has its own special language, and part of learning math is learning what the math terms mean. Many children with ASD can learn math patterns and calculations. They can skip count, learn addition and subtraction facts, memorize multiplication tables, and fill in graphs. Sometimes they need visual strategies and/or manipulatives, and they sometimes learn to use the calculator for various math functions. The difficulty arises with word problems or when they are asked to estimate rather than calculate. One boy asked me, "Why guess when you can know?"

Many schools have adopted math programs aimed at helping children think in divergent mathematical ways. The programs present several math operations at once, and the curricula are built in a spiral format. The idea is that children can learn to think about math and then come back to each topic at more and more complex levels. These programs are generally a nightmare for children with ASD as well as their parents. "I was as frustrated as my child because I did not know what a number sentence was," one parent complained.

> Carolyn truly has a mathematical mind. She loves math and had a wonderful teacher for first and second grade who helped her understand the complicated math program. Still, Carolyn does not always do well on math tests. Why? Carolyn inadvertently skips problems. She cannot always stay organized in her work and does not always answer the math questions in order.

Writing—Motor Component

The writing process is often quite difficult for children with ASD. It is common for children with ASD to have motor planning problems. They may struggle with gripping pencils, sequencing letter formations, spacing words, and forming letters that are conventionally sized. The very act of paper-and-pencil work may be a chore for them.

> Alex couldn't learn to write until he was 10 years old, though he could read, spell, and use the computer keyboard. Now, as a teenager, he makes some of his letters in an idiosyncratic way, but his writing is generally legible. Working independently, he fills the page with large letters and may write vertically as well as horizontally.

Writing—Formulation and the Blank Page

Children with ASD may look at the blank page in their daily journal and have no idea about what to write. Probes and particular topics may be somewhat helpful, but open-ended ideas may be too abstract and nonspecific. Often the children don't know how to start writing and seem to view the writing process as separate and distinct from oral language. They may get stuck because they are missing a fact or detail. Most typical children will find something to say if asked to describe a favorite food or book. This probe may stymie a child with ASD, who will agonize over whether pizza or spaghetti is her favorite because sometimes she likes one and sometimes she likes the other.

> Audrey, a very bright girl with ASD, started refusing to go to school and was showing signs of anxiety. After trying behavioral interventions, motivators, and bribes to no avail, her parents and teachers finally discovered that the problem was journal writing at the beginning of the day. In Audrey's mind, there was something that she was "supposed to write" and she couldn't figure out what that was. Her teacher's idea that this was an opportunity for the class to write about whatever they wanted was too general for Audrey. The problem was solved when Audrey was allowed to write the exact same thing in her journal each day. For months she wrote, "My name is Audrey. My teacher's name is Ms. Johnson. My school is Edison. I am a girl." Once journal writing was finished, she could go on with her day at school.

Narrative Writing

Storytelling is a skill that typical children begin to develop in their preschool years. Very young children will refer to names of people or characters and assume that the listener knows who they are talking about. A 3-year-old may tell her grandmother that she went to Eva's house yesterday, unaware that her grandmother has no idea that Eva is a girl in her music class. As children grow older, they realize the need to give a listener background information. They develop the idea of story sequence and that a story has a beginning, middle, and end. These skills are developed over a period of years, continuing into adulthood. Oral narratives are often interactive, with the listener asking questions for clarification.

Written narratives have linguistic conventions that are different from oral narratives. For example, a child may say, "Joey said, 'That ball is mine.'" When writing, the child may use the following construction: "'That ball is mine,' said Joey." Typical children pick up literary conventions through reading books.

Children with ASD are often not aware of the needs of the listener or reader. They may have difficulty constructing a main idea and separating irrelevant from relevant details in their narrative. Literary conventions are confusing to them, and they try to use patterned sentences whether or not they fit the situation. Because they tend to be concrete thinkers, many children with ASD are uncomfortable with fictional writing because it is not real.

> David, a fourth grader with ASD, was having trouble creating narratives at school. He had, however, extensive knowledge about Greek mythology. He could write the story of Medusa and could even insert some of his own phrases into the narrative. After some resistance, he rewrote the story by changing the names of the characters. Later he again rewrote it, this time changing the setting and some of the details. After several rewrites, he began to see how to make the story funny. The story maintained its basic structure, but David was on his way to creating his own stories.

Rote Learning

Although many children with ASD have excellent rote memory skills, one of the core characteristics in the ASD learning style is difficulty associating bits of information. Just as we can memorize a poem, the "Pledge of Allegiance," or a song in a foreign language without understanding the words, children with ASD can often absorb words and patterns without true comprehension. Some nonverbal or preverbal children with ASD memorize the way to McDonald's and get upset if their parents take a different route. Some learn the alphabet but can only recognize the letters in order.

There is debate as to whether there is value in rote learning. Should we encourage children to learn the states and their capitals when they have difficulty asking for a drink of water? In my view, we can use rote learning as a framework to develop other needed skills. We can add new information to the framework and teach children to make the associations.

> One young boy with ASD was fascinated with maps and knew all the streets in Chicago and their corresponding block numbers. As he grew up, he was able to direct his parents to particular locations, and when he later learned to drive, he never got lost.

Rote learning can also be a social asset. Although they may recognize a child's deficits, people are usually impressed with a child's rote recitation of dinosaur names from the Jurassic era.

> Daniel was the source of information for his classmates whenever they had a question about animals. He knew the names and habitats of hundreds of obscure animals, and his information was invariably correct.

Discrepancies in Skills and Abilities

Although students with ASD may be able to handle certain parts of the academic curriculum and may even excel in some areas, they may struggle with basic curricular concepts. During the elementary and middle school years, children are expected to be generalists and gain experience and knowledge in a wide variety of topics. There are opportunities in high school to go into greater depth in some areas, but the requirements for graduation include courses in all academic disciplines.

As students enter adulthood, their interests and talents can lead to vocational or career paths. The students just have to make it through the school system first.

> Mike was the pioneer student in his school district to be in a full inclusion program. His one-to-one aide and his parents dedicated many years to getting him through school. It wasn't easy. Mike was a talented cartoonist and was also very interested in woodworking. He learned the basics of cartooning from copying the work of Bruce Blitz. Norm Abram of *New Yankee Workshop* was Mike's idol. His high school program allowed him to take woodshop over and over again, and he also took classes in graphic arts that introduced him to computer animation. We arranged a part-time job in a graphic arts and printing company, and now Mike is pursuing further training at a technical institute. He still has great difficulty with classes that are outside his field, but he is getting good grades in his art and graphics courses.

Visual-Motor Challenges

While some children with ASD have good visual skills and are able to draw quite well, many others find visual motor tasks quite challenging. They may see details but have difficulty organizing them into a whole.

> When I was visiting Drew's second-grade class, the teacher asked the children to draw a map of the classroom. Most children were able to draw representations of bookshelves near the walls, tables and chairs in the middle of the room, science materials in the back near the windows, and the door near the front. Drew's drawing was very revealing. He put in a lot of the furniture and materials, but they were randomly scattered on the page. He also worked hard at labeling his pictures, but many of the words were upside down or backwards.

Many students with ASD get overwhelmed if there is too much information on a page. They literally don't know where to look first. They may not be able to copy a sentence from the board because each time they look up, they have a hard time finding the next word. They also have trouble figuring out where on their papers they should write the words they see.

> Paul had learned his math facts quite early. By age 4, he could add one- and two-digit numbers, and mentally subtract with ease. He had also memorized the multiplication tables to 12. When his first-grade teacher introduced the "Mad Math Minute" using simple addition facts up to 10, Paul had a major meltdown. The written task consisted of a page with 50 problems, and Paul had difficulty focusing on them one at a time. This slowed him down considerably. He wanted to stop and erase if his numerals didn't look exactly right or if he had inadvertently written a *2* backwards. Also, the children had to stop working when the minute elapsed, and Paul could not stand to leave any problems unfinished.

With all the difficulties described in the previous sections, it is amazing that any children with ASD can adapt to the school setting and learn a range of academic skills.

Social Learning Differences and Theory of Mind

The *DSM-5* identifies social communication and social interaction as core deficits in ASD. These include deficits in social–emotional reciprocity, deficits in nonverbal communicative behaviors used for social interaction, and deficits in developing, maintaining, and understanding relationships. Simon Baron-Cohen (2002) espoused the theory that male brains are organized to systematize, while female brains are better at empathizing. He and others characterize autism as the "extreme male brain." An fMRI study from UCLA (Dapretto et al., 2006) revealed reduced brain activity in the mirror-neuron system in the prefrontal cortex of individuals with ASD who lacked the ability to imitate others' facial expressions. In another study (Tabuchi et al., 2007), researchers were able to genetically engineer mice that were less social than their peers. While neuroscientists necessarily study the effects of brain mechanisms on specific aspects of social functioning, Pelphrey and Carter (2008) theorized that primary impairments in joint attention, action understanding and imitation, and early language functioning may give rise to higher-order deficits in some aspects of social interactions.

While science is still a long way from providing answers to the complex problem of social–behavioral differences in those with ASD, it is obvious that we see prominent differences in social understanding and behavior across the spectrum. Many children with ASD are affectionate and seek attention from their families and other children; however, they lack the smooth, continuous awareness of others and the ability to take another's perspective. Parents of very high-functioning children note the egocentric way their children view the world. One parent described it this way: "For my son, it's his way or the highway. It is all black and white with no shades of gray."

> Darryl, an adult with ASD, enjoys sending away for free promotional toys and buying children's items on sale. When his mother insisted that he clear out his room, he began bringing his treasures to me for my prize box or to add to my therapy materials. It was a win–win situation. He got to look at toys that he was clearly too old for, and I had the best-stocked prize box in the office. One day, as he was emptying the latest acquisitions into my prize box, another therapist came by. "Do you think that I could have a few of those things for my prize box?" she asked. Darryl glared at her and said loudly, "I don't think so!" and turned away. Later, when we talked about the effect of his social interchange, he was remorseful. He grabbed my prize box, sought her out, and proceeded to give her the items he had just given me.

True social competence depends on several elements:

• Flexible and ever-changing perceptions of ourselves and others

• Constantly taking in new information

• Making associations and comparisons with what is known about a particular person and about people in general

Most people spend their lives working on social skills. We inadvertently hurt people's feelings, say the wrong thing, or wonder how to approach someone about a thorny problem. For those with ASD, social exchanges are minefields that can blow up at any moment, and they rarely understand why.

> The father of a boy with ASD recognized characteristics of ASD in himself while his son was going through diagnostic evaluations. He was a minister, but churches never asked him to stay on for the long term. He gave wonderful, thoughtful, inspiring sermons, but he could never figure out the delicate church politics and inevitably offended the wrong person.

Early Social Learning

In typically developing children, evidence of social learning appears quite early. Infants respond to and mirror their caregivers' faces. They respond to voices and novel actions, and follow people with their eyes. Approximately 25% to 30% of children who are later diagnosed with ASD have typical early social development, only to regress in the second year of life (Rogers, 2004). Most, however, have subtle or apparent signs of social difficulties in their first year. These signs are easy to miss, since most—but not all—children with ASD achieve early developmental motor milestones on time. Sometimes the infants and toddlers are described as being "too good;" they are happy on their own and don't demand much attention. Others are "fussy babies" who aren't easily soothed. Some are "serious babies," who seldom smile in a social way. Some infants later diagnosed with ASD smile, but as one mother told me, "I was never sure what she was smiling about. It seemed disconnected." Many parents had suspicions that something just wasn't right, but it was easy to rationalize their fears away. They went for hearing evaluations because their children weren't responding to being called. They made adjustments to their children's sensitivities and figured out ways to make daily life go smoothly. They avoided situations they knew would be difficult for their children. They listened to the advice and/or critical comments of their families and wondered if they were just spoiling their children.

Because there is so much variability in the presentation of symptoms in preverbal or nonverbal children, it is helpful to look at specific behaviors on a continuum of frequency of occurrence. The Early Social Behaviors rating scale, located in the appendix to this chapter, can be used to evaluate early social behaviors in children. Although there is some variability in typical development, these social behaviors should develop by 9 to 12 months of age.

Joint attention is the ability to engage in interactions involving two individuals and an object. The infant needs to monitor the parent's attention to himself as well as monitor the parent's attention to the object they are both observing. This collaboration of two individuals is the basis of shared interests and experiences. Most typical 9-month-old children can engage in this social skill, but it is less frequently seen in those at risk for ASD.

Most typically developing infants are soothed by close proximity of the caregiver and by the caregiver's touch. They lean in comfortably when being carried or held. It is common for parents of children later diagnosed with ASD to report that their children were difficult to soothe, or that they had trouble relaxing to latch on to nurse. Some of these infants seemed happier when left alone in their crib.

Parents feel that the initial bonding that occurs with their infant has largely to do with eye contact. Newborns have been shown to look at faces whose eyes are open, and to look longer at faces whose gaze is direct rather than averted, but only when the faces are oriented in the upright position (Farroni, Csibra, Simion, & Johnson, 2002). In reviewing the brain research related to eye-gaze, Grossmann and Farroni (2009) concluded that the brain is tuned to notice gaze information from upright faces, but that as the infants develop, they learn to extract gaze information in other head positions. However, only frontal faces with direct gaze stimulate the brain to interpret eye contact as a communicative signal.

An infant's first smile is a joy to behold. Facial expressions and body positions and actions clearly communicate early emotions in a typical infant. Parents of many children later diagnosed with ASD often find their children hard to read. These children may seem overly serious and aloof (underreactive), or they may be sensory seeking or quick to cry (overreactive).

Imitation is a basic building block for the development of social reciprocity and empathy (Decety & Meyer 2009). When a baby imitates sounds or actions, she is reenacting her perception of what another person is doing. The baby learns to meet the expectations of others and to expect what others will do in response.

A baby's understanding of the relationship of a finger-point and eye-gaze to its target is important for language development (Baldwin & Moses, 1996). If the caregiver points and labels the object or emotional expression, the baby learns to make the association between the object and its name. This ability is enhanced if the caregiver first makes direct eye contact with the baby and talks to her while pointing. Some children who are later diagnosed with ASD have difficulty with these processes.

Early gestures are the basis for reciprocal communication in the preverbal child. In typical development a baby learns to affect another person's actions via direct gestures (such as reaching for an object) or symbolic gestures (such as raising arms to indicate "up"). The adult then responds to the gesture, and the interaction is completed. Children later diagnosed with ASD use gesture less frequently.

They often communicate by taking an adult's hand and placing it on the object they desire or by leading the adult to the place they want to go. One dad commented that his child used him as a "big robot slave" to get things he couldn't reach on his own. Caregivers should seek further evaluation and early intervention if there is concern about any of the items identified on the Early Social Behaviors rating scale.

> Percy had an older brother who was diagnosed with severe autism and an older sister whose development was typical. Understandably, Percy's parents scrutinized his every action from the day he was born. Percy's brother had been delayed in every developmental milestone, and the family was elated that Percy sat and crawled on time. They were worried, however, when Percy did not reach for the toys on his walker and when he stared at the flickering light coming through the blinds. By 7 months, Percy was enrolled in early intervention and later received an ASD diagnosis. Though his presentation was quite different from that of his brother, Percy's family was sensitive to the early social signs of ASD.

Higher-Level Social Learning

The demands on social interaction are not static and change throughout the lifespan. Parents train their young children to help them meet social customs. They teach them to greet and take leave of people even before they can talk. Waving "bye-bye" is a very early social behavior in typical 1-year-old children. Young children learn to share and say "Please" and "Thank you." They are taught not to hit or bite others. In preschool, children learn how to be part of a group and how to take turns. They work out social roles in their pretend play. Robert Fulghum's humorous book *All I Ever Really Needed to Know I Learned in Kindergarten* (originally published in 1986) contains many truths that reveal how we learned to get along in life. Children with ASD, however, even those who are quite high functioning, show deficits in critical social skills when compared to typical peers.

Theory of Mind

Children with ASD characteristically lack the ability to take the perspective of others during interactions. Baron-Cohen, Tager-Flusberg, and Cohen (1993); Wellman (1993); and others have studied how children with ASD differ from typical peers in developing *theory of mind* (ToM), a term referring to the ability to make sense of behavior related to mental states. (The term *mind blindness* has been used to describe difficulty with ToM.) ToM involves judging what another person believes to be true, what a person wants or desires, or what a person knows. It also involves judging whether someone is joking or teasing or whether she truly means what she says. Understanding one's own emotions and perceptions and those in others is essential to ToM.

The development of ToM is truly complex and involves many systems, not the least of which is language. Tager-Flusberg (1993) wrote that language is crucial in communicating "contents" of the mind of others and is the lens through which we view the child's developing ToM.

Wellman (1993) studied how ToM develops in typical children. He and his colleagues found that infants from birth to 6 months cry, smile, attend to faces, imitate, become attached, and interact reciprocally. Older infants begin attributing mental states to others and recognize mental states in themselves. They show us that they understand others' mental states through gaze, gesture, and joint attention. In the second year, children start to understand that others have personal experiences with objects in their personal space. They can find things that others have hidden. They know that an adult can reach something that they can't. They know that if Daddy puts on his coat, he is going outside. As language develops, children understand more about states that are absent or that exist in the past or the future. For example, a child at this stage can anticipate that if he hits his sister, she will cry and Mommy will be angry. They also use words to represent mental states, such as *sad, happy,* or *frightened.*

Wellman (1993) also found that 3- and 4-year-olds can understand that thoughts are held by other people. The Sally–Anne false belief test is a well-known assessment for determining a child's ability to understand what someone else believes to be true (false beliefs). This test depicts a little scenario that is acted out with puppets or with real people.

Sally and Anne are seated at a table. Sally has a basket in front of her, and Anne has a box in front of her. Sally puts a marble in her basket and leaves the room. While she is gone, Anne takes the marble and puts it in her box.

The question is then asked: When Sally comes back, where will Sally look for her marble?

Typical 3- and 4-year-old children can understand that Sally *thinks* the marble is in her basket because she *doesn't know* that Anne moved it. Studies of children with Down syndrome who function cognitively at the 3- and 4-year-old level can also understand this. Children with ASD, however, do not perform as well on this task and tend to reply that Sally will look in the box because that is where the marble "really is." Children with autism required nearly twice as high a verbal mental age to pass false belief tasks than did other subjects (Happé, 1995).

> I decided to try this task with Ben, a youngster with ASD, and his dad. We set up the Sally–Anne task with a ball, a basket, and a box. Dad put the ball in the basket and left the room. Ben switched the ball to the box. I then asked Ben, "Where will Dad look for the ball?" Ben answered, "The box." Thinking that perhaps the question form was the problem, I rephrased it. "Dad thinks the ball is in the _____." "The box," replied Ben. So we had Dad come in and asked, "Dad, where is the ball?" Dad made a great show of saying, "It's in the basket. I put it there myself." "No, it's not," said Ben, and he showed Dad that the ball was in the box. We then tried the routine again, thinking that this time, Ben would understand. He kept saying that Dad would look in the box, because that was where the ball really was. Finally, when Dad left the room again after having put the ball in the basket, I said to Ben, "Let's trick Dad. He put the ball in the basket and we're moving it to the box. We'll trick him." When it was framed as a trick, Ben finally understood.
>
> As we get older, we are expected to have a greater understanding about people in general and the reactions of particular people. I recently fielded a phone call from a graduate student with ASD who had just had an unpleasant altercation with her mother. "I just don't get it," she told me. "My mom expects me to know stuff that she didn't tell me. She says I should just know. How can I know if she doesn't tell me?"

Hobson (1989) believes there are "prewiring" capacities for perception of and responsiveness to the bodily expressed attitudes of other people. More recent neurological and genetic research is supporting this notion. Carver and Cornew (2009) proposed the hypothesis that a complex neural system underlies social information gathering and that the component parts of this system emerge separately and gradually through the course of development. Mind blindness and poor ToM development may be, according to some, a primary deficit in ASD. It is a deficit with a combination of strands, however. Visual perception, body awareness, sensory integration, associative and executive functions, and language all play a part in the ability to perceive mental states.

Language, Conversation, and the Development of Social Skills

Typical children seem to have innate capacities for social learning; while they need to be taught specific skills, the impulse to use these skills comes from within. Children with ASD also need specific social skills instruction, yet they do not seem to possess the innate social impulse to use these skills to interact with others. Some children with ASD seem to want social contact, but it is usually on their own terms or to satisfy their own needs.

> Clyde has learned to ask questions about other people, but he really doesn't care to listen to the answer. He'd rather bring up a topic of interest to him.

Language is a major currency in social skill development, and social use of language is affected by gestalt processing. Gestalt processing reduces flexibility in comprehension and expression. Literal interpretations may lead to misunderstandings. Gestalt processors have difficulty discerning the nuances of meaning and intention. They may have difficulty combining language patterns to express what they really want to say. They may also have difficulty listening to what is said and figuring out the meaning at the same time.

> Darryl and I watch videos to analyze people's interactions and to get him to understand the plot of a story. When I stop the video and ask what just happened, he often repeats the last thing that was said and can't tell what led up to it. He can repeat the sentence but doesn't know what it means in the context of the story.

Having a social conversation taxes the abilities of even the most verbal individuals with ASD. The items in Table 2.1, discussed below, are just a fraction of the communication skills necessary for smooth social conversations.

Social Precursors

What is going on in the environment? Are we at school, in the park, in an office? Who is the person I'm talking to in relation to me? Is it a peer, a teacher, my boss? Each scenario would need to be approached in a different way.

> J.J., a young adult with ASD, loved to greet people he saw at work. He often read the names on their nametags and would say, "Hi, Dave," as he walked by. When the head of the company walked by, J.J.'s well-intentioned greeting of "Hi, Mort," was perceived as being rude. "Everyone" knew that the boss was a formal person and wanted to be addressed as Dr. Doe. Everyone knew but J.J. Once J.J. was told how to address the CEO, he never again made that mistake.

Topic Introduction

Is the topic appropriate to the place and the listener? How do you start talking to someone? Do you ask a question? Do you make a comment?

Table 2.1
Factors That Influence Communication

1. Social precursors	9. Intonation and loudness
2. Topic introduction	10. Conversational repair
3. Topic maintenance	11. Literal interpretation of language
4. Conversational transitions	12. Appropriateness
5. Listening behaviors	13. Small talk
6. Interrupting politely	14. Social customs
7. Feedback	15. Humor
8. Turn taking and social reciprocity	

> Mike learned that no one in high school wanted to talk about Thomas the Tank Engine, so he learned to inhibit his impulse to start a conversation about the train. When he went to college, we suggested that Japanese animé may be a topic that some other students would like to talk about, so Mike joined the Animé Club. When I asked what the club members do, Mike told me that someone brings a video or DVD and they all watch it. "Do you talk about the story?" I asked. "No," said Mike. "We just watch it from beginning to end." It appears that Mike has found his group.

Many children with ASD just begin talking, and the listener has to try to figure out what they are talking about. Parents may know what the reference is because they know the child's experience, but the child does not realize that others have not shared his experience.

> Austin came into school one day saying, "The bus driver said 'Beat it. Get off the bus.'" His teacher was alarmed, but the other children told her that nothing had happened on the bus that day. Austin was reciting the script from the movie *Home Alone 2*. We helped Austin use the phrase, "In the movie . . . ," to introduce the topic.

Topic Maintenance

A conversation with someone with ASD can turn on a word. You may be talking about a toy car and suddenly find yourself listening to a list of car makes and models. The problem may be that it is hard for the person with ASD to figure out the topic, so she responds to a detail or a word that takes her in another direction. If you think about it, you can follow the connection, but it makes the social interchange quite odd. Because of their difficulty in following the topic, many people with ASD keep returning to their own favorite topics.

> *The Simpsons* television show is a favorite of many teens with ASD. I often try to broaden the teens' fund of knowledge by bringing up current events or social issues, many of which have been subjects of *The Simpsons* segments. I thought I was having a wonderful conversation about religion with one boy, when I realized that he was quoting Homer and Bart from the TV show.

Conversational Transitions

Typical conversations flow freely from one topic to the next and sometimes return several times within an interchange of a few minutes. Typical speakers indicate transitions and topic changes with phrases such as "That reminds me" or by asking a question such as "Did you hear about . . .?" The timing of conversational transitions is important, and nonverbal cues like nodding or eye-gaze shifts may accompany the transition. This task is difficult for even the most verbal people with ASD.

> Marty was working on topic maintenance. He'd practiced staying on topic for four to five interchanges. One day he had something important to tell me and asked, "Can I change the topic now?"

Listening Behaviors

People who work with children with ASD often complain that they can't tell whether the children have not heard what they said, are ignoring them, or do not understand. Many times these children have heard just fine and will respond or do what was asked after a few moments. "Good listeners" display certain behaviors that are absent in those with ASD. These behaviors include nodding, showing eye-gaze, joint attending, shifting attention, or giving a quick verbal response ("okay," "yes," "mm-hmm"). Sometimes it takes longer for a child with ASD to respond because it takes her longer to process what she heard.

> Sean's parents were frustrated that he would not respond to the simplest verbal requests the first time. When asked to get his shoes, Sean would have a vacant stare. His parents would repeat their request over and over until Sean finally moved to get his shoes. They felt that he understood, but he just wasn't listening to them. Then they tried an experiment. They made their request once and then waited. Sure enough, after nearly a minute, Sean went over to get his shoes. Maybe it took him that long to process the request and organize himself to comply, but his parents now knew that he heard and understood even though he didn't appear to.

Interrupting Politely

Parents of toddlers complain that they can never talk on the phone without their children constantly interrupting and demanding attention. Gaining someone's attention in an appropriate and polite way is a skill that typical children eventually learn but few with ASD have mastered. The art of interrupting depends on reading the person's body language, using nonverbal cues to call attention, and using polite forms such as "Pardon me" or "Excuse me." It involves understanding the needs and situation of others.

> Darryl would come into the office and immediately start asking questions of the office staff in a loud voice. He took no notice of whether they were on the phone, talking to another person, or engrossed in work. In his mind, he was being friendly and communicative.

Feedback

When two people are in a conversation, they each need to show the other that they have understood what was said and what was meant. Listening indicators such as nodding or saying "Uh-huh" are only part of it. Feedback also involves asking follow-up questions, paraphrasing what the speaker said, making appropriate comments, and, in many small ways, showing the speaker respect and regard. You can imagine how difficult this task must be for even the most able people with ASD.

> When the father of a child with ASD was himself diagnosed with ASD, his wife told me this story. As many couples do, they fell into a pattern of talking while they were washing dishes or straightening up after they had put the children to sleep. For years, the wife had been quite frustrated that her husband didn't respond appropriately to her concerns and

problems when she talked to him at the end of the day. She knew he cared, but he just didn't show it. After the diagnosis, the wife realized that her husband could not do two things at once. He could not do the dishes and attend well to conversation at the same time. Now if there is something serious they need to discuss, they choose a quiet place with no distractions and concentrate solely on talking and listening.

Turn Taking and Social Reciprocity

Young children learn social turn taking through structured play and games. Usually an adult must do the initial teaching of this skill and enforce it when disagreements occur. As we mature, turn taking takes on subtler forms and is known as *social reciprocity*. Reciprocity may occur within a conversation, but it also occurs in the grand scheme of social interactions. It involves knowing that you need to give as well as take in a relationship. It means understanding that when you see a person with her arms full of packages, you should hold the door open for her. Reciprocity is the currency of social niceties that improves relationships with others (e.g., bringing cookies for the morning coffee break at work).

Robby understood about presents and birthdays, but when he was asked to choose a present for a girl in his class, he chose something he liked—a big dinosaur—and then did not want to give it to her.

Arthur went to a church group every Wednesday evening where the members each brought some food to share. Arthur never brought anything. He just didn't think about it. The members, realizing that Arthur lacked some social graces, finally asked Arthur to bring a bottle of soda to the next meeting. Arthur was happy to do so, and he brought a small bottle of soda, just for himself. The others realized that they had to be more specific with Arthur and asked him to bring a 2-liter bottle of soda to the next meeting. Again, Arthur was happy to do so. Even after that, unless he was asked directly, he never thought to bring anything on his own.

Intonation and Loudness

Those with ASD often have difficulty monitoring the loudness of their speech and judging how loudly or softly to speak in given situations. Their prosody or intonation patterns may have a sing-song quality, or they may speak in a monotone. While they may say the right thing, the message that they convey may contradict their words. Volume and intonation are so automatic that they are hard to bring under conscious control.

Alex often appears to be shouting, even when I am sitting right next to him in a quiet room. With a cue, he can tone it down, but invariably in a few minutes he is talking loudly again. Alex has been working on varying his intonation pattern, and he can do it while reading aloud, but he still has trouble in conversation.

Conversational Repair

We all have said the wrong thing at one time or another. We've also misunderstood what someone has said or meant. To make amends, we apologize for the misunderstanding, clarify what we meant, or ask the other person for clarification. These language functions present difficulties for those with ASD.

In a social language group for young teens with ASD, Shauna told her friends that her favorite color was pink and that nearly all her clothes were pink. When Peter said that he did not like pink and that he wouldn't be caught dead in pink, Shauna started to cry. Peter was mystified. He didn't care if Shauna liked pink, but Shauna thought he was criticizing her. When an adult tried to mediate and get them to repair their conversation, Peter couldn't understand why repair was needed. He said, "I just told the truth. I hate pink. She likes it. So what?" Shauna couldn't separate herself from her choice and wouldn't budge either. She told Peter that if he didn't like pink, he was not her friend.

Literal Interpretation of Language

Idioms and figures of speech present problems for those with ASD. The idea that you can say one thing and mean another is confusing, particularly in a social situation that requires a quick response. People with ASD tend to interpret statements and directions in their most concrete ways, understanding black and white but not shades of gray. Their confusions are humorous in the retelling, but they are often embarrassing when it happens.

> The teacher was getting irritated because Audrey moved so slowly. "Come on, Audrey," she said. "Get your math book out now. Step on it!" Audrey did just that.

> My husband was instrumental in helping J.J., a young adult with ASD, obtain a good job, complete with benefits. J.J. was so grateful that he thanked my husband profusely each time he saw him. After a while, it began to get on my husband's nerves, and he asked me what to do about it. "Tell him that you are happy that he likes his job, but that he need not thank you over and over. Tell him to say thank you only once a day," I suggested. J.J. followed my husband's suggestions, and the problem was solved. After several weeks, however, my husband got a voice-mail message from J.J. "I'm sorry, Dr. Kupperman," he said. "I think I thanked you twice yesterday."

Appropriateness

We all must learn that appropriate behavior and communication vary in different situations and with different people. Topics that may be appropriate with peers may not be appropriate at work or at school. We learn how to dress and act appropriately for the occasion. Many people with ASD wish for a "rule book" that would outline what they should or should not do or talk about. Unfortunately, because the rules are so subtle and vary so widely, such a book would probably have a thousand pages.

> I had just heard a wonderful, insightful presentation by a well-known man with ASD at a national convention. Later, as I was standing with some colleagues at lunch, he came up close to us, pointed his finger at my sandwich, and with no preamble asked loudly, "Was that sandwich free, or did you have to pay for it?"

> There is an entire discipline devoted to appropriate behavior in a public restroom. Since most individuals with ASD are males, and since most of the therapists and teachers who work with them are females, I thought it would be a good idea to understand the rules that govern the men's room. My male resources told me that there are unspoken rules as to where to stand, where to look, and whether it is okay to acknowledge another guy. The rules are different for younger boys at school vs. adolescents vs. college students. The best advice came from a firefighter who spent many days and nights with his male colleagues. He stated that it was always appropriate to use the stall rather than the urinal.

Small Talk

Have you ever gone to a party where you knew no one? How did you start a conversation? What did you talk about? How did you pick a likely person to talk to? Navigating this social scene presents many challenges for those with ASD of all ages. Young children must learn that bodily functions or family arguments are not great topics for the lunch bunch. Teens with ASD need to realize that a monologue on laundry detergents may not be of interest to everyone at school. They need to learn how to add appropriate comments to ongoing conversations.

> The lunchroom supervisor overheard this conversation between a boy with ASD and his peer buddy. "I hate the smell of this chili," said the peer buddy. "It makes me sick." Taking his cue from the word *sick*, the boy responded. "I got sick last night. I had diarrhea, and it got all over and. . . ." He went on and on without missing one gross detail.

> Austin is not at all interested in sports, but because it is the hot topic in his peer group, his parents make sure that he knows if the home team won or lost the big game. He doesn't know how to comment about the game, however. He might say, "The Bears lost yesterday. Losing is okay. Some teams lose."

Social Customs

Social customs develop in cultures and ethnic groups, in regions of a city, in schools, in families, and in peer groups. In some groups, it is customary for men to hug, but in others it is taboo. Some families are very vocal about their complaints and don't hesitate to discuss personal issues, and others are very private. When trying to help a child with ASD observe social customs, we need to be aware of the child's cultural background and the family's preferences.

> Mikhal, a teen with ASD, had gone to a Jewish parochial elementary school. The high school that provided the best program for him was a Catholic school that required that he take religion classes. Mikhal, who took his religion very seriously, made sure all of his teachers knew he was Jewish and that he didn't believe what they believed and that was okay. His teachers all knew because Mikhal informed them each and every school day.

Humor

Many people with ASD develop a sense of humor. They may find physical mishaps or blunders funny yet may not easily understand the references in puns. Typical children begin to learn about puns through knock-knock jokes and riddles. Children with ASD learn that they are supposed to laugh at the end of the joke, but they don't know why. In addition, they may not understand that humor must be shared.

> It took a lot of explaining before Wade understood why it was okay to laugh when the Three Stooges fell down but not when the principal slipped on the ice on the sidewalk.

> The knock-knock joke made up by a child with ASD and hyperlexia was:

> *Knock, knock*

> *Who's there?*

> *T*

> *T who?*

> *T U V*

> Actually, that child made up 25 such jokes, but he couldn't do one for Z because nothing follows Z.

I will be having a conversation with Al and without apparent reason, he'll start chuckling to himself. When I ask him why, he'll often say that he is thinking of a funny scene in his favorite movie, completely without reference to the topic of conversation. "It's okay," he tells me. "It's just humor."

By recognizing and understanding the learning-style differences in those with ASD, we can devise effective strategies to help them learn language and communication, reading and math, and social competencies. With natural neurological development and with effective, focused treatment, most people with ASD improve as they get older. Their learning-style differences, however, remain constant.

Chapter 2 Appendix

Early Social Behaviors Rating Scale

The earliest social indicators are easy to miss because they are reduced or absent in children who are later diagnosed with autism. Evaluate the child at 9 months. Indicate how often the child displays each behavior. If the child obtains a rating of Never or Seldom on any item, consider it a red flag and seek further evaluation.

	Never	Seldom	Sometimes	Often	Usually
Joint Attention • If a toy, book, or food item is presented, will the child look at it along with an adult?					
Proximity • Will the child tolerate or seek closeness to an adult or another child?					
Eye-Gaze • Is the child drawn to looking at adults' faces? • Does the child look at someone who is trying to engage him/her?					
Body Language • Does the child's body posture and position communicate his/her state of mind? • Does the child show interest, joy, fatigue, or irritability with his or her demeanor?					
Imitation • Does the child imitate actions, gestures, or sounds?					
Reciprocity • Does the child engage in back-and-forth actions or play? • Does the child give and take food or a toy? • Does the child try to continue a simple game like peek-a-boo?					
Following the "Point" • Will the child direct his/her attention to something an adult points to in a book (close by) or in the distance? • Is the child aware that the adult wants him/her to look?					
Gesture • Will the child use a gesture to indicate a desire or need? • Will the child raise his or her hand to indicate "up"?					

© 2017 by PRO-ED, Inc.

Chapter 3

Intervention Strategies Begin With the Child

There are many issues to think about when developing strategies for working with children with ASD. The problems are complex and the choices are not always straightforward. There are many treatment options for children with ASD. How can parents, SLPs, teachers, and therapists choose strategies and develop tactics for a particular child with ASD? It is not an easy task.

Starting with the child may seem obvious, but when a child is diagnosed with ASD, the immediate reaction is "What can we do about it?" Knowing that early intervention is important, families are eager to find treatments. Using the Internet, parents quickly get up to speed on intervention programs and begin to search for therapists and practitioners. While it is true that treatment can begin before the child is thoroughly assessed, it is best to stop, take a breath, and take a good look at the child. Since this is a spectrum disorder, by definition children do not all have the same presentation. Each child has a unique set of strengths and weaknesses. Symptoms may be mild or severe. Behaviors may occur with varying rates of frequency. Comorbid symptoms may be present or absent. Remember that this is a child with ASD who is in many ways the same as any other child his age. Characteristics of ASD may be problematic, but they are human characteristics, often recognizable in some form in all of us.

The Child's Family

Many parents divide their child's life and their own lives into two sections: before and after the ASD diagnosis. For some parents, their reaction to a diagnosis is relief. They finally have a name for their child's puzzling behaviors. In their heart of hearts they knew that something was not right. Now that their suspicions are confirmed, they know they have not caused the behaviors and they are not inept parents. They can get to work developing intervention strategies. For other parents, the news is devastating. They recognized the difficulties but hoped their child would grow out of them. They mourn the loss of their dreams for a healthy, typical child. They too begin to develop intervention strategies, but their mission is often to find that elusive cure.

Regardless of where parents begin, they are on the ASD journey. Along the way there will be frustrations and triumphs, tears and laughter, and an emotional roller coaster involving their circle of family and friends. The most important thing to remember is that their child is just the same the day after the diagnosis as he was the day before the diagnosis. The child does not know or care that there is now a diagnosis and a label. That child has the same toothy grin, the same sleepy smell, the same furious temper, and the same special rituals. It is time for parents to chart their course and assemble their crew.

A Team Approach

During or after the ASD diagnosis process, parents seek out advice, counsel, evaluations, and treatment from a variety of professionals. Within the first year, most families have had at least three consultations in addition to evaluations by early intervention programs or by their school district.

My message to parents is to listen to everything that any professional tells them and filter that information through what they know about their own child. They must gain confidence in their own ability to judge what is best for their child since they know their child better than anyone else. What professionals have to offer is expertise, information, research, and experience with many children.

My message to professionals is to listen to the parents, since they live with their child day in and day out. Professionals must show parents that they are knowledgeable, but open to input. They must put aside their biases and work in the best interests of the child and the family. They must recognize that they are not experts at everything and should make referrals when necessary. Because there are no easy answers as to what to do for children with ASD, it is best when parents and professionals embark on this journey together.

What do you need to know to plan an intervention strategy? A diagnostic label, especially one as broad as ASD, is not enough information to plan intervention for a particular child. The measures described in Chapter 1 are designed to determine whether the child's presentation warrants an ASD diagnosis. We need to know much more about how the child learns and functions in order to design and apply intervention strategies.

A psychiatrist, psychologist, developmental pediatrician, neurologist, or SLP with expertise in the field of ASD may make the original diagnosis. The intervention plan is usually designed by providers such as SLPs, OTs, and special educators. Each one will do an initial evaluation, either independently or as part of a team. The evaluation may consist of a structured or informal observation and, if the child is able, formal tests.

Initial Evaluation

Evaluating children with ASD is a daunting task. Each child is unique. Behavior may be challenging. Parents may be stressed. Nothing may go as planned. It is often helpful to have a format to ensure that key information is obtained. Use the Child Evaluation for Autism Spectrum Disorder form provided in the appendix to Chapter 3 to help organize your information and observations. Send the Intake Information and Medical/Developmental History sections (Parts 1 and 2) to the parents, and have the parents return the form before the initial evaluation meeting. The team should use the Formal Testing form (Part 3) to consider which types of formal tests are appropriate. They can use the guidelines in the Chapter 3 Appendix for structuring observations and for providing feedback to the family.

Intake Information and Medical/Developmental History Forms

Information can be gathered using the Intake Information and Medical/Developmental History sections (Parts 1 and 2) that the parents or guardians fill out. Send the forms to the parents/guardians via email, fax, or snail mail when the initial evaluation appointment is made, and request that they complete and return them before the appointment. The information will be valuable in planning the evaluation. Review any reports of previous evaluations or treatment summaries provided by the parents/guardians. No matter how much information is gathered beforehand, it is helpful during the evaluation to ask the child's caretakers to "tell their story," cite their concerns, and explain why they are seeking this evaluation. Be an active listener, and use the forms as a springboard for further questions.

Formal Testing

Formal testing should be completed, if possible. Several sessions may be needed. In some settings the evaluation may be performed by a team of professionals, either as a group or in series.

Some young children need time to warm up to, or acclimate to, a new person in a new setting. In that case, begin the evaluation by talking to the parents for a short time, and then have them facilitate the interactions with the child. Other children need attention immediately. In that case, focus on the child first, and talk to the parents later. A written list or picture schedule often works to help the child make transitions between activities. A favorite activity can be put at the end of the list as a "reward" for completing the tasks.

It is often helpful for the parents to stay in the room during formal testing. They know their child best and often can be helpful in gaining the child's cooperation. Rely on the parents to provide tangible rewards and to signal when breaks are needed. Sometimes the child is distracted by the presence of their parents. In that case, parents can be close by, in an observation room or just outside the door, so they can be on call when needed.

Standardized tests are given in a prescribed way, and scores are compared to norms based on same-age peers. Some tests are criterion referenced. Scores are compared to a predetermined set of standards. There are specific tests to measure all aspects of language, motor, and sensory functioning and academic readiness and achievement. There are also cognitive tests, using either verbal or nonverbal means, to estimate a child's intelligence.

It is important to remember that children with ASD do not learn in a typical developmental sequence. Chapter 2 describes how they may excel in some aspects of language, cognition, or social learning, but may have great difficulty with other concepts that typically develop earlier. Some may identify colors, numbers, letters, and shapes, but not body parts or farm animals. They may recite video scripts, but not be able to tell their own names. Others may figure out how to open a complicated child safety lock, but be unable to do a simple puzzle.

Test Format

It is important to select tests that best illustrate a child's strengths and weaknesses. Single-word receptive or expressive vocabulary tests may sample a child's strengths in a way that a more general language test would not. The stimulus phrase used on various test items may affect the child's ability to respond. Because their language learning is so specific, some children may respond to the stimulus "Touch the ____," but not "Show me the ____," or "Where is the ____?" Some reading comprehension tests rely solely on question forms that may be difficult for children with ASD. They may respond better to tests with matching tasks or a fill-in-the-blank format. Some children do better with items using photographs, and others do better with simple drawings. In some cases, the child can actually perform the task but does not understand the verbal directions or is not able to respond within the time constraints of the test.

Test Organization

Many standardized tests are organized so that each successive item is more difficult. In many presentations, a child must correctly respond to a set number of test items in a row to achieve a basal (or base score). The child then must miss a set number of items in a row to achieve a ceiling (the point at which the test is discontinued). Children with ASD can become frustrated when they think they have missed an item. Many do not like to guess. They either know the answer or they don't, and they may not want to continue beyond their comfort zone.

Often, parents are confused about their child's test results. One child scored at the 2-year-old level on a standard language test but knew many more complicated words than the average 2-year-old; on the other hand, the child was not really communicating with those words and couldn't ask for more juice the way other 2-year-olds do. Another child's cognitive standard score was 75, in the below-average range, yet he could do math problems in his head at age 4.

Test Administration

In my experience, some higher-functioning children with ASD become quite adept at test taking. They actually love the process, and their scores are quite high. The problem is that they do not function as well in real life. Others do not do as well as they potentially could because of anxiety about their test performance or because they are unfamiliar with the examiner or the therapy room. Parents and the examiner must help a child feel comfortable and motivate the child to perform. Lists, visual schedules, rewards, and bribes are sometimes successful. If a child is not able to sit at the table for the duration of the formal test, the test can be administered on the floor or while the child is standing next to the table. Frequent sensory breaks may be necessary. The pacing of the presentation of the test items should meet a child's needs. Some children need extra time to process what they hear. Others need more rapid presentations so that they do not lose attention. In order to get a more complete picture of a child's abilities, some examiners will present test items in the standard way but will probe later to see if the child can perform similar tasks in a different format.

Parents are present during most of my evaluations, either in the same room or watching behind a one-way mirror. As an examiner, I find this helpful in so many ways. Parents already know some tricks to get their child to cooperate. They know the subtle signals that indicate whether the child is just not tuning in or whether she needs to use the toilet. They can tell me whether the child's behavior is typical or whether the child is more or less responsive than usual. It is also eye-opening to the parents to see how their child responds to the testing. Sometimes they are amazed that their child can answer, and sometimes they are dismayed at the difficulties.

Parents can also provide valuable background information. One parent commented, "I'm not surprised that Stuart did not respond to the questions about the lawn mower. We live in a big-city high-rise apartment. I'm sure he's never seen a lawn mower before." That comment offered the opportunity for me to explain that typical children can respond to items with which they have had no direct experience because they are able to pick up concepts and vocabulary from the background or from books or television. Children with ASD have greater difficulty doing that, so direct experience is much more important for them.

Test Results

Regardless of the problems with standardized testing, the tests can yield valuable information about a child's capabilities and weaknesses. The results of testing can be a road map for developing intervention strategies. They can indicate what a child is expected to do at a certain age and help in developing strategies to fill the gaps.

Tables 3.1–3.3 show a variety of testing results for three different students with ASD. Table 3.1 shows the results from the *Wechsler Intelligence Scale for Children–Fifth Edition* (WISC-V; Wechsler, 2013) for a student, GQ. In GQ's test scores, the composite scores give a skewed view of his abilities. The subtest scores provide a better picture of strengths and weaknesses. In the verbal comprehension subtest, GQ was capable of defining isolated words presented and was able to see concrete relations among words. When presented with more abstract language or required to comprehend social situations, GQ lacked the ability to use language within a social context as required in the comprehension subtest. On the memory subtests, GQ did well on rote tasks, but when higher-level associations and cognitive shifting were required on the letter–number sequencing task, difficulty with attention and impulsivity interfered with his ability to retain and manipulate information presented orally.

Table 3.2 shows the results from the *Test of Semantic Skills–Primary* (TOSS-P; Bowers, Huisingh, LoGiudice, & Orman, 2002) for the student JT, age 4 years 0 months. In JT's test scores, one very high score in the Stating Categories subtest skews the composite totals and makes it appear

Table 3.1
Test Results for GQ, a Student With ASD[a]

GQ, age 9-2

Index scale	Composite	%ile	Interpretation
Verbal Comprehension	87	19	Low average
Visual Spatial	74	4	Borderline
Fluid Reasoning	73[b]	4	Borderline
Working Memory	74	4	Borderline
Processing Speed	73	4	Borderline
Full Scale	72[b]	3	Borderline

Subtests	Scaled score
Verbal Comprehension	
Similarities	10
Vocabulary	8
Information	7
Comprehension	5
Visual Spatial	
Block Design	6
Visual Puzzles	7
Fluid Reasoning	
Matrix Reasoning	6
Figure Weights	6
Picture Concepts	5
Working Memory	
Digit Span	10
Picture Span	8
Letter–Number Sequencing	1
Processing Speed	
Coding	4
Symbol Search	6

[a]*Wechsler Intelligence Scale for Children—Fifth Edition* (WISC-V; Wechsler, 2013).
[b]May be minimal estimate, as GQ has difficulty completing timed tasks.

that expressive function is much higher than receptive function. It is important to note that JT had been working on categories in therapy. Because categories had been specifically taught, the score is probably not representative of overall functioning.

Even when using checklists completed through observation and parent report, scores may reveal areas of strength. The results from the *Rossetti Infant-Toddler Language Scale* (Rossetti, 2006)

Table 3.2
Test Results for JT, a Student With ASD[a]

JT, age 4-0

Subtest	Standard score
Identifying Labels	99
Identifying Categories	107
Identifying Attributes	80
Identifying Functions	90
Identifying Definitions	86
RECEPTIVE TOTAL	90
Stating Labels	104
Stating Categories	133
Stating Attributes	100
Stating Functions	83
Stating Definitions	98
EXPRESSIVE TOTAL	106
TOTAL TEST	98

[a]*Test of Semantic Skills–Primary* (TOSS-P; Bowers, Huisingh, LoGiudice, & Orman, 2002).

and the *Hawaii Early Learning Profile* (HELP; Warshaw, 1992–2006) for the student DH are shown in Table 3.3. This child is minimally verbal, but his skills are not evenly delayed. His play skills are a relative strength at the 18-month level on the Rosetti, his social–emotional profile is at the 19-month level on the HELP, and his gross motor skills at the 24-month level on the HELP are not considered delayed.

Despite the scientific basis for the creation of test items, the statistical analyses, the reliability and validity measures, and the normative data gathered, giving formal tests to children with ASD and interpreting the results may be more of an art than a science. If formal testing is not feasible, valuable information can also be gleaned from careful observations of the child and parent/teacher reports.

Observations

Observational data can be gathered directly by watching a child in a variety of situations or gathered indirectly via reports by family, caregivers, and/or teachers. The ADOS, described in Chapter 1, is a very reliable semistructured observation designed for diagnostic purposes. It determines whether the child meets criteria for an ASD diagnosis. Further observational data are necessary to plan interventions, however. A child's behavior may vary in different settings. Some children do well with adults in a quiet setting but look quite different when they are in a noisy group of peers. Others become reticent or anxious during testing because they fear making mistakes, yet are warm and communicative with their siblings. In an ideal world, it would be wonderful to observe a child in natural interactions at school and at home, in addition to in the evaluation setting. When it is not possible to observe a child at school and at home, we need to rely on parent, caretaker, and

Table 3.3

Test Results for DH, a Student With ASD[a, b]

DH, age 30 months

Subtest	Age performance
Interaction/Attachment	12 months
Pragmatics	12 months
Gestures	12 months
Play	18 months
Language Comprehension	12 months
Language Expression	12 months

Subtest	Age equivalency	Percent delay (0%–29% is not a delay)
Cognitive	15 months	50
Communication	14 months	>50
Gross Motor	24 months	20
Fine Motor	15 months	50
Social/Emotional	19 months	37
Self-Help/Adaptive	12 months	>50

[a]*Rossetti Infant-Toddler Language Scale* (Rossetti, 2006). [b]*Hawaii Early Learning Profile* (HELP) (Warshaw, 1992–2006).

teacher reports. Always ask the parents if the child's behavior in the evaluation is typical of what they see in other settings. Observe the child's interactions in the office waiting room as well as in the evaluation room. Allow the child some downtime, to watch the child's actions when he or she is not directly engaged. Use the questions in Part 4 of the Appendix to Chapter 3 to guide your observations.

Here are some examples of information to gather through observation.

- During the evaluation, was the child calm or excitable, attentive or distractible?

- Could the child regulate himself, or did he need an adult to help? Was the child able to be soothed by his parents? What worked or didn't work?

- Did the child visually reference the adults? Did she look at something that was pointed to? Did he engage in eye contact? Did the child show various facial expressions?

- How did the child respond to various approaches by the examiner—verbal, demonstration, hand-over-hand?

- Did the child's parents use specific words or gestures to elicit responses?

- What materials (if any) did the child gravitate to? Did the child show competence in using the materials? Did the child show pleasure when engaging in the materials?

- What was the nature of his spontaneous communications—words, pointing, hand-pulling?

- Could the child attend to anything for a period of time? Was there joint attention?

- Could the child's attention be shifted using a verbal cue, or were visual prompts needed?
- Did the child understand and/or comply with requests?
- What did the child do when not directly engaged?
- Were there restricted or repetitive behaviors, and if so, did they interfere with completing a task or attending to a toy?
- Was the observed behavior typical of the child?

Observations at Play

In addition to materials used in formal testing, it is helpful to have a few special toys and activities available for children functioning at various levels. These materials can be used to judge learning styles and response patterns.

My bag of tricks for young or lower-functioning children includes a ball ramp, balloons to fly, long-lasting bubbles from Gymboree, an alphabet puzzle, sponge blocks, a pop-up book, a lift-the-flap book, a reaction toy (a jack-in-the-box, a busy-box, or the Don't Wake Daddy game by Hasbro), and a radio-controlled car. For children who are interested in letters and numbers or who are reading and spelling, I have a basket of plastic magnetic letters and/or I introduce them to a text-to-speech app on an iPad that says or sings the words that have been typed. I teach older children to play the card game Blink or a game on the iPad to see how quickly they pick it up.

Observations in Conversation

It is always interesting to engage verbal children, adolescents, and adults in conversations about their special interests. You can see how they react when you add information, change the direction of the conversation, or contradict them. You can see how they answer a variety of questions and how long they stay engaged in the conversation. Look for these behaviors as the conversation goes along:

- Was eye-gaze appropriate?
- How did the individual initiate a conversation (e.g., asking a question, making a request, introducing the topic, launching into a monologue)?
- Was the topic of interest to others in the conversation, or did the individual talk only about idiosyncratic interests?
- Did the individual stand too close or too far from the conversational partner?
- Was the intonation pattern monotonous or singsong?
- Did the individual speak too loudly or too softly for the situation?
- Did gestures and body language match the verbal message?
- How did the individual indicate that he or she was listening to others?
- Did the individual appear to share enjoyment in the conversation?

Darryl, an adult with ASD, has a wealth of information about trivia, but it is hard to listen to what he has to say. He is a tall person, and he often stands with his feet apart and his belly pushed forward, pointing with his index finger as he speaks loudly. This combination of behaviors makes the listener feel besieged rather than engaged.

Observations in the Classroom

If it is possible, an observation in the child's classroom is always enlightening. Seeing a child in a group of children is quite different from an observation in a one-to-one setting.

- Did the child initiate interactions with other children?
- Did the child respond to the approaches of others?
- Did the child respond to group instruction?
- Did the child follow classroom routines and/or follow the rules of a game?
- Could the child complete a task independently?
- Describe the child's attention and/or distractibility patterns.
- Describe any behavioral issues and how they were handled.
- What accommodations have been put in place to help the child?

> Recently I evaluated several children who were gestalt processors of language but had very few other symptoms of ASD. When I saw them individually and compared them to children who are more severely affected, they looked quite good. When I observed them in their classroom and compared them to their typical peers, the symptoms were more obvious. Although they were responsive to the teachers, they rarely interacted verbally with the other children. They seemed to be on the fringes of the classroom activities, rather than being direct participants. When they did try to participate, their questions and comments were often slightly off target.

Observations Using Checklists and Questionnaires

Checklists or questionnaires filled out by parents, caregivers, or teachers can yield useful information. There are published checklists, rating scales, and questionnaires, such as the *Children's Communication Checklist–Second Edition* (CCC-2; Bishop, 2003), for obtaining observations of pragmatic, semantic, and nonverbal communication. Many professionals use one of their own design and may include these questions:

- What are the child's eating and sleeping habits?
- How does the child communicate wants and needs?
- Are there sensory sensitivities?
- What works to teach the child something new?
- What does the child like to do?
- What frustrates the child?
- What is soothing to the child?
- Is there a special song the child likes, or does the child hate it when people sing?
- What routines have been developed at home or at school?
- What happens when these routines are changed?
- Does the child have any unexpected strengths?
- What is most challenging or worrisome about this child?
- What is delightful about this child?

It is a mistake to focus only on what the child cannot do. It is important that checklists or questionnaires gather information about positive attributes of the child as well as outline deficit areas. The positives can be used as building blocks when designing strategies. The observation tools can help give family, professionals, and educators a balanced view of the child and a starting place for therapy.

> One teacher wrote that she had been limiting her barely verbal preschool student's choices of play materials because she felt he was "stimming" on looking at letters, numbers, and words. Then one day he took the days of the week cards and arranged them in order. At first she thought it was a fluke, so she mixed up the cards and the child arranged them in order again several more times. When she carefully observed what he was doing with letters, numbers, and word cards, she revised her intervention strategy to include this unexpected strength. As a result, his meltdowns became less frequent and his whole school experience improved.

Feedback, Support, and Planning

An important part of the evaluation process is the discussion and planning that occurs when the initial evaluation is completed. In some settings, separate feedback appointments are scheduled after the formal tests are scored and the reports are written. It is always good, however, to ask the parents whether they have any questions before they leave the evaluation. Sometimes their questions can be dealt with right away, but at the very least, the examiner should be sure to respond to their questions in the written report and during the feedback session. While offering a specific diagnosis is important, it is equally important to help the parents/guardians plan the next steps. Be sure to point out the child's strengths and opportunities rather than focusing only on the deficits and challenges. Beware of offering false hope, but know that providing realistic, positive action steps will be very supportive. Many parents have gathered information on the Internet, but they need help in determining the veracity of the information and interpreting which recommendations apply to their child. Use the questions in Part 5 of the Child Evaluation for Autism Spectrum Disorder in the Chapter 3 Appendix to guide your feedback, support, and planning consultations.

Learning Styles

As described in Chapter 2, the conventional wisdom is that children with ASD are concrete learners (Prior & McGillivray, 1980). They learn what they see or directly experience. They may need many examples before they can generalize or make inferences from what they have learned. Children with ASD tend to learn in specific situations and may not transfer that knowledge into a new context without instruction. They also need to be shown how to go from the general to the specific. They need to be shown how a general rule applies to the specific problem before them. These children tend to need direct teaching. Since they may not be as aware of their environment as typical children, they miss incidental learning opportunities.

The conventional wisdom does not apply to all children with ASD, however. Just as all humans have unique learning styles, so do children with ASD. Some are better at visual learning, and others remember everything they hear. Some children need many repetitions; other children need to be shown only once or twice. While some children with ASD patiently do the same thing over and over until they master it, others are easily frustrated. Some need time to process what they are shown or told, and others need quick presentations. Some get confused if the visual field is too busy; other children get bored if the pictures are too simple. While some work best with background noise or music, other children with ASD are too distracted by extraneous noises.

Not only does *one size not fit all* but *one size might not even fit one*. A single child's style may vary with the type of learning. One child learned to open child safety locks through incidental observation and trial-and-error problem solving, but that same child needed many repetitions before he could accurately complete a form board puzzle. Another child with ASD could write wonderful essays, but he struggled with basic algebra concepts.

Changes Through the Lifespan

To make things even more complicated, because of neurological maturation, pruning periods, and the creation of new circuits, the ability to learn certain concepts changes throughout life (Huttenlocher, 2002; Westermann et al., 2007). Typical preschoolers can learn scientific principles such as floating and sinking through observation and experimentation, but third graders understand these principles from the perspective of water displacement. High school students can derive a formula to calculate whether an object will float or sink, while shipbuilders need to understand the complexities of creating a heavy vessel that floats.

For children with ASD, readiness to learn new concepts and skills changes as they mature (Karmiloff-Smith, 2007). A child who is unable to match pictures despite many trials may quickly learn when the task is reintroduced several months later. Also, many children with ASD do not always perform a skill consistently, making it difficult to meet the behavioral criterion for mastery. They seem to lose interest in the task and may not do it again for weeks.

Once a child's learning style is analyzed, teachers, parents, and therapists can devise strategies to accommodate the style. Generally children with ASD do learn and improve as they get older, though the degree of improvement is dependent on what they are "given" neurologically in combination with the treatment and education they receive (Karmiloff-Smith, 2007). In general, their learning style remains a constant, even as they learn many new skills and concepts. There are individuals with "best outcomes," who navigate independently in society, do well in school, get college degrees, hold jobs, and even marry and have children. To most observers, they seem perfectly typical. If you are that person's parent, teacher, therapist, or spouse, however, you understand how the individual learns and what accommodations she must make to get through each day.

> Tim Page is a well-known music critic and culture writer for national newspapers and magazines. As an adult, he realized that he had an autism spectrum disorder. He discovered that his strengths, his learning style, and his difficulties in social understanding were part of a pattern. He wrote eloquently about his foibles, his all-encompassing interests, and his struggles throughout life in an article in the *New Yorker* (Page, 2007). He credits Emily Post's etiquette book with helping him develop the social behavior that did not come naturally.

Response Patterns

Children with ASD communicate their understanding in different ways. They can look, nod, gesture, point, grunt, make a sound, say a word, choose a picture, repeat a phrase, or create a sentence. They can fetch an object, move to a particular spot, wiggle, wave, smile, screech, cry, or turn away. They may write or touch the computer screen or hit the keys. The list can go on and on. For preverbal or nonverbal children, you may need to observe very carefully to see a response. They may need hand-over-hand or operant training to learn to indicate in a standard way. Others learn to gesture through finger-play songs. Sometimes the response pattern is skewed. Children may say "no" when asked a yes/no question, even though they mean "yes." Older children might answer multiple-choice questions better than open-ended questions.

Angie's mother reported the following daily conversation with her daughter.

Mom: Do you want breakfast now?

Angie: No. (Mom knew she was hungry.)

> Mom: What do you want to eat?
>
> Angie: Want to eat. (an echoed phrase)
>
> Mom: Do you want an egg?
>
> Angie: No.
>
> Mom: Do you want a waffle?
>
> Angie: No.
>
> Mom: Do you want egg or waffle?
>
> Angie: (reaching for the waffle) Waffle.

In the above interchange, Angie did want the waffle. Some children's response patterns are such that they will always choose the last thing said, whether they want it or not. In such a case, the conversation may go like this:

> Mom: Do you want egg or waffle?
>
> Child: Waffle.
>
> Mom: Do you want waffle or egg?
>
> Child: Egg.

This response pattern can be quite frustrating, but there are ways around the dilemma. The parent could show the child both objects and have him physically choose one. Then the parent could ask the question again and help the child respond. Another tactic would be to present a desired object with a very undesirable foil ("Do you want waffle or Brussels sprouts?").

Some children's response patterns are ritualized. For a time Joe insisted that the listener repeat the last thing he said. The following exchange occurred as Joe sat among a pile of his favorite books.

> Joe: I want *Green Eggs and Ham.*
>
> Me: *Green Eggs and Ham.*
>
> Joe: I want *Great Day for Up.*
>
> Me: Okay.
>
> Joe: (louder) *Great Day for Up.*
>
> Me: I know you want it.
>
> Joe: (getting insistent) *Great Day for Up. Great Day for Up. Great Day for Up.*
>
> Me: You have it in your hand.
>
> Joe: *Great Day for Up.* (beginning to have a meltdown)
>
> Me: Okay, Joe. *Great Day for Up.*
>
> Joe: I want *Cat in the Hat.*

To Joe, my repeating his phrase was affirmation that I had heard it and acknowledged it. The only way he knew that was if I said his exact words. Then he could go on.

These examples show that response patterns may need to be identified, taught, and/or recognized in terms of what they mean to a child. Children may be taught to give picture symbols to request or respond, but is the response pattern the act of giving or the choosing of the picture? It may be either or both.

> Some time ago, Dylan was quite good at choosing between two pictures on Laureate's First Words computer program. He loved to do it for a short time each session. Choosing the correct picture meant the funny creature would appear, motivating him to continue. His first response pattern was to point to the picture on the screen. He was not as happy

when I tried to teach him to use the mouse. Most children these days have never seen a mouse. They touch the screen on their tablet or use the touchpad on their parents' laptops. Laureate responded by creating First Words apps.

Response patterns may have language, motor, and social components. A child who is dyspraxic may need an augmentative or alternative communication device. A child with motor-planning problems may have difficulty circling the correct answer on a worksheet. Many children with ASD may need a script to respond to a question or a social greeting. Establishing a response pattern in various situations is one of the keys to implementing a strategy, whether the pattern arises from the child or is directly taught.

Stimulus Patterns

All very young children develop responses to particular stimulus patterns. Parents of infants quickly learn that saying something in a particular intonation pattern will elicit a smile and that singing a song in a certain way will prompt the child to gesture. Many children with ASD need a particular stimulus to perform or respond (Sundberg & Partington, 1998). Behavior therapists teach a child to respond to a specific stimulus phrase, and once the response is established, they systematically introduce other phrases to prompt the same response.

Bedtime rituals are particular stimulus patterns that help a child prepare for sleep (the response). The stimulus pattern may become long and complex, but the key is that it is the same pattern each night. A typical bedtime ritual may be taking a bath, brushing teeth, reading a story, singing a song, and having a goodnight kiss in bed. For typical children, there can be some variations within the pattern. Bath toys may be varied, and the song and book may be different each night.

> Darla, a 6-year-old with ASD, had a very specific bedtime ritual. She needed five bath toys—no more, no less. She had to have pajamas with blue flowers. Darla's mother had bought 10 sets in several sizes to accommodate her. She had to read *Goodnight Moon* twice. Later she added *Good Night, Gorilla* to her ritual. Darla had a special blanket and pillow. When all went well, she fell asleep quickly, but if one of the elements was missing, she had difficulty getting to sleep.

Most stimulus patterns are simpler. A child may not be able to answer *wh-* questions but may be able to fill in the blank. Parents are great sources for knowing the stimulus patterns their child needs. They know what their child can do if the circumstances are right. They worry that their child's capabilities will be underestimated if asked to respond to an unfamiliar stimulus.

Children with ASD do better in structured classrooms than they do in less structured classrooms. If you observe an early childhood special education class and compare it to a typical preschool class with children of the same age, you will notice that the special education class is much more structured. The teachers are trained to give clear, specific directions (the stimulus) and help the children follow through (the response). Each activity has a clear beginning and end. In a typical classroom, although there is a daily schedule, the stimuli are much more varied and may come from other children as well as from the teacher. The children respond in a creative and flexible way.

Children with ASD, because they seek patterns in order to learn, begin to anticipate certain stimuli at certain times.

> Ned knew the therapy routine. After he greeted me, I'd ask which card game he wanted. He would answer, and then I would ask, "Where are the card games?" He would reply, "In the black box." I drew as much conversation as I could out of putting the box on the table and getting the games out. It was a very adaptive routine. Ned got to do his

> favorite game for 5 minutes while answering questions and/or making comments about the game. One day, Ned's mother asked an important question just as therapy was about to start. The routine was interrupted. Ned, however, went on with it anyway. His mother and I heard him say, "What card game do you want? My Word. Where are the card games? In the black box. Where should I put the black box? On the table. Where's My Word? I'll find it. I found it. Okay. My Word." Ned played both sides of the interchange—the stimulus patterns and the responses.

Sometimes it is hard to know when the stimulus pattern is functional for a child and when it needs to be changed so the child can move on. Much can be learned by observing and listening to the child.

> I spent 10 minutes before a session looking for a particular toy that Jorge needed for his transition routine, but I couldn't find it anywhere. When Jorge came into the therapy room, I anticipated a meltdown. I said, "Sorry Jorge. No Woody doll. It's lost." Jorge looked at me, picked up a stuffed seal, and went through his routine as if nothing had happened.

Smooth social interactions depend on anticipating what a person will say and knowing how to respond. Developing a repertoire of responses to stimulus patterns is very useful to people with ASD as they try to navigate the social world. For example, it is useful to know that when someone asks, "How are you?" that person is not expecting a detailed account of your troubles with an ingrown toenail.

> Adrian is a wonderful teenager with ASD. We have known each other since he was a terrifyingly wild 3-year-old. He can now make himself understood in a conversation, though his verbal skills are limited. He is a responsible, well-behaved young man who is working hard on developing his reading skills. Over the years, I frequently greeted him by saying, "Hi, Adrian. What's happening?" Recently, he walked into the therapy room grinning. Before I could say anything, he said, "Hi, Phyllis. Nothing is happening."

Identifying stimulus patterns that are helpful to children with ASD, building flexibility in responding to a variety of stimuli, and judging how to respond to stimulus patterns are important when developing intervention strategies.

Strengths

Strengths are abilities that can be used in a variety of situations. In planning intervention for those with ASD, it is crucial to describe strengths as well as to identify weaknesses. Individuals with ASD may have excellent memory skills, artistic abilities, or reading or math skills. Strengths, even though they may be surprising or precocious, are different from savant skills. Savant skills are isolated from the rest of the individual's functioning.

> In the movie *Rain Man*, Raymond was portrayed as an autistic savant. He could calculate rapidly, but he could not use the math skills in a functional way. He could count toothpicks, but he could not use money to make a purchase.

Strengths can be used to develop weaker areas and to scaffold remediation strategies. If a child is good at doing a U.S. floor puzzle, that skill can be used to foster social interactions with peers. Precocious reading abilities (hyperlexia) can be used to improve weaknesses in language.

There is a school of thought that holds that children with ASD should be helped to follow typical developmental trajectories and meet prescribed educational standards. If a child has strengths beyond what is expected at his age, those strengths are often ignored or even discouraged

(National Research Council, 2001). For example, preschool children with ASD who are reading are often not provided with written supports, since typical preschool children are not expected to read yet. Since one of the hallmark characteristics of ASD is uneven development (National Research Council, 2001), these children often do not develop in a typical sequence. By ignoring strengths, teachers and therapists miss a valuable entrée into a child's world. In the end, the child needs to develop strengths as well as weaknesses to reach his full potential. Further development and utilization of a child's strengths should not be overlooked in the intervention strategy. One of the strengths could eventually become a vocation.

> O's mother emailed that her son with ASD, who had graduated from college a few years ago, had found the perfect job. He was a quality-control technician for a small chemical company. The precision and perfectionism that slowed him down and caused frustration in elementary school was now a valuable commodity.

> Although J.J.'s music degree and his skill as a violinist did not result in a music career, it offered him wonderful avocational opportunities. He plays in several community orchestras and is asked to perform at various social functions. As a result, he gains social status and gives pleasure to others.

Special Interests, Fascinations, and Obsessions

Some individuals with ASD develop encyclopedic knowledge about unusual topics. They use their strengths to learn about something that catches their attention.

> For some inexplicable reason, many young boys with ASD become fascinated to the point of obsession with Thomas the Tank Engine. They learn the unusual names of all the engines, study the product brochures, and memorize British scripts, dialogues, and books. Along the way, they learn to identify colors and numbers. Another positive outcome is that many typical peers are also interested in the trains, providing a shared context for their first social imaginary play schemes.

Because interests may become obsessions, and obsessions can interfere with thought processes and learning, the child may need help in managing obsessions. Merely limiting the obsessive behavior or redirecting the conversation away from interests or fascinations can increase anxiety and generally is counterproductive. On the other hand, it can be hard to find a functional use for unusual interests, such as wood paneling, vacuum cleaners, retail malls in the United States, and the locations of the corporate headquarters of foreign car manufacturers. Some suggestions are to broaden the scope of the interests, to use them as motivators and/or rewards, or to use them as subject matter in math problems or short stories.

Fears, Aversions, and Sensitivities

Some children with ASD are sensitive to loud noises and/or music. Some are unusually fearful of a host of common things in their environment. Others can't stand to have anything messy on their hands. In most cases, it is hard to prepare them, comfort them, or talk them through their fears because of their language difficulties. An intervention strategy could circumvent these problems, work to alleviate fears, and/or desensitize sensory issues.

> Andy loved to go to the supermarket with his mother. He enjoyed looking at all the signs and the products. One day as they entered the store, Andy started screaming in fear. His mother finally figured out that he was frightened by the bats that were hanging from the ceiling to promote a Batman movie. "But, Andy," his mother said, "those bats aren't

real." "Yes, yes, real bats," cried Andy. After Andy had calmed down, his mother asked the store manager if he could take a bat down to show Andy that they were not real bats. "See, Andy," his mother said. "They're not real. They are just paper." "Real paper," said Andy.

While it is sometimes possible to determine the source of fears or aversions, usually the child can't explain why he is frightened. Sensitivities may have their source in neurological differences (Williams, Goldstein, & Minshew, 2006). Decisions about intervention strategies need to take the child's perspective. Those working with the child need to seek common threads or patterns in the behavior to figure out how to help the child cope.

Aaron loved vacuum cleaners. He didn't seem to mind the loud noise, and he would check out the vacuum cleaner whenever he visited someone's house. He even knew the make and color of all of his neighbors' vacuum cleaners. He became upset, however, whenever he heard static on the radio, in a sound system, or on a cell phone. His parents were puzzled. Why did he like noisy vacuum cleaners and hate the quieter static? The common thread seemed to be predictability. Aaron knew that the vacuum could be turned on and off. He could control the switch, and he knew when the sound would start. Static was unpredictable and random, and could not be easily controlled. We labeled the static as "unpredictable," a word that gave him a comforting way to deal with the randomness of the sound. "There's that unpredictable static," he would say.

Social Skills

Even though difficulty in social functioning is a core deficit in ASD and research points to differences in brain organization that affect social functioning, there is a wide spectrum of social abilities in individuals with ASD (Baron-Cohen et al., 1999). In addition, social abilities may not necessarily parallel higher language or cognitive functioning. Some very bright verbal children have a great deal of difficulty interacting with others and may not respond to overtures by others. Some children with limited language and poor academic skills may show awareness and responsiveness beyond what would be expected.

Although it is not an ASD, Williams syndrome is a genetic disorder characterized by an overly social personality combined with developmental delays, learning disabilities, and attention deficits. In both Williams syndrome and ASD, the amygdala and structures in the prefrontal cortex in the brain show abnormal function in fMRI studies, though the abnormalities are different (Baron-Cohen et al., 1999; Meyer-Lindenberg et al., 2005). These studies illustrate the complexity of neurological functioning in social processing. Therefore, in planning strategies for children with ASD, social reciprocity and social functioning should be assessed both in conjunction with other skills and as a separate entity. Strategies for social skill development will vary with ability level, age, and the demands of the environment.

Ben is a young adult with ASD. As a child, he had a great deal of difficulty with academic learning. Ben had repetitive behaviors and struggled to communicate, yet he has always been interested in other people and his social judgment is quite good. At school Ben was friendly to everyone, and he always knew which teachers were retiring each year. Now he travels to visit family on his own and drives his own very cool car. While Ben is not loquacious, his conversations are pleasant and thoughtful. He is quite reliable as an employee, and he gets himself to his job and to therapy on his own and on time.

A number of years ago, a mother called to talk to me about her grown son with ASD. She was proud to share that he had been in a fraternity in college and had recently graduated. He had even decided to spend a year in South America so he could become fluent in

Spanish. He lived with a family there, and from all reports, things went well. However, he still had social challenges. Soon after he returned from South America, a family friend stopped by. As she eagerly questioned the young man about his experiences, he turned and left the room. His mother was embarrassed. Later, when she asked him why he had been so rude, he replied, "I don't find that woman interesting." An effective intervention strategy would certainly include learning about perspective taking.

Parent Insights

Parents have intimate knowledge about their child that is not available from any other source. They know whether their child has difficulty falling asleep. They know how hard it was to toilet train their child. They know about favorite foods, what happened on family vacations, and how the child reacts to different members of the family. Parents, however, often have difficulty looking at their child with an objective eye. Their perspective is colored by love for the child, fear for the future, tremendous responsibility, worries for their other children, daily frustrations, and lack of sleep. Yet parents have much to offer in the development of strategies for their child. They can help set realistic, functional priorities for working with their child that will help in every aspect of life. For instance, they can let the professional know if they need a strategy for getting dressed independently or for decreasing head banging.

> Florence resisted getting dressed each morning before school. She had set ideas about what she wanted to wear and often chose clothing that was inappropriate to the season, too small, or in the laundry. Her mother tried stocking her closet with a variety of appropriate clothes, but Florence often wanted an item that wasn't there and was distraught until it was found. Her mother frequently gave in and let Florence wear what she wanted (e.g., pink flip-flops in the snow). Once Florence was dressed and off to school, it took her at least an hour to settle down. Strategies were devised and some worked for a few days, but sooner or later Florence circumvented them all. Florence's parents were at their wits' end and realized they needed help. They asked the school to send a consultant to observe the morning uproar and devise a strategy that would work for their family and their own special child.

Parents are in the best position to keep us focused on their child's needs. For example, for team meetings, some parents bring a picture of their child and place it in the middle of the conference table. Others have a set of pictures on the cover of their notebook. If the discussion seems to be straying away from the child's needs, some parents subtly or not so subtly draw everyone's attention to the adorable pictures.

The Family, School, and Community

Although the first step in devising a strategy is to take a careful look at the child, the child does not exist in a vacuum. The child is part of a family, may be a student at a school, and lives in a community. Each of these social contexts is unique and affects the child in a multitude of ways.

Family

The traditional family of the 1950s is no longer status quo. Gender roles have been redefined and redistributed. With these changes come new challenges. Traditional family support systems may not be available. Extended families—grandparents, aunts, and uncles—may live far away. Neighbors lead busy lives and may not be around to lend a hand. Day-care providers may be hired so that parents can work to support the family, but such providers might not provide the needed emotional support.

As strategies are being developed for treatment of the child with ASD, family characteristics need to be considered. The stress of the diagnosis as well as the stress of dealing with a child with ASD are great. Coping with the reality of the situation is a long-term process with many emotional ups and downs. The professionals on the team will want to review information gathered on the Child Evaluation for Autism Spectrum Disorder forms provided in the Appendix to Chapter 3 and schedule regular parent meetings and/or phone calls to help support the family as needed.

We have seen a number of families where one twin has been diagnosed with ASD. Some families have other children who are close in age. We recently met a child with ASD whose older brother had just been diagnosed with juvenile diabetes. Others have had crises with elderly parents. Another family was in the midst of a bitter divorce. One mother had just received confirmation of a diagnosis of breast cancer at the same time that her child was being evaluated. It is amazing that these families can get up each morning and face the day, let alone plan strategies for their child with ASD. The resilience and determination of most families is truly inspiring.

Because there is a genetic component in some types of ASD (Veenstra-VanDerWeele & Cook, 2003), family history is important. Some parents accept the diagnosis fairly easily because their nephew, cousin, or grandfather also has ASD. Family members may have very different strategies for treating their children, but at some level it is comforting to know that someone else in their family is dealing with similar issues. For some with a family history of ASD, however, their greatest fear was that they too would have a child with ASD and the news is devastating. They don't have the luxury of slowly learning about the disorder and what they are in for. They often think of the worst possible outcomes.

What is the nature of the support systems?

- Are close family and friends nearby and available to help?
- Does the family have service providers who provide support?
- Has the family contacted the local or national autism society?
- Have the parents participated in support groups with other parents of children with ASD?
- Have the parents communicated with other parents via online message boards or Facebook groups?
- Do the parents understand what public services are available?
- Have the parents contacted local early intervention agencies, local public school programs, and/or private programs?
- Are the school programs and private agencies supported administratively and financially well enough to provide the needed services?
- Does the family have the means to pay for help?

Some families' reaction to their child's diagnosis of ASD is to seek support from various sources immediately. They may be very proactive and vocal about their needs. Other families are much more private in their struggles. They don't want to burden others and need to work things out themselves first. Both of these approaches and all the variations in between are valid. More often than not, it seems that the two parents have different ways of developing a support system. One partner may need to talk it out with whoever will listen. The other partner may not want the well-meaning but uninformed advice of others. He or she would rather seek information from professionals or the Internet. Each must learn to respect the other's viewpoint so that they can go forward in developing intervention strategies for their child.

School

Support systems are necessary for school districts as well. A commitment by the school district to provide state-of-the-art training for teachers and paraprofessionals directly affects each child and family. Staff who have resources for consultation and networks for finding materials and techniques can do their best work with the children and in turn provide support to parents and other professionals.

Support does not mean complete agreement. If a parent wants to try something that a therapy provider does not agree with, the provider can listen carefully, give an honest opinion, and then be there for the parent as the journey takes that turn. If a therapist recommends a technique that a teacher does not feel would work in her classroom, a planning meeting could be held to determine how to proceed so that both understand the goals and strategies.

> Anton's mother wanted to try a special diet for her son. Even though his teacher did not agree with this treatment approach, and even though it meant some extra work at snack time, the teacher agreed to support the mother's efforts. She set up a system that ensured Anton would get his special snacks and avoid eating foods not on his diet.

Community

Community agencies are resources for a myriad of services, but they, too, need the support of local, state, and federal government sources; private foundations; and donors for financial viability. There is nothing more dispiriting to service providers or more detrimental to families than to develop needed service programs and then have to abruptly discontinue those services because the funding source disappears. Support for community agencies and organizations also comes from the ASD awareness initiatives that inform the general public about ASD. If people are aware, they can support legislators who vote to fund programs for ASD, they can be sympathetic to the mother whose child is having a tantrum in the supermarket, and they can provide jobs in their businesses for individuals with ASD.

> Years ago when Adam, a child with ASD, ran out the door of the supermarket as his mother was checking out, she yelled to the person coming in, "Grab him. He's deaf!" She knew that people would understand that a deaf child couldn't listen to words of warning. If she had said, "Grab him. He's autistic!" people would not have known what she was talking about. These days, it is likely that people would understand. They may have seen many specials about autism on television. They may not know what to do specifically, but they would have heard the word and would have known that action needed to be taken. The community cannot be supportive if they are not informed.
>
> Not long ago, Alan wandered away from his high school group while on a field trip to a busy metropolitan train station. His parents and the police were alerted, and an all-out search was begun. Hours later, he was found miles away in a trendy women's clothing store by an alert saleswoman, who recognized the symptoms of ASD and called the police.

There has been an initiative to provide information and training to law enforcement agencies and local police departments. They are taught to recognize symptoms of ASD, the best ways to approach a person with ASD, and especially not to misinterpret or overreact to an individual's lack of response to an officer's directive. Parents are encouraged to inform the local police that a child in their household has ASD in case their young escape artist manages to go off on his or her own.

Working Together

Support systems for family, school districts, and community are interdependent. Ideally, all are on the road together. Sometimes parents take the lead, sometimes teachers initiate ideas, and sometimes therapists and medical professionals show the way. Families join and raise funds for special interest groups that in turn provide them with services and support. Citizens support political candidates who develop legislation that will benefit their children. National groups such as the Autism Society of America, Autism Speaks, or the American Pediatric Association (APA) provide information that trickles down to individuals in the community. Government agencies such as the National Institutes of Health (NIH) or the Centers for Disease Control and Prevention (CDC) inform the direction of research and intervention. Autism centers at hospitals and universities carry out basic research that may someday provide answers to the puzzle, but they need the support of families to participate. This is not an ideal world. Conflicts arise. Egos are bruised. Self-serving decisions are made. If good support systems are in place, however, the focus can remain where it should be—on the children with ASD.

The Web of Support Systems

In planning strategies for children with ASD, the support systems should be carefully analyzed. Without support, even the best strategies will fail. Figure 3.1 shows examples of available support systems.

A wise person once said, "The only answer to '*you should* . . . is *yes, but* . . . .' " We all know what we SHOULD do, BUT we have a lot of reasons and rationalizations for why we cannot or won't do what we should. A good strategy does not just list the "shoulds." It is a road map of how to carry out the intervention, using the resources available and providing the support necessary to make it happen. Using the support systems of the family, the school, and the community, the strategy is built and carried out step by step.

Figure 3.1. The web of support systems.

Goals and Objectives

> An acquaintance was telling me about two friends who each have a child with autism. The mothers were comparing notes about upcoming Individualized Education Program (IEP) meetings. They were prepared, with long lists of questions and ideas for goals for the next year. "My husband never does this," one griped to the other. "The only question he ever asks is . . . ." The other mother jumped in and both said in unison, "Will my child be able to live independently?"

Before specific strategies are chosen, long-term goals and short-term objectives need to be identified. Goals are more general and may take a long time to achieve. Objectives are the small steps necessary to achieve the goals and may be met in a year or less. Goals may address daily living, communication, academic, sensory–motor, and/or social needs. Parents, teachers, or therapists may suggest goals.

What are the long-term goals and short-term objectives for the child?

- Are the goals in various settings compatible with one another?
- Are the goals reasonably achievable?
- Can progress toward the goals and objectives be measured in meaningful ways?

If the child is served by an early intervention program for children from birth to 3 years of age, an Individual Family Service Plan (IFSP) is generated and meetings are held to update the goals and objectives. If a child is enrolled in a public school district program beginning at age 3, an IEP is generated. If an adult is a client of a program or agency, an adult service plan (ASP) is generated for that individual. Private practitioners and agencies generate goals for their services that may or may not overlap with the IFSP, the IEP, or the ASP. See Table 3.4 for examples of goals and objectives for children with ASD.

There are some tools that may help the families of children with ASD develop all-encompassing goals and develop plans to carry out these goals. Two of the most popular are PATH (Planning Alternative Tomorrows with Hope; Pearpoint, O'Brien, & Forest, 1991) and MAPS (Making Action Plans, http://www.inclusion.com/maps.html). These tools help families articulate their hopes and dreams for their children. Tools like these give families a chance to step back from the daily work and take a look at what the future might hold. The use of these tools encourages families to think on a larger scale and incorporate many people in the process.

Jim's PATH team formulated the following dreams:

- Self-Help: driving, living independently
- Employment: possibly computers, detailed work, professional expertise
- Social Skills: effective communication and social interactions
- Social Life: have friends, be a part of the community, integrated into extended family, possibility of marriage and family

To move toward those dreams, in one year Jim:

- Used the telephone appropriately without personal identification number (PIN) or supervision
- Found common interests with a friend
- Hung out with friends in a kid-only space
- Had a reciprocal conversation about his needs/wants

- Worked toward inclusion
- Did things with his brother and had a good time
- Participated in a sporting event (martial arts, football)

Table 3.4
Examples of Goals and Objectives for Children With ASD

IFSP Goals for DH (age 30 months)

DH will consistently respond to requests to "come here."

DH will use gestures and vocalization to protest, call others, and indicate a desire for a change in activities.

DH will imitate patting a doll, show shoes, imitate housework activities, and use 2 toys together in pretend play.

DH will point to 2 action words in pictures and identify 3 body parts on self or a doll.

DH will imitate consonant and vowel combinations.

IEP Goals and Objectives for DH (age 36 months)

Goal: to increase receptive and expressive vocabulary for age-appropriate words, to increase length of utterance for requests, and to answer specific social questions

Objective 1: DH will identify and name with verbal approximations new words in the following categories: toys, animals, TV/video characters, and people.
- Criterion: 3 to 5 new words in each category
- Frequency: per quarter

Objective 2: DH will request desired items using the carrier phrase, "I want _____, please."
- Criterion: 80%
- Frequency: per quarter

Objective 3: DH will answer social questions, such as "What's your name?" and "How old are you?"
- Criterion: 90%
- Frequency: per quarter
- Progress toward the goal will be measured by checklists and charts.

IEP Goals and Objectives for NG (age 3–11)

Goal for Language Arts—Listening/Speaking: Given at least 3 categorical themes (e.g., foods, clothes, animals), NG will sort at least 10 items in the correct area and respond with the appropriate function of the category (e.g., "eat apple") 3 out of 4 times with a single cue.

Short-term Objective/Benchmark 1: Given at least 3 categorical themes (e.g., foods, clothes, animals), NG will sort at least 10 items in the correct area with a visual model and verbal prompt.
- Evaluation Criterion: 3 of 4 attempts
- Evaluation Procedure: observation log
- Schedule for Determining Procedure: semester

Short-term Objective/Benchmark 2: Given at least 3 categorical themes (e.g., foods, clothes, animals), NG will sort at least 10 items in the correct area with a single cue.
- Evaluation Criterion: 3 of 4 attempts
- Evaluation Procedure: observation log
- Schedule for Determining Procedure: semester

Short-term Objective/Benchmark 3: Given at least 3 categorical themes (e.g., foods, clothes, animals), NG will sort at least 10 items in the correct area and respond with the appropriate function of the category (e.g., "eat apple") with a visual model and verbal prompt.
- Evaluation Criterion: 3 of 4 attempts
- Evaluation Procedure: observation log
- Schedule for Determining Procedure: semester

Short-term Objective/Benchmark 4: Given at least 3 categorical themes (e.g., foods, clothes, animals), NG will sort at least 10 items in the correct area and respond with the appropriate function of the category (e.g., "eat apple") with a single cue.
- Evaluation Criterion: 3 of 4 attempts
- Evaluation Procedure: observation log
- Schedule for Determining Procedure: semester

Even if families do not go through a formal process such as PATH or AutismMAPS, they can still take some time to see the bigger picture.

> Eric is a young man who is severely affected by autism. His family left no stone unturned in finding therapists and schools to work with him, but he has never learned to talk and his abilities are limited. Eric is a likeable person, but he is subject to temper tantrums. He had been dismissed from several programs because of his unpredictable and sometimes dangerous behavior. Throughout adolescence, Eric lived at home with the help of a caretaker. He had grown to the size of a football player, dwarfing his petite mother and slender father. His father's hopes that Eric would someday live independently were not to be fulfilled. His father, however, created another vision. He sought funding to transform a nearby single-family home into a supported living facility. With the help of a consultant, the house was outfitted with adaptive equipment and safety devices to make it suitable for Eric and eventually other residents to live there with trained staff. Eric could now live near his parents, remain within his community and near extended family and friends, and access programs where he is known and understood.

> Eric's father did not stop there. Through his experience, he realized that in his state, services for adults with disabilities were woefully lacking. Eric's father formed a charitable foundation that raises money to support agencies that develop living facilities, programs, and support systems for adults with ASD and other disabilities.

Through all these processes, all the participants have input in devising goals, articulating measurable objectives, determining strategies, and identifying tactics that will work for a child. Here again, the child's particular learning style must be taken into consideration and goals and objectives must be changed to meet the child's current reality. Everyone involved in the treatment, education, and care of the individual with ASD should be aware of all the goals so that strategies and tactics can overlap in all settings.

Strategies and Tactics

After looking at the child, family, school, and community and developing long-term goals and short-term objectives, it's time to look at strategies that will point us in the appropriate direction. Strategies are general methods or approaches used to achieve long-term goals. Tactics are specific activities or tools used with a child to meet measurable short-term objectives.

> **Strategies:** general methods and/or approaches used to achieve goals
> **Tactics:** specific activities or tools used to meet the measurable objectives

There are strategies that are set programs, with trained practitioners who use prescribed tactics. Other strategies borrow bits and pieces of programs as they apply to a particular child. Some strategic plans use programs simultaneously and some in sequence. Sometimes strategies are entirely unique to the individual child.

> One family began behavioral intervention soon after their child was diagnosed with ASD. They hired an applied behavior analysis (ABA) consultant to set up a home program for 15 hours per week. When their child was 3 years old, they continued the behavioral strategy but also enrolled their child in an early childhood special education program with supportive services and developed an IEP.

> Another family identified language development and social communication as their primary goals and supplemented their school program with private speech and language therapy, Floortime, and playgroups at home.

Yet another family added music lessons and drama club to their child's program to strengthen his talents in those areas.

One way to look at strategies is whether they are "bottom-up" (inside-out) approaches or "top-down" (outside-in) approaches. In bottom-up strategies for children with ASD, tactics are aimed at developing specific skills and then helping the child to generalize those skills, discern rules, and formulate schemas. These approaches provide experiences and modeling in specific situations, and help the child internalize them so that they generalize to other situations. Using the tree-versus-forest analogy, this is the "Tree, tree, tree, tree—aha, lots of trees together are a forest" approach. In top-down strategies for children with ASD, tactics are aimed at presenting general rules or methods and then showing the child how to apply these rules and methods in specific situations. This strategy provides instruction from the outside in. In the tree-versus-forest analogy, this is the "Here is a forest and in it are oak trees, spruce trees, and maples" approach.

Some commonly used programs for children with ASD are listed in Table 3.5 and are categorized as primarily top-down or bottom-up. Some can also be found in *The Source for Treatment Methodologies in Autism* (Richard, 2000); in *Autism: Teaching Does Make a Difference* (Scheuerman & Webber, 2002); on the Autism Speaks Web site (www.autismspeaks.org); and the Autism Society of America Web site (www.autism-society.org). Also refer to Volkmar et al. (2014) for the American Academy of Child and Adolescent Psychiatry Practice Parameter for the Assessment and Treatment of Children and Adolescents With Autism Spectrum Disorder.

In looking at specific programs for individuals with ASD, parents and professionals are encouraged to do careful research into efficacy for a particular child. The guidelines discussed in Chapter 1 about the science of ASD apply to intervention strategies as well, although controlled studies of treatment outcomes are few and far between. Behavioral interventions have been studied most extensively, but the group results may not apply in the case of an individual child. Because of the nature of the spectrum, certain interventions may be appropriate only after children gain particular skills.

Table 3.5
Commonly Used Programs for Children With ASD

Top-Down Programs

- *Applied Behavior Analysis* (2nd ed.) (ABA) (Cooper, Heron, & Heward, 1987)
- *The Verbal Behavior Approach* (ABA-VB) (Barbera & Rasmussen, 2007)
- Discrete Trial Teaching (DTT) (Bogin, Sullivan, Rogers, & Stabel, 2010)
- *The STAR Program* (2nd ed.) (Arick, Loos, Falco, & Krug, 2015)
- Picture Exchange Communication System (PECS) (www.pecs.com)
- TEACCH Program (www.teacch.com)

Bottom-Up Programs

- Floortime; Developmental, Individual Differences, Relationship (DIR) approach (www.floortime.org)
- Relationship Development Intervention (RDI) (Gutstein, 2009)
- Theraplay (www.theraplay.org)
- Social Stories (http://carolgraysocialstories.com/)

Combined Programs

- HANDLE (www.handle.org)
- Pivotal Response Treatments at UCSB Koegel Autism Center (http://education.ucsb.edu/autism)
- SCERTS (www.scerts.com)
- Early Start Denver Model (Rogers & Dawson, 2009a, 2009b, 2012)

Other factors also need to be considered. The success of a treatment program is largely dependent on the skill and the personality of the practitioner administering the program. It is very important to network with other parents and professionals and benefit from their experiences and recommendations. Meet with the practitioner. Have a trial session. Determine if the child will respond well to that person. Be wary of exaggerated claims for success. Make sure that the goals of the program jibe with the goals identified for the child. Remember that no one program does it all.

Physiological, Biochemical, and Medical Strategies

There are a number of strategies aimed at altering the neurological or biochemical makeup of a child's body. These go along with theories about what causes ASD or are aimed at specific symptoms apparent in children with ASD. Since the cause of ASD is still unknown, the field is open to a wide variety of theories and treatments. It is difficult to carry out large double-blind studies on human subjects, so the efficacy of these treatments is hard to determine. Professionals should specifically inquire about the use of alternative or complementary treatments and be prepared to discuss their risks and potential benefits (Volkmar et al., 2014). Approach these strategies with caution, and search for scientific evidence as described in Chapter 1 (NYSDH, 1999).

OTs and developmental optometrists may use a variety of treatments aimed at affecting the sensory and regulatory systems of children with ASD. These include a variety of listening programs (auditory integration training), sensory integration techniques, and vision training. Some researchers are looking into the molecular biology of the child or are seeking connections between the digestive and neurological systems. (See www.autism.com/index.asp.) Some are using medications that affect the neurotransmitters in the brain. Since supporting evidence is not definitive for these treatments, parents need to weigh potential benefits against risk factors to decide whether to try these strategies for their child (McDougle & Posey, 2002).

Most families of children with ASD try physiological or biochemical treatments at some point (Green et al., 2006). Many feel that sensory and regulation strategies used by OTs are beneficial to their children despite the lack of good efficacy studies. Families may try gluten-free and casein-free diets and find that sometimes children have fewer digestive disturbances and feel better on this diet. Other parents see no benefit at all. Specific medications seem to ameliorate some symptoms, allowing for better school performance in some children. Medications may be offered to children with ASD when there is a specific target symptom or comorbid condition (Volkmar et al., 2014). These treatments, though they may be helpful for some, are not cures for ASD and should be used judiciously.

Intensity of Intervention

Research points to intensity of intervention as a powerful factor in the success of treatment for children with ASD (National Research Council, 2001; Sheinkopf & Siegel, 1998). While some programs recommend up to 40 hours a week of intensive intervention, it is generally accepted that 25 hours per week year-round is a best practice to effect improvement in children with ASD. This intervention need not be restricted to one program, however. Skilled teachers, educated parents, experienced therapists, and loving caretakers and family members can all contribute to the focused intervention. It is also true that not all children with ASD need such intensive intervention. A mildly affected child may be better engaged in play with peers than in intensive behavioral therapy. Some children may become overstimulated and frustrated by the intense demands placed upon them and may need more time alone to integrate what they are learning.

Because of variables in family constellation, level of education, and family situations, studies have failed to demonstrate differences in outcomes in home-based versus school- or clinic-based programs of similar intensity (Wolery & Garfinkle, 2002). Some families may have the means to provide a separate room and hire trainers to come into the home. Other families with siblings or working parents would find it distracting or impossible to schedule a home program.

Custom-Tailored Intervention Strategies

There are many reasons for custom-tailoring an intervention strategy:

- There is no one available in the child's hometown who is trained in a particular program.
- The cost is prohibitive.
- The child's pattern of strengths and weaknesses does not fit with the structure of the program.
- The child is not ready to benefit from the program.
- The child has already mastered the skills targeted in the program.
- The child has responded well to methods that are not part of the program.
- There is a philosophical bias toward creating something specially designed for this particular child.

Whatever the reasons, the vast majority of children with ASD are involved in custom-tailored programs. Interestingly, even when set programs are used, it has been found that children only participate in them for an average of 1 to 2 years (Greenspan & Weider, 1997b; Jacobson, Mulick, & Green, 1998; Koegel, Koegel, Shoshan, & McNerney, 1999; Mahoney & Perales, 2005; Rogers, 1996).

In custom-tailoring a program, the steps outlined above—evaluating the child, the family, school, and community resources—are the starting points. Goals and objectives are developed, and possible strategies are discussed. Then the work begins. It may be that a behavioral, top-down strategy is used for achieving one goal, while a play-based, bottom-up strategy is used to achieve another goal. Computer-based learning may be used for achieving an academic goal, while scripting of social language may be used to learn to play games with other children.

Goals may be hierarchical or they may address a particular behavior or need.

> J.T., a $5\frac{1}{2}$-year-old-boy, was obsessed with Webkinz. He thought about the computer games constantly. In his social language group with another boy, his goal was to develop the ability to play reciprocally and have balanced give-and-take interactions. We designed a program based on his interests and needs. J.T. was able to teach the other boy how to play a real live version of Wheel of Wow, adjust to the changes suggested by the other boy, and together create a game that was fun for both of them.

Another way to custom-tailor a program is to add elements to the set program. Sometimes the methods used in the set program can be adapted to incorporate the gains made in other areas.

> Noor's family developed an ABA home program, with talented trainers and a good consultant. She also was enrolled in an early childhood special education program and in individual speech and language therapy for an hour per week. Nevertheless, she was minimally verbal. One day, her mother brought the pictures that Noor was trying to learn to label in her ABA program. Rather than use the standard stimulus "What's this?," the therapist modeled the sentence "It's a car. It's a _____." Soon Noor began to fill in the cloze sentence. Her excited mother brought this idea back to the ABA trainers, and as they incorporated this method, Noor began to label pictures spontaneously.

Early Intervention and School Strategies

Children with ASD are often diagnosed before the age of 3. Many children begin intervention through the early intervention birth-to-three system in their state. Pediatricians or concerned parents themselves can initiate an evaluation through an agency in their region. Birth-to-three programs are termed Part C Programs, and a list of state agencies that coordinate these services is available through the National Early Childhood Technical Assistance Center Web site (www .nectac.org).

In the early intervention system, much of the treatment is home based, and it follows a clinical model for providing services. Goals and objectives are very specific to the individual child, and individual therapists work closely with families to develop strategies and tactics. A child may receive the services of an SLP, an OT, a developmental therapist, and perhaps a PT. The case manager may request an evaluation by a developmental pediatrician, a neurologist, a psychiatrist, or a psychologist. Regular meetings are held, usually in the family's home, and systems are put in place for collaboration. Ideally, all the services begin soon after the child is identified, and everything works smoothly. In the real world, sometimes therapists cannot be found, there may be turnover in providers, and the home may not be the best place for treatment. Nonetheless, research supports the idea that early treatment improves outcomes for children with ASD (Dawson, Ashman, & Carver, 2000; Harris & Handleman, 2000; Kasari, Gulsrud, Freeman, Paparella, & Hellemann, 2012; Landa, 2007; McGee, Morrier, & Daley, 1999).

At age 3 the child is no longer eligible for early intervention services, and a transition is made to public school programs. During this transition, many of the parameters of service delivery shift. Services are provided at school. One major goal of the school program is to prepare a child for learning and developing within a classroom setting. The child must fit into a program rather than the program being designed around the child. Individual goals, objectives, strategies, and tactics are identified, but the focus is helping the child to access classroom procedures. Support services of speech and language therapy, occupational therapy, physical therapy, and social work may be delivered within the classroom (push-in services), or the child may be taken from the classroom for individual or small-group sessions (pullout services). In most school districts, a family may opt for support services alone, enrollment in an early childhood special education class with other children with special needs, enrollment in an "at-risk" program, or a combination of services. Some school districts have typical preschool classes in which a few children with special needs are included, and some have blended early childhood special education classes with typical classes staffed by a team of teachers.

Parents sometimes find this transition difficult. They miss the close connection with service providers and the opportunity for daily input. Parents put their child on a bus and entrust him to a whole new group of people. They may not receive the same number of minutes of support services they had in early intervention. They have many of the same feelings that any parent has during transitions ("Is my child ready for preschool/kindergarten/high school/college?").

Most parents come to understand that a school program is necessary for a child's progress, but a school program cannot do it all. The parent may need to provide other services as well. Set programs may continue. Parents may seek outside therapies to supplement services. They may find recreational programs or organize playgroups so that their child has access to typical children. Parents continue to set priorities and strategize, taking into account the resources available to meet their child's goals and objectives.

Dylan's parents were understandably nervous when he turned 3 and was about to enter an early childhood special education program. He was diagnosed with ASD and dyspraxia, and he was not talking. He liked to "run the show" with his early intervention therapists, and he seemed bright and alert. Dylan's therapists had found a number of visual-motor tasks that he could complete if he was approached in a certain way. How would he do in a classroom? Would he be able to demonstrate his strengths? Would the teachers be able to handle this strong-willed young boy? Indeed it was a rocky start. Dylan wouldn't sit, wandered the room opening doors, and resisted engagement. Gradually, however, the teachers put strategies and tactics in place, and when his mother came to observe after 2 months, Dylan was sitting at a table with other children and completing his tasks independently. Dylan is still enrolled in some outside therapies, but his mother is very encouraged that he learned to fit in to a required classroom routine as well as he has.

Lyle was a verbal, intelligent 4-year-old with ASD. He knew a lot about maps and globes. The early childhood special education class was too restrictive for his needs, but his school district did not have other options. His parents enrolled him in individual speech and language therapy and occupational therapy through the school district, and they tried several typical preschools in the area. Each time, teachers were not equipped to deal with his rigid behavior and his inability to respond in a group. Finally, Lyle's parents found a park district program that would take him with the help of an aide provided by the Special Recreation Program affiliate. With support, Lyle was able to participate with his typical peers.

As children get older, school options change. Over the years, strategic educational philosophies have changed as well. While isolated special education classes had been the norm in the past, the educational pendulum swung to mainstreaming, to inclusion, and then to a full inclusion model in the 1980s and 1990s. All of these options provide access to general education classes to some degree; see Table 3.6 for an explanation of each term.

Though there are some who feel that full inclusion of children with disabilities is a civil right, the law as outlined in the Individuals With Disabilities Education Improvement Act of 2004 (IDEA 2004) does not require inclusion. Rather, it requires that a child be educated in the least restrictive environment (LRE) and that the analysis of this environment begin with general education placement. There should be a continuum of placements considered, and the decision should be driven by the IEP. IDEA 2004 provides the rights to a free and appropriate public education (FAPE), appropriate evaluations, participation by the parents and student in decision making, and procedural safeguards.

Gilbert was minimally verbal, but he had some academic skills. At the request of his parents, the school reluctantly agreed to a full inclusion program with the support of a full-time aide. There was little in the class that Gilbert could do at grade level, but materials were adapted for him, and it was thought that he was benefiting from being there. His classroom behavior was good much of the time, but once, in frustration, Gilbert

Table 3.6
School Options

Mainstreaming: the selective placement of special education students in one or more regular education classes with the idea that the students must keep up with the regular class requirements.

Inclusion: the education of each child to the maximum extent appropriate in the school and classroom he or she would otherwise attend. Support is brought to the child, and the requirement is that the child benefits from the class. Modifications in curricular expectations may be made.

Full Inclusion: the education of all students in the general education classroom all of the time. All support services are brought to the child, and the child is removed only when appropriate services cannot be provided in the regular class.

threw a book across the classroom, hitting another child in the head. The school decided that inclusion was no longer safe for Gilbert and the other children. Rather than place him in a self-contained special education classroom, the family opted to homeschool him for several years until a special school placement was found to meet Gilbert's needs.

Dirk was mildly affected by ASD. His behavior had always been a bit different. He had difficulty socializing, but he made it without assistance through the primary grades. He had wonderful teachers who could accommodate him as a matter of course. Dirk's school troubles began in middle school. The demands of changing classes, keeping organized, and adapting to the demands of different teachers was too much for him to handle. He could do the work, but he couldn't always remember to turn in the assignments. Dirk brought everything home each day and worked another several hours with his parents to make sense of what had been presented. He could not study for tests on his own and needed help in organizing and completing long-term projects. Dirk's teachers were not concerned. They could see that Dirk was trying hard, and he was achieving Bs and Cs. Those grades were not good enough for Dirk, however. He knew he could get As, and anything less was a failure in his eyes.

What does IDEA 2004 mean for children with ASD? It means that each educational path is different. It means that each year the needs and options are reevaluated. It means that there are no ready answers, no straight lines to success, and no rest for weary parents.

Family-Centered Intervention

While it is true that the child's needs and goals should be paramount, the family's needs and goals may truly drive the course of treatment. If parents and teachers or parents and professionals get into a "them versus us" mentality, then the intervention program, no matter how good it is, will suffer. In order for the family to be able to take suggestions from the teacher or other service provider, the professionals need to be able to take suggestions from the parents. Everyone needs to be an equal member of the team.

When my colleagues and I are training new clinicians to work with parents, we show them that they do not need to be an expert at everything. The children we work with are difficult, and some days everything will go wrong. New clinicians may feel that the parents will be critical of them. They feel incompetent if a child is uncontrollable. On the contrary, most parents take comfort in the fact that they are not the only ones who have difficulty managing their child. If a child's behavior is especially off-target, we may ask the parents to join us, ask their advice, and together find ways to reengage the child. Often the parent will share that the child has been out of sorts all day and that it has been a tough day all around.

Sometimes parents need support as much as their child. In a clinical setting, with the parent right there, it is easy to let the child play for a while as you address the parent's need.

Bea's family lived in town near her aunts, uncles, and many cousins. Bea had a hard time with self-regulation, had frequent temper tantrums, and needed a lot of help to settle down. At $4\frac{1}{2}$, Bea still used a pacifier at naptime and bedtime, a practice that bothered one of her aunts. The aunt was giving Bea's mom a hard time about it, and Bea's mother, who was already feeling besieged about Bea's behavior at home, needed advice, counsel, and a place to vent. By spending a few minutes with Bea's mom, I probably did the most therapeutic thing that could have been done for Bea.

Although a family may not be quite as accessible in the school setting, a team relationship is still possible. Teachers and parents can communicate by email. Parents can give teachers a heads-up if their child didn't sleep well and is likely to be tired. Teachers can send out a "good news" message about what the child did or said. Keeping the lines of communication open so that parents and school staff understand each other's stresses and limitations helps everyone stay on the same page.

Procedural Safeguards

What happens when parents and school districts disagree or when parents need to understand their rights in regard to school programs? IDEA 2004 has outlined procedural safeguards regarding mediation and due process hearings. Parents have also taken school districts to court at various levels. In most cases, a parent advocate or special education lawyer can help a parent negotiate with the school district so that the needs of the child are met in a cooperative manner. The best lawyers and advocates do their homework ahead of time so that everyone knows the positions of the other party before the IEP meeting, and compromises can happen without confrontational battles. When IDEA was first put in place, due process hearings were more common. Although legal action is still a recourse, there is greater understanding that a legal battle drains energy and resources away from the real work with a child.

> Many lawyers who develop special education specialties are themselves parents of children with disabilities. This background gives them insight into the family's needs as well as expertise in the law. One parent felt that a private special school would better serve her child, and she knew that the school district was reluctant to outplace children. She was ready to battle. Her lawyer, however, mediated behind the scenes. He contacted the school lawyer and laid out the reasons for why the parent wanted her child to be placed out of the district. When it came to the meeting, the private-school placement was a done deal. Although the school district believed that they could continue to serve the child well, they agreed to the alternative placement. So the parent did not need to say anything negative about the district program, there were no recriminations, and the child's best interests were served.

A Team Approach for Success

Because there is so much new information about ASD these days, no one person can possibly keep up with all of it. Parents and professionals can share articles, ideas for intervention, and strategies that may be appropriate to their children. Through the years, parents have brought in articles and breaking news and we have become allies in keeping up with what is happening in the field of ASD.

The family is the key to assembling the team for the child. They choose physicians, arrange for evaluations, choose service providers, and go to school meetings. Although some parents feel that they are the least qualified to play the role of case manager and team leader, they are really the only ones who can do it. Parents can be helped to see that, although the professionals can give insight and direction, parents are truly the experts about their unique and wonderful child. The professionals who are part of the team need to help the parents develop the communication skills necessary to keep it all together. Parents often keep a big notebook with reports, test results, goals, and important schoolwork. Some also write journals or make scrapbooks. For some harried parents, it is all they can do to keep the piles of paper in a big box. Whatever system works for a family, all the information and the strategies that are developed constitute the story of the child's life, and through the story we can devise tactics to help the child move forward.

Chapter 3 Appendix

Child Evaluation for Autism Spectrum Disorder

TO THE PARENT/CAREGIVER: Please take the time to complete Parts 1 and 2 of this form and return them to us a week before your initial evaluation meeting. This information will help us get to know your child and better understand your concerns about your child before your appointment. It will help us plan the evaluation to fit your child's needs. You may wish to add a descriptive paragraph to address concerns not covered in the forms. You may bring snacks, reinforcers, or digital devices to help motivate your child to participate in the evaluation. Thank you.

Part 1: Intake Information

Date _____

Child's name _____ DOB _____ Age _____ Sex _____

Parents/Guardians

Names: _____ _____

Relationship to the child: _____ _____

Occupations: _____ _____

Marital status: _____

Primary address: _____
                     Street   City   State   Zip

Secondary address (if applicable) _____

Phone numbers: Home _____

                        Cell _____ (name _____)

                        Cell _____ (name _____)

Email _____ (name _____)

Email _____ (name _____)

Child's physician _____ Phone _____ Fax _____

Physician's address _____
                       Street   City   State   Zip

Medical insurance _____ ID# _____ Group # _____

Primary policy holder _____

Please describe your concerns about your child. Why are you seeking evaluation/services at this time?

_____

_____

_____

_____

_____

Part 2: Medical/Developmental History

Pregnancy, Birth, and Neonatal History:

Length of pregnancy _____

Please describe any complications and/or other factors that may have occurred during pregnancy (e.g., infections; toxemia; surgeries; medications; use of drugs, alcohol, tobacco).

_____

_____

Please describe any complications or problems during birth (e.g., use of forceps, umbilical cord around neck, slowed heart rate, hypoxia).

_____

_____

Birth weight _____ lb. _____ oz.

Did the infant have any breathing problems after delivery? If yes, please describe.

_____

_____

Was the infant in an incubator and/or the NICU? _____ If yes, the number of days _____.

Did the infant have any sucking or feeding problems? If yes, please describe.

_____

_____

How many days was the infant in the hospital? _____ days

Did the infant return to the hospital within the first 6 months? If yes, please explain.

_____

_____

Please describe the infant's nature during the first 6 months (e.g., quiet, fussy, alert, difficult to calm, good/poor sleeper)

_____

_____

_____

_____

Developmental History:

When and why did you first become concerned about your child's development?

_____

_____

What is most challenging or worrisome about your child?

_____

_____

Motor Milestones: Fill in the age that the milestone was accomplished, or indicate whether any milestone was late in developing.

Sitting alone, unsupported _____   Crawling _____   Standing alone _____

Walking alone _____   Self-feeding with spoon _____

Undressing/dressing _____   Toilet training completed _____

Communication:

What languages are spoken in the home? _____

What is the child's primary language? _____

Fill in the age at which the milestone was accomplished, or indicate whether any milestone was late in developing.

Babbling _____ First words _____ Word combinations _____

Responded to name _____ Followed simple directions _____

Did your child lose early words? _____ If yes, at what age? _____

Does or did your child echo phrases or repeat scripts? _____ If yes, please describe.

_____

_____

Does your child use gestures? _____

Describe how your child communicates wants and needs.

_____

_____

Social Communication:

Does your child: look at your face? _____

look at what you are pointing to? _____ share attention to book, toys, or activities? _____

initiate or respond to social interactions with adults or peers? _____

maintain appropriate eye contact? _____ understand and show facial expressions? _____

share imaginative play? _____ show interest in making friends? _____

Describe your concerns about your child's social communication.

_____

_____

_____

Restricted/Repetitive Behaviors:

If your child engages excessively in repetitive motor movements, use of objects, or idiosyncratic speech patterns, please describe.

_____

_____

If your child insists on the same routines, is inflexible about change, adheres to rigid rituals, or has temper tantrums, please describe.

_____

_____

If your child is intensely focused on certain interests or objects and has difficulty shifting to other interests or objects, please describe.

_____

_____

Describe activities that frustrate your child or that your child avoids.

_____

_____

If your child has unusual sensory sensitivities, sleep issues, or food avoidances, please describe.

_____

_____

What works?:
What works to teach your child something new?

_____

_____

What is soothing to your child?

_____

_____

What routines have been developed at home or at school?

_____

_____

What happens when those routines are changed?

_____

_____

Is there a special activity or song that your child enjoys that gets your child engaged?

_____

Strengths and Talents: Please describe what your child can do well (e.g., musical abilities, precocious reading, spelling, memory skills, artistic talents, physical abilities, puzzles, math, computers, apps).

_____

_____

_____

Describe activities that your child likes to do.

_____

_____

What is delightful about your child?

_____

_____

Medical History: Please list any significant medical history, including ear infections, high fevers, hospitalizations, injuries, and/or surgeries and the ages at which they occurred.

_____

_____

Is your child taking any medications? If so, please list, and explain the reason.

_____

_____

Are the child's immunizations current? _____

Have you sought consultations/evaluations with medical specialists (e.g., neurologists, geneticists, developmental pediatricians, psychiatrists, psychologists, speech/language pathologists, occupational therapists)? If so, please list and **attach copies of any relevant reports you wish to share.**

_____

_____

_____

_____

Family History:

Is your child biological or adopted? _____

Does the child with ASD have siblings? If so, please list them below.

Siblings: Name   M/F   Age

_____   _____   _____

_____   _____   _____

_____   _____   _____

_____   _____   _____

_____   _____   _____

Please list all the people who live with the child.

_____

Please list any additional significant caretakers who are with the child on a regular basis.

_____

Are there any members of your immediate or extended family who have not been diagnosed but who have recognizable traits of ASD, or who have been diagnosed with ASD, developmental disabilities, communication disorders, or learning disabilities? If so, please describe.

_____

_____

Has your family experienced any significant difficulties, stressors, or serious illnesses that may affect the child?

_____

_____

Intervention and School History:

Please attach any relevant reports and/or IEP documents you may wish to share.

Has your child received services through the Early Intervention Birth-to-Three Program? If so, list services, providers, and dates of service.

_____   _____

_____   _____

Has your child received therapies and/or behavioral interventions? If so, list services, providers and dates of service.

_____   _____

_____   _____

Does your child attend school or day care? If so, list school name, type of program, and grade level.

_____

_____

Have the teachers reported any concerns? If so, please explain.

_____

_____

Additional Information: Is there any additional information that would assist us in evaluating your child?

_____

_____

_____

_____   _____

Person completing this form   Relationship

Part 3: Formal Testing

TO THE EVALUATOR: Because of the wide range of abilities in children with ASD, specific tests in each evaluation area need to be carefully chosen. Because children with ASD may demonstrate uneven skills, analyze responses to particular subtests or test items rather than merely reporting total test standard scores. Keep copies of the test forms for comparison with future evaluations. Some children may be unable to participate in formal testing.

Types of tests to be considered for formal evaluations: (Write the tests you are considering in each category.)

Checklists for ASD diagnoses and/or autism diagnostic observation scale

Behavior rating scales

Speech and language evaluations

Tests of cognitive abilities

Motor, sensory, and adaptive ability scales

Reading decoding and comprehension tests (if appropriate)

Tests of academic abilities

Tests of social communication

Part 4: Observations

TO THE EVALUATOR: Use these guidelines to help you determine what to look for during the evaluation, in a conversation, and in the classroom or peer group. Write your observations in the space below each question. Include examples and/or explanations.

OBSERVATIONS DURING THE EVALUATION

During the evaluation, was the child calm or excitable, attentive or distractible?

Could the child regulate himself, or did he or she need an adult to help? Was the child able to be soothed by the parents? What worked or didn't work?

Did the child visually reference the adults? Did he look at something that was pointed to? Did he or she engage in eye contact? Did the child show various facial expressions?

How did the child respond to various approaches by the examiner—verbal, demonstration, hand-over-hand?

Did the child's parents use specific words or gestures to elicit responses?

What materials (if any) did the child gravitate to? Did the child show competence in using the materials? Did the child show pleasure when engaging with the materials?

What was the nature of the child's spontaneous communications—words, pointing, hand-pulling?

Could the child attend to anything for a period of time? Was there joint attention?

Could the child's attention be shifted using a verbal cue, or were visual prompts needed?

Did the child understand and/or comply with requests? Give examples.

What did the child do when not directly engaged?

Were there restricted or repetitive behaviors, and if so, did they interfere with completing a task or attending to a toy?

Ask the parents if the observed behaviors are typical of what they see in various situations. Ask them to describe the child's typical behaviors.

OBSERVATIONS IN CONVERSATION

Was eye-gaze appropriate?

How did the child initiate a conversation (e.g., asking a question, making a request, introducing the topic, launching into a monologue)?

Was the topic of interest to others in the conversation, or did the child talk only about idiosyncratic interests? Give examples of topics.

Did the child stand too close or too far from the conversational partner?

Was the child's intonation pattern monotonous or sing-song?

Did the child speak too loudly or too softly for the situation?

Did the gestures and body language match the verbal message?

How did the child indicate that he or she was listening to others?

Did the child appear to share enjoyment in the conversation?

CLASSROOM OR PEER GROUP OBSERVATIONS

Did the child initiate interactions with other children?

Did the child respond to the approaches of others?

Did the child respond to group instruction?

Did the child follow classroom routines and/or follow the rules of a game?

Could the child complete a task independently?

Describe the child's attention and/or distractibility patterns.

Describe any behavioral issues and how they were handled.

What accommodations have been put in place to help the child?

Part 5: Feedback, Support, and Planning

TO THE EVALUATOR: Use these guidelines to structure the feedback session and to bring up topics related to support systems and planning. Make sure that the parents'/caregivers' questions are addressed. These topics should also be included in the written report.

- Offer a diagnosis. Explain why the diagnosis is appropriate, and support your thinking with test data, observations, *DSM-5* guidelines, and research.

- Point out the child's strengths and positives.

- Explain the child's challenges.

- Carefully gauge the reaction to the diagnosis. Some families are relieved to have a label for the symptoms they have seen, while for others the diagnosis of ASD confirms their worst fears. Allow time for the family to absorb the information and frame their questions.

- Provide information about community resources, local and national autism organizations, and support groups. Offer a list of online resources, books, articles, online message boards, and Facebook groups.

- Provide evidence from scientific studies about the efficacy of treatments the family may wish to explore.

- Help the family identify support from close family and friends.

- Help the parents plan the next steps specific to their child. Remember that each child with ASD is an individual and there is no one-size-fits-all magic program.

  * Has the child been involved in treatment and/or school programs? Help the family assess whether additions and/or changes need to be made.

  * Does the child need further assessment from medical specialists or service providers?

  * Help the family understand what public services are available and which services may be covered by insurance.

  * For school-age children, help the parents understand the educational options and the rights and protections offered by the Individuals With Disabilities Education Improvement Act (IDEA). (See discussion in Chapter 3.)

  * Include recommendations in the written report for specific strategies and tactics that parents can use at home and that they can share with teachers and other service providers.

 Chapter 4

Intervention Tactics

Once you've established goals and objectives and the strategies to reach the objectives, it's time to select tactics. This chapter covers intervention tactics in detail. Tactics are used to implement the strategies to reach the objectives.

The challenge in suggesting tactics for children with ASD is the children's wide range of abilities. A tactic dealing with nonverbal communication, for example, would be quite different for a preverbal or nonverbal child as compared to the tactic for a verbal child. Even something as specific as teaching *what* questions varies from very simple to complex. To make this chapter usable and practical for SLPs, teachers, and parents working with particular children with ASD, tactics are divided into eight groups—basic skills, language, classroom, reading, writing, math, thinking, and social skills.

In each group of tactics, individual tactics are numbered. For many tactics, three levels of examples for activities are provided. Keep in mind that a particular child may need tactics between the levels suggested. Many of the tactics are interrelated. The Appendix to this chapter contains a summary chart listing all of the tactics in the first column and related tactics in the second column.

The suggestions in this chapter are intended as jumping-off points rather than prescriptions. Many of the tactics are based on the principle of using strengths to address weaknesses. The content of activities should be based on each child's unique interests and on what is required in the child's life.

Here is an example of how to choose tactics to achieve a particular goal and objective:

Goal: Charlie will write a logical narrative.

Objective 1: Charlie will write a logical paragraph.

Under *Language,* choose these tactics:

Language 14	Teach sequencing.
Language 15	Teach about attributes and descriptors.
Language 16	Teach explaining and describing.
Language 17	Teach how to create narratives and dialogues.

Under *Writing,* choose these tactics:

Writing 1	Decrease blank-page anxiety.
Writing 3	Use guided writing.
Writing 4	Demonstrate story organization.

Under *Basic,* consider these tactics:

Basic 1	Use visual patterns.
Basic 6	Follow the child.

After incorporating particular activities suggested under the tactics, the objective "Charlie will write a logical paragraph" would include:

Sequencing prewritten sentence strips (Language 14b)

Using adjectives in describing activities (Language 15b)

Describing a past event (Language 16c)

Retelling familiar stories (Language 17b)

Dictating a story to a "scribe" (Writing 1b)

Using Charlie's special interest in elephants as the topic (Basic 6)

Using a visual template for a five-sentence paragraph (Basic 1 and Writing 4a)

- topic sentence
- three details
- closing sentence

Basic Tactics

These tactics address the common learning style of children with ASD as described in Chapter 2. They are basic to the way we approach intervention with many of these children. Not all children with ASD need all the tactics. Look at the assessment of a child's particular learning style, strategies, and goals, and choose tactics with the best fit.

BASIC TACTIC 1: USE VISUAL PATTERNS

Children with ASD may be visual learners. Use visual, graphic, and written patterns. These patterns are concrete and tangible, and they don't disappear into thin air like verbal words do. Not all children are attracted to the same type of visual material, however. Some children like line drawings because they are less confusing. Others find that line drawings are too abstract and difficult to interpret. Some children like photographs because they are more like real objects. Others are attracted to cartoons or illustrations with exaggerated features. Children with hyperlexia or those with a fascination for letters and numbers may ignore everything but the words or letters on a picture. Take into account a particular child's differences in perception and focus.

> Every time Jerry saw a particular photo of the family car, he identified it as "McDonald's." After careful scrutiny with a magnifying glass, we did indeed find a very tiny McDonald's sign in the corner of the photo.

Use the same set of pictures, graphics, or written words until the child is successful at identifying or using it. Then carefully select other pictures of the same objects or words in a different font so that the child can begin to generalize.

Think about it. What distinguishes a picture of a boy from a picture of a girl, or the picture of a cat from a picture of a dog? A child with ASD may need to be specifically taught what features to look for.

BASIC TACTIC 2: TEACH VOCABULARY

Children with ASD have difficulty picking up new vocabulary from the background stream of language. They may also understand a particular word in one context but not automatically understand its meaning in another context. Teach vocabulary specific to each activity.

> Even though we had practiced prepositions and Sylvie could put the block behind the box, she did not know what to do when told to stand behind Jon.

Beware of words with multiple meanings and idiomatic language.

> April was tapping her fork on the table. When her dad told her to "knock it off," April did just that.

BASIC TACTIC 3: USE SIMPLE GRAMMAR

Typical language learners benefit from a language-rich environment with an abundance of verbal explanations, expansion, and elaboration. Since children with ASD learn language primarily through gestalt processing, they are often confused by too much language, particularly in new or upsetting situations. Simplify the grammatical structure of questions and explanations and speak slowly.

> My difficulty in going to France with my high school–level French extends to language processing as well as to misunderstanding questions. If I am calm and people speak slowly and simply, I can usually understand. If I am lost and I ask directions, anxiety reduces my comprehension significantly. I find myself scanning the language for the words for left and right and relying on gestures. The direction giver, sensing my confusion, tries harder by using more words of explanation, which makes me even more confused.

> When Andrew first came into our center for an evaluation, he took one look at the waiting room and reception desk and started wailing. "He thinks it's a doctor's office," his mother explained. She tried to tell him that he wasn't getting a shot and that this would be fun. But the more she talked, the more agitated Andrew became. When I showed him a Thomas train and said, "More Thomas. Come," he settled down long enough to come into the playroom.

BASIC TACTIC 4: USE EXAMPLES AND DEMONSTRATIONS

Children with ASD may not feel the need to engage in pretend play, greet a friend, ask a question, or sit at a table. Adults make the decision to teach new skills that they feel children need to learn. Just telling children that it is nice to say hi or wave when you come in the door doesn't usually carry over into everyday life. They need to practice greeting people in many different settings. They usually cannot go from the general to the specific. Instead, demonstrate and give many examples so that eventually they can go from the specific to the general. Broaden the scope of the examples across environments, so they know the response is expected everywhere.

> Tommy was learning about categories. He learned many unusual animal names. He could say that a cheetah and an orangutan were animals and a cricket and a praying mantis were insects. When asked to name some animals, however, he could only think of three.

BASIC TACTIC 5: REPEAT, REPEAT, REPEAT

Often children with ASD need many repetitions before information is fully absorbed into long-term memory. They may memorize scripts by seeing the same video, or the way to the grocery store by taking the same route many times. There is comfort in repetition and in knowing exactly what to expect in an often confusing world. One reason computer programs are attractive is because they are predictable and exactly the same each time. Most children move on from repeating the same script or sequence of events when they feel they have mastered it. As adults, we often feel that we have to constantly present something new, but children with ASD need things to be the same. We can find a balance by repeating, repeating, repeating, and then planning for change.

BASIC TACTIC 6: FOLLOW THE CHILD

Join in the child's activity when the child cannot respond to what is being presented, then gradually draw the child into new interactions. Follow the child, and take advantage of teachable moments. Some of my most productive sessions with children with ASD have been those I have not planned. Sometimes a child will come with a favorite toy and that will become the object to use to stimulate a request, pretend with, hide and find, tickle, or swing in a sheet.

> Josh brought his NASCAR collection to our session one day. We discussed the numbers, the sponsors, the drivers, and the races. It became the basis for a game that he made up. We practiced asking questions, taking turns, and having a two-way conversation.

> Brianna had been going through a prolonged negative phase. Her best word was "no," and the more adults tried to intervene, the more negative she became. We followed her lead and made no requests. At first she did very little, but soon she began to draw the adults into interactions with her.

BASIC TACTIC 7: USE CLOZE SENTENCE FORMATS

Wh- questions are particularly difficult for most children with ASD. Even the most concrete *what* questions can be confusing because the word itself is intangible. While children are learning how to answer *wh-* questions, use cloze sentence formats to clarify the communication. Instead of asking *Where did the class go today?*, use the sentence *The class went to the* _____. Modeling the proper pronoun in a cloze sentence is a bit of a problem, but using gestures and intonation markers usually helps. For example, if you want to know what a child wants to eat, the cloze sentence model is *I want to eat* _____. If you prompt the child by using the word *say*, the child will often repeat *Say I want to eat bananas*. A written sentence strip or a nonverbal gesture may be more helpful.

> Mark was playing in his room when his finger got stuck in one of his toys. When he yelled, his mother called to him and asked "What do you want?" When she got no response, she tried a cloze sentence. "Mark, tell me: I want the _____." Mark was then able to say "I want the finger."

Decks of question cards are also useful because they ask the question on one card and give the answer on another. Many children with ASD memorize the questions and answers verbatim at first and then can go on to learn different answers to the same questions.

BASIC TACTIC 8: GO FROM CONCRETE TO ABSTRACT

One of the primary functions of human language is to communicate abstract ideas. Word combinations stand for concepts that have no existence in the real world. While high-functioning individuals with ASD can eventually come to understand abstraction and inferential thinking, they come to it through direct experience and concrete examples. A child can learn the concept of kindness by being shown specific ways of being kind: sharing toys, helping someone, using polite words. Sometimes these examples need to be even more concrete. For example, "When you let Sammy play with your truck, you were being kind." Use many concrete examples to develop an abstract concept.

> When Nick was 3, he loved to do the United States floor puzzle. He knew the names of all the states and their capitals and could put the puzzle together quite quickly. When his family took a road trip and crossed the border from Illinois to Indiana, he became upset. He thought that Indiana should be yellow, since that was the color of the Indiana puzzle piece. Even years later, the idea that a map is a representation of something as vast as the United States was hard for him to grasp.

BASIC TACTIC 9: USE ROTE LEARNING

If a child truly learns something, the new information and ideas can be associated with previous knowledge, compared, contrasted, and used flexibly. Rote learning is often viewed as pure memorization without much understanding or application. Since children with ASD can often memorize bits of information but have difficulty associating the new information with previous knowledge, teachers question whether these students have truly "learned" the material. We all have learned some information in a rote fashion. We learned the multiplication tables and the list of presidents of the United States. We learned that $E = mc^2$ but few of us can explain what it means. It is better for children with ASD to be introduced to information and to learn to repeat it back than not to present the information (Heward, 2003). Use rote-learning abilities to expose children to vocabulary, ideas, and concepts that may become useful to them later.

Michael loved to study the encyclopedia on the computer. He especially liked the videos and graphics. Michael learned Martin Luther King Jr.'s "I Have a Dream" speech. He learned that John F. Kennedy said, "Ask not what your country can do for you, but what you can do for your country." And over and over again, he watched Neil Armstrong's first step on the moon. When Michael was in second grade, he was included in general education with a paraprofessional assistant. When the teacher showed a slide of an astronaut in a space suit, Michael said to his paraprofessional, "That's Neil Armstrong. He walked on the moon on July 20, 1969." When asked to repeat it to the rest of the class, the children were amazed. It was the first thing Michael had ever said in class. As a follow-up, Michael's mother helped him set up a demonstration using flour, paprika, and rocks to show how craters formed on the moon. Michael recited the script—directly from the TV science show *Beakman's World*. Everyone was very excited until it came time for the test. Michael could not answer a single question about the moon on the test. The teacher wondered if Michael really "knew" anything about the moon. What good was this rote learning? When a new assessment was created using cloze sentence formats and Michael's scripts, he did well. The question of knowledge, though, still remains.

BASIC TACTIC 10: USE LISTS AND SCHEDULES

Children with ASD often have difficulty with executive function. They have difficulty planning and carrying out tasks. They do better when given organization for a particular task, a sequence of events, and a plan for the day. Lists and schedules are very important tools and can be used throughout the day. Many teachers use picture schedules to structure the school day. Even non-readers often do well with simple lists because the lists are tangible. Many parents carry small writing boards so they can quickly write the schedule like "1. Bank, 2. McDonald's." Lists and schedules help introduce the concepts of *first* and *then*. Tantrum behavior is dramatically reduced when a child can delay the strongly desired activity and do what is asked of her first.

Shelly was obsessed with a ball ramp toy. If it was in the room, she wanted to do nothing else. If it was not in the room, she kept looking and asking for it. We made her a very short list: 1. Brown Bear book, 2. ball ramp. We drew simple line drawings to go with the words. At first Shelly would look at the book for a few seconds and then was allowed to run two balls down the ramp. We gradually increased her time with the book. She learned that if the ball ramp was on the list, she could count on playing with it. In later sessions, the list contained two activities before the ball ramp. Eventually, Shelly participated in activities for 45 minutes before playing with the ball ramp. The list tactic helped Shelly cope with other obsessions across a variety of settings. The written list helped her put obsessive thoughts aside so she could concentrate on other tasks.

BASIC TACTIC 11: DEVELOP BEHAVIOR SYSTEMS

Many children with ASD benefit from structured behavior systems. Even when a child is not involved in a discrete-trials or applied behavioral analysis program, behavioral tactics can be helpful. The following steps of a behavioral tactic have been used successfully to modify particular behaviors:

1. Write the goal and objective stated in a positive way. Say what the child will do, rather than identify the behavior to be extinguished.

> Because Marty wandered around with his food at snack time at school and dinnertime at home, the target behavior is "Marty will sit and eat at the table for 3 minutes."

2. Make a chart and write the objective at the top.

3. Set up a positive reward system. Stars can be earned but cannot be taken away.

Many families use a simple five-square star chart with a picture of a small reward at the end. Figure 4.1 illustrates a simple star chart.

> If Marty doesn't sit at the table, the adult can say, "Oh, well. No star now. Maybe next time."

4. The reward pictured should be something the child wants. Allow older children to negotiate the number of stars needed to earn the reward.

> Marty liked the toys from the movie *Cars* and was motivated to add to his collection.

5. Guarantee success. Make sure the target behavior can be achieved and the stars can be earned in a day or two at first. Modify the target behavior or the number of stars needed so the child will learn that her efforts will be rewarded.

BASIC TACTIC 12: DEVELOP TEAMWORK

Children with ASD do not automatically transfer learned information and behavior from one environment to the next. A child with ASD may learn a routine at school but may not use it at home. Teachers, parents, and therapists need to communicate with each other. Everyone needs to know which prompts elicit the desired responses and how to prepare the child for success. It is important to work as a team to facilitate transfer across environments.

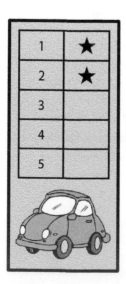

Everyone who knew Alex described him as a visual learner. He was a precocious reader and loved dictionaries and cookbooks. Despite his strong visual skills, Alex had great difficulty recognizing faces. Alex knew me very well. He could differentiate me from the other women at the therapy center. He recognized me at events in the community. One day, however, when I came to his school, he did not know who I was. He wasn't prepared to see me in that environment and could not reconcile my face with the school. We learned to prepare him for situations ahead of time so he would know what to expect and transfer this very basic knowledge to a different environment.

Figure 4.1. A chart for a positive reward system.

BASIC TACTIC 13: DEVELOP COMMUNICATION SYSTEMS

Implement a communication system for parents, school personnel, and outside professionals. If families, therapists, and teachers can work hand in hand, the benefit to the child is enormous.

> Daniel's parents held periodic "Daniel meetings" at their home. They invited everyone who worked with him and provided delicious food as an added incentive. Teachers, therapists, tutors, and Daniel's parents found it very helpful to share ideas in an informal way. Between meetings, participants used email to keep everyone up to date and to raise questions and concerns.

BASIC TACTIC 14: EXPAND THE CONTEXT

Those with ASD tend to learn in particular situations, and conscious efforts are required to transfer new skills into different contexts. A behavior or language pattern developed in a therapy setting needs to be practiced in the classroom, at home, and in the community in a variety of activities and with a variety of people. We need to help individuals with ASD realize that games learned with their siblings, for example, can be played with classmates. They need to learn that rules at school (e.g., use a quiet voice) also apply at home.

> One of our basic rules is, "If someone speaks to you, you must answer." Kate would do it well in the therapy room and at home with her parents, but she was complaining that too many people at school were talking to her and she didn't want to answer all the time. Her mother and I persisted, explaining that she must respond everywhere. "Oh, no," Kate exclaimed with glee. "What about stranger danger? If a stranger speaks to me, I don't have to answer!"

BASIC TACTIC 15: HAVE FUN

Children with ASD are first and foremost children. Although life with them can be difficult and filled with many challenges, they can be charming and loving and funny. It is important to find joy amidst the sorrow and laughter through the tears.

> One adolescent with ASD often tells me, "People like humor. They like to laugh." And then he asks in all seriousness, "Why?"

> Carolyn's mother saw that Carolyn had dropped nails on the floor close to where her younger sister was playing. She asked sternly, "Carolyn, where did those nails come from?" Carolyn looked at the box and answered, "From China."

Apply the basic tactics to specific interventions for language, reading, writing, math, thinking, and social skills. Although each area is discussed separately in the subsequent pages, it is important to remember that these skills overlap. Gestalt processing of language affects reading comprehension and interpretation of social communication. A writing assignment may have a social component as well as a written language goal. Identify specific elements in each of these areas to meet the unique needs of each child with ASD.

Language Tactics

The language tactics are presented in a general hierarchical order, and three levels of activities are suggested for each tactic. Children with ASD, however, seldom follow expected hierarchies as they may gain higher-level skills before they accomplish skills that seem to come first in typical development (Prizant, 1983). Pick and choose tactics that best fit a child's needs. Receptive and expressive tactics are considered together since children with ASD often seem to acquire these skills simultaneously (Wynn & Smith, 2003).

LANGUAGE TACTIC 1: TEACH REFERENCING AND INDICATING

A basic form of early communication is the ability to refer to a caregiver and draw another person into eye contact; to indicate by a gesture, point, or vocalization; and to follow another person's point or gesture. An early sign of ASD is the child's lack of response when his name is called.

Language Tactic 1a

Engage the child in a reciprocal action, such as peek-a-boo. Place a scarf over your face, and show the child how to pull the scarf down to get a surprising sound ("boo") or a physical action (tickle).

Language Tactic 1b

Show the child how to indicate to an adult that he wants something out of reach. The indication may be gestured or verbal, but the goal is for the child to initiate engagement with the adult.

Language Tactic 1c

Teach the child to look at his communication partner for an appropriate time, indicating he is listening. Many times a child with ASD is actually listening but does not reference the speaker in a way that indicates he has heard. Show the child how to nod or to say "uh-huh."

LANGUAGE TACTIC 2: TEACH LABELING

Many verbal children with ASD develop good labeling skills, though they may not be able to put words together to form two-word phrases. Other children may comprehend common labels of both nouns and actions but may not be able to respond verbally. Labels can be simple (names of foods or body parts) or complex (systems used in the biological sciences to classify plants).

Language Tactic 2a

Use physical prompts to help the child point to body parts, pictures, or computer programs or to fetch or give objects. At this basic level, figuring out the child's best response pattern is an important part of this tactic.

Language Tactic 2b

Practice verbally labeling items in a book or in the environment. Use the same set of pictures or items until the child can label most of them easily. Use cloze sentences to help the child label an item when it is not physically present. For example, say, "Grandma gave you a _____. Let's go get it."

Language Tactic 2c

Teach higher-level labels (mammals, reptiles, marsupials) using sorting tasks, worksheets with multiple choices, or computer programs.

LANGUAGE TACTIC 3: EXPAND VOCABULARY

Typical children gain vocabulary very rapidly after the age of 2, and by age 6 they may use 2,500 to 5,000 words and may comprehend as many as 20,000 or more words (Stahl, 1999). Many verbal children with ASD can learn new vocabulary rapidly, but they must be specifically taught through association and repetition.

Language Tactic 3a

Teach receptive identification of specific vocabulary. For example, when teaching color words, help the child differentiate and identify colors by putting the concept into action, such as asking the child to roll the blue ball down the ramp.

Language Tactic 3b

Teach vocabulary within a context. Frame experiences with particular words and later reinforce those words with pictures and stories. For example, help the child notice the weather. At recess or before getting in the car, say, "It's windy. Feel the wind." Help the child associate the real wind with the picture of wind when talking about the weather in circle time at school. More than one child with ASD has associated the word *windy* only with the picture of the puffy blowing cloud.

Language Tactic 3c

At a higher level, some vocabulary is specific to various school subjects, professions, activities, or social groups. It is important to teach the lingo. A child can't talk about baseball unless he knows the terms *fly ball*, *home run*, or *double*. It is common for children with ASD to be able to list names of teams but not understand the game at all. A key part of education is teaching vocabulary. For example, if the student needs to name or identify the parts of the U.S. government for a test on the U.S. Constitution, teach the vocabulary by matching words to definitions, using synonyms, and using words in context.

> Alex loves to peruse the dictionary. He chooses three words at the beginning of each session and learns the definitions. He noticed that there were words with two pronunciations, such as *console*, and he wanted to know what those kinds of words were called. A quick look on the Internet taught us that these are called *heteronyms*, and Alex loved that word. In subsequent sessions he found other heteronyms, and he never fails to tell me with a big grin that "bow" has a heteronym.

LANGUAGE TACTIC 4: TEACH HOW TO COMMUNICATE WANTS AND NEEDS

Sometimes at the basic level, children with ASD need to be shown that they can want something. They may put forth no effort to do anything without an outside prompt. The tactic is getting them to understand their desire and then to communicate it in any way they can. Others communicate by signs that caregivers learn to recognize, such as the "I-need-the-potty dance." Tantrums are a form of communication but do not always have the desired result. At a higher level, children can learn to discern between wants and needs.

Language Tactic 4a

> Teach the child some basic signs, gestures, or sounds to indicate a desire. Engage the child in a physical activity, such as swinging in a sheet. Set up a pattern, such as "ready-set-go," until the child anticipates the action. Then delay the start of the activity until the child gives an indication to continue. The sign for "more," a grunt, a word approximation, or a picture symbol can be used. The emphasis is on the communication of the desire, rather than the act of talking or giving. The reinforcement is that the desire is fulfilled.

Language Tactic 4b

Use patterned sentences or cloze sentence formats. Vary the sentence patterns, for example, "I want the _____," "Give me the _____," or "Please get the _____." This tactic avoids the question form, and the last example avoids the pronoun as well. Question forms and pronouns are problematic for many children with ASD.

> Sometimes the children learn this tactic all too well. Carla watched me search my bookshelf and said, "Phyllis, you want the _____?" Dutifully, I filled in the blank.

Language Tactic 4c

At a higher level, help adolescents understand the difference between desires and needs. For example, students can understand that although they want to watch television, they need to do homework. A chart such as the one below is useful in outlining requirements and options.

IF (requirement)	THEN (option)
I finish my homework.	I can play a video game for 15 minutes.
I take a shower.	I can wear my yellow shirt.
I pass the social studies test.	I can take woodshop next semester.

Don't underestimate the importance of the ability to articulate wants and desires. Some adolescents have spent their lives learning to do what others tell them. They literally don't realize that they can have long-term desires. When transition teams ask them what careers they would like to pursue, they have no clue.

> Ben doesn't much like his job as a bagger at a supermarket. When I asked him what he'd rather do, he couldn't think of anything. Finally he said, "Maybe I could work at Target."

LANGUAGE TACTIC 5: TEACH REQUESTING

While a child may say what he wants, the adult decides whether or not to grant the request. In typical development, the idea of requesting occurs very early. It is expressed in the look a toddler gives just before he goes somewhere he knows he shouldn't be. It requires awareness of who is in charge. The concept of asking permission of an authority needs to be directly taught to those with ASD.

Language Tactic 5a

Teach the child to look at the adult to gain approval for a desired action. For a child with ASD, this is not a skill that comes naturally and it must be practiced. Teach the child to wait for a key word before acting. For example, before jumping on a trampoline, teach the child to wait for the adult to say, "Go." In effect, this is asking permission before starting.

> Dylan had free rein of the therapy room during his initial evaluation. He spent many minutes going back and forth between the children's computer and the "work" computer, clicking the optical mouse on each and watching the lights go on. During his first several therapy sessions, he needed to be taught that the "work" computer was off-limits. Dylan did very well for several months, but one day he stood next to the "work" computer and looked at his mother and the therapist as if to ask permission to touch the mouse again.

Language Tactic 5b

Teach the child to use polite forms to request rather than demand. Egocentric demands need to be moderated so that they become interactive communications. The child also needs to learn that a request can be denied or negotiated.

> One young boy wanted to play a computer game as part of his session. He asked politely, and he and the therapist negotiated the plan that he would play one level of the game and then would go on to other things. Everything was quite clear to both parties at the beginning. After he played the game, however, the boy did not want to stop. When reminded of the request and the negotiation, he said, "Yes, but I changed my mind."

Language Tactic 5c

Teens with ASD often feel that they do not need to request things because they always have good reasons for doing things. For example, the adolescent must be helped to understand that he needs to ask before borrowing his father's laptop, even though he may have to wait until his father gets home. A visual chart with clear explanations and limits is often helpful.

LANGUAGE TACTIC 6: PRACTICE PROTESTING

In typical development, protesting is developed to a fine art during the period known as the "Terrible Twos." In children with ASD, the tactic of protesting is useful in developing the child's sense of self. It is as if the child were saying, "I am a person and I don't want to _____." Some children with ASD protest by hitting themselves or others or by having tantrums. An adult's first impulse is often to stop the behavior rather than to address the protest. If the adult helps the child protest in a more communicative way, she can then better address the reason for the protest.

Language Tactic 6a

Teach the child the sign or gesture for *stop, no,* or *all done,* both receptively and expressively. You can also use a written word or picture symbol. It is important to acknowledge the protests so the child does not have to resort to more dramatic behaviors.

Language Tactic 6b

Practice verbal patterns such as "I don't like _____," "I don't want _____," or "No more _____." Pair dislikes with likes in a concrete or visual way. For example, "I don't like hot dogs; I like cheese" or "I don't like blue shoes; I like pink shoes."

Language Tactic 6c

Practice polite protest language ("No, thank you"). Teach the child to suggest alternatives to what he does not want to do. Look for the child's reason for protesting. Is the child protesting something new, difficult, or unexpected? Does the child not understand? Is the child overwhelmed or is the child testing the limits? The response to the protest is driven by the perceived reason.

> Josh learned to protest very politely. The problem was that he protested doing anything slightly new, different, or not of his own choosing. If asked to try a new game, he often said, "No, thanks" and wouldn't budge. Why was Josh protesting so much? His mother and I realized that he was anxious about not knowing how to do something or failing to do well. It worked better to demonstrate a new activity before asking Josh to participate. We also modeled an alternative to his initial protest—"I'll try."

LANGUAGE TACTIC 7: OFFER CHOICES

Some children with ASD have difficulty making choices because they don't understand the concept of *either/or.* Others feel that only one of the choices is the right choice and they don't want to choose the wrong one. Some might always choose the safe, known choice, and some might be unclear of their options.

Language Tactic 7a

First teach the child to choose just one. Start with two or three desired foods or toys and help the child pick one. When naming the items, emphasize the word *or.* Add a foil (a known undesired food or toy) and help the child avoid that choice.

Language Tactic 7b

Some children are paralyzed by thinking there is always a perfect choice. When presented with choices of no real consequence, they take forever to pick one. Start with choosing from two identical objects or actions. Then move to two similar but neutral objects or actions. For example, prior to a pencil activity, have the child choose between two identical pencils. Then have the child choose from two similar but not identical pencils. Similarly, when leaving, the child could choose to go out the right door or the left door when both doors open to the same hallway.

Language Tactic 7c

At a higher level, teach the parameters of making choices. Show the individual with ASD how to identify and evaluate options. For example, when planning to drive to the mall, he might consider whether to choose:

- the most direct route
- the route least likely to have a traffic problem
- the most familiar route
- the route that avoids the freeway

Evaluate the pros and cons of each decision and make the choice based on what is most important to the individual.

LANGUAGE TACTIC 8: TEACH HOW TO FOLLOW DIRECTIONS

At the basic level, following one- or two-step directions depends on understanding prepositions. Children with ASD who are scanning language for nouns and verbs may not tune into little words such as *on* or *in*. At a higher level, the individual may not process adjectives or adverbs. Following directions may involve vocabulary specific to the topic. Many students have particular difficulty following directions in math. As directions become lengthier or more complex, memory skills also affect following directions.

Language Tactic 8a

Teach the child to follow one- and two-step directions that do not contain prepositions, such as "Get the ball" or "Clap your hands." If possible, have the child give directions as well as follow directions.

Language Tactic 8b

Systematically add prepositions, adjectives, adverbs, and dependent clauses to the directions. For example, work up to "Get the little, striped ball on the second shelf, and quickly hide it under the blue cardboard box on the round table." Then add negatives to the directions. For example, "Do not open the box until Dad comes home." Many children with ASD only process the "open the box" part of that direction.

> Finn and his family played the "Boss Game," in which they took turns giving a series of increasingly lengthy and complex physical directions. For example, "Touch your head four times, jump backwards, clap twice, and sit on a blue chair." When the same directions were given to the whole group, Finn watched what the others were doing. Although that was a pretty good tactic for a child with ASD, our goal was to help him follow directions independently. We changed the game so that each participant received separate directions to follow and remember until the boss said, "Go!"

Language Tactic 8c

Following verbal and/or written directions to complete math, social studies, or science assignments requires higher-level language. First, introduce vocabulary used in the text. Then identify implied and explicit directions. For example, in "Do problems 1–5 on page 60. Show your work," the child must understand that "1–5" means 1, 2, 3, 4, and 5, and he must figure out what "work" to show. The child with ASD may know the answer, but he might not be able to express how he knows it.

LANGUAGE TACTIC 9: TEACH CAUSE AND EFFECT

The idea that one action causes another is difficult for those with ASD. They may not understand the relationship between two events, and the language to describe this relationship is abstract.

While they can learn the patterns of *if/then, why/because,* or *why/so,* the two sides of the cause-and-effect equation often do not match.

> Arlene was shown a picture of a girl who was crying because she fell and skinned her knee. When I asked Arlene why the girl was crying, she replied, "Because she was wearing a blue dress."

Language Tactic 9a

In developing the cause-and-effect tactic at the basic level, avoid the *why/because* question form. Children with ASD generally have difficulty with the abstract quality of *why* questions. At the basic level, children need to learn physical cause and effect ("If you jump off the high slide, you will get hurt"). Teach the child to demonstrate how one physical act causes something to happen. Reaction toys (jack-in-the boxes, car launchers) are good ways to start. Use the child's noise or word (the cause) to create a big effect. For example, a child's noise can cause you to let go of a balloon so that it flies around the room.

Language Tactic 9b

Many typical 3- and 4-year-old children go through a phase of constantly asking *why* questions, such as "Why is the sky blue?" or "Why do dogs have tails and we don't?" Children with ASD may go through this phase at a later age than typical children. Help them understand the abstract concept of *because* by first teaching *if/then.* Most parents and teachers rejoice when children with ASD understand *if/then,* since this concept can be used to understand behavioral consequences ("If you put on your shoes, then you can go outside").

Language Tactic 9c

Understanding cause and effect is key to both higher-level reading comprehension and understanding social relationships. For example, "Why did a character in a book (or a person in real life) react in a particular way?" Students with ASD need a lot of coaching to understand this concept. Provide many examples of abstract and social cause-and-effect relationships, and practice articulating reasons.

> Anthony was doing very well in school. He was getting an A in reading comprehension because he got 90% correct on all of his quizzes. When his mother looked at the quizzes to see what questions he got wrong, she noticed that he missed the inferential question on each quiz. He could answer the factual questions or questions about what happened in the plot, but he could not answer why something happened or what caused it. He could not guess the reason for a reaction.

LANGUAGE TACTIC 10: TEACH LANGUAGE CONCEPTS

Verbal children with ASD develop language in a sequence that varies from that of their typical peers. Usually when children with typical language reach the age of 4 to $4\frac{1}{2}$, they become ready to learn language concepts such as opposites, categories, absurdities, same/different, what does not belong, and what goes together. They learn to use pronoun referents and plurals. Teach each concept directly, practice, and then put each concept into a context. Present each concept in several different ways. For example, when teaching absurdities, show a "What's wrong" picture and ask, "What's wrong?" or "What's silly?" The child may say, "The traffic lights are the wrong colors." The child may later create a negative sentence, such as "The traffic light shouldn't be pink." Finally, ask the child to state how it should be. For example, "The traffic light should have red and green."

Language Tactic 10a

On a nonverbal level, have the child put together a puzzle depicting opposites or associations. Teach the child to sort pictures or objects by category; for example, put the animals in the animal box and the cars in the car box.

Language Tactic 10b

Teach the child to describe concepts with verbal phrases. Depending on the child's language ability, these phrases can be simple or complex. For example, when introducing opposites, the child can first say "big" and "little." A child with more language can say, "If it's not big, it's little." Then teach the child to say "The opposite of *big* is *little*."

Language Tactic 10c

Higher-level language depends on the concepts of association, categorization, part-to-whole, and so forth. Teach the student to see relationships in the curricular material at school. Lists and charts are helpful. For example, show the concept of continents versus countries visually with maps and charts, and match the countries to their continents using lists and worksheets.

LANGUAGE TACTIC 11: MAKE ASSOCIATIONS

Making associations is a key tactic in learning. Students with ASD have difficulty associating new information with previous knowledge. At a basic level, help children see that toys represent real objects. Once they have sufficient language, teach them to use similes to draw comparisons.

Language Tactic 11a

Symbolic play helps a child develop associations to real life. While a child with ASD may engage in toy play, he often needs to be directly taught how to pretend. The child may pour water into a cup, but he may not pretend to have a tea party. Use common, everyday experiences within the child's life as a basis for play. For example, teach the child with ASD to pretend to drive a toy car and make a car noise. Show the child how to feed a baby doll a bottle, cover it up, and put it to sleep.

Language Tactic 11b

Teach the child to narrate his play and associate the play scheme with something he has done at home or in the past. For example, when playing with a toy giraffe, help the child say, "I saw a big giraffe at the zoo." When playing with pretend food, help the child say, "I baked cookies with Grandma at home."

Language Tactic 11c

Show the student how a concept in science, for example, resembles something in his experience. Blow up a balloon and let it fly around. Show how this resembles the way a jet engine works. Show the student how multiplying by 5 (a new concept) is the same as adding 5 of the same number (a known concept).

LANGUAGE TACTIC 12: TEACH HOW TO ANSWER QUESTIONS

Individuals with ASD frequently have difficulty with *wh-* questions. One way to assess which question patterns are difficult for the child is by using *The WH Question Comprehension Test* by Vicker and Naremore (2002). This test presents 10 each of *who, what, where, when, why,* and *how* questions. Children with ASD frequently have difficulty with *why* and *how* questions. They tend to respond to questions literally, not perceiving the intent of the questions. They tend to be uncomfortable with questions that do not have precise answers.

Language Tactic 12a

Where questions are a good place to start because the child can respond without words. Teach the child to point, fetch, or show answers to "Where is the ball?," "Where is your nose?," or "Where is Mommy?"

Language Tactic 12b

Packs of *wh*-question cards, with the question on one card and the answer on the other, are good tools for practicing how to answer a variety of question types. While the child with ASD may like to learn the specific answers shown on the cards, show him that other answers are also possible.

After practice, most children generalize the ability to answer these concrete questions. Teach the child to answer a variety of questions using cloze sentence formats, gradually fading the prompts.

Language Tactic 12c
Demonstrate and write answers to questions requiring inference or conjecture. Teach the child with ASD to start those answers with "maybe" to distinguish conjecture from fact.

> Austin and I were reading a book about astronauts. When I asked him why he thought that people wanted to explore space, he couldn't find the answer in the book. Hoping to get him to think of an answer on his own, I modeled the word maybe as a cue for his answer. He looked at me disgustedly and said, "Maybe, maybe. I don't like that word maybe." He wanted things to be precise and concrete. No maybes allowed.

LANGUAGE TACTIC 13: TEACH HOW TO ASK QUESTIONS
Asking questions is not the opposite of answering questions. It is a more complex task. You must figure out what you need to know, whom you should ask, and how to formulate the question. Question asking may serve to initiate conversation or to keep the conversation going.

Language Tactic 13a
A young child with ASD may ask a question by making a statement with an upward inflection ("I can have juice?"). A question may be a request or a statement of the child's desire or need. Model inverted question forms and provide plenty of practice.

Language Tactic 13b
The next level of question asking involves another person. In a dyad or small group, teach the child to ask, "Do you want to play _____?," "Which color do you want?," or "What video game do you like?"

Language Tactic 13c
High-level questioning involves understanding the social purpose of the question, how the question should be phrased, and whether it is appropriate to ask. Directly teach what question to ask and how to ask the question. Although rules for question asking may be too rigid and/or broad, avoiding certain types of questions can prevent embarrassing situations. For example, avoid questions about bodily functions, race, ethnicity, or disability, as a general rule. Teach the young adult with ASD to listen to the answer to his question and follow up with another question related to the topic.

> During lunchtime at work, J.J. didn't know what to talk about, so he would try to initiate a conversation by asking questions about everyone else's food. "What kind of yogurt is that?" "What is in your sandwich?" or "What is written on your Snapple cap?" Although these questions seem innocuous on the surface, they were beginning to get on everyone's nerves. A rule was made that there would be no more questions about food. J.J. could ask a question about the topic people were discussing. For example, if someone asked another worker, "How was your vacation?" J.J. could follow up by asking, "Where did you go?"

LANGUAGE TACTIC 14: TEACH SEQUENCING
A basic executive function is the ability to organize in a logical order. Language sequencing is a necessary skill for creating narratives and for having effective conversational interchanges. Devise tactics with a variety of objects, stories, lists, or written materials.

Language Tactic 14a

Use nesting cups or boxes to teach the child to sequence by size. Use pictures to sequence a story. Teach the words *first* and *then*. Help the child organize a task in 1–2–3 order.

Language Tactic 14b

There are a number of tactics for nonverbal and verbal sequencing. Use computer games, iPad apps, worksheets, and objects to teach the child to pick out the sequence pattern in a series. Have the child organize sentence strips into a sequential story. Encourage the child to retell the order of plot elements in a familiar story. Teach the child how to give directions or to tell others how to complete a task.

Language Tactic 14c

Sequencing skills are necessary for creating oral and written narratives, describing past events, and engaging in conversation. Written templates and scaffolds help the student create a story with a logical sequence. Use a dry erase board to help the student write brainstorming ideas. Show how to organize those ideas into a story or essay. Help the student figure out what the listener or reader needs to know first in order to understand.

LANGUAGE TACTIC 15: TEACH ABOUT ATTRIBUTES AND DESCRIPTORS

Children with ASD may have difficulty following directions using adjectives and adverbs. Conversely, they may tune in to the details rather than the main idea. It is helpful to develop tactics to address both sides of the problem.

Language Tactic 15a

Emphasize the words for attributes in giving directions to the child with ASD. Have the child choose an object from its description ("Give me the animal that has no legs"). Demonstrate how to categorize pictures or objects by attributes (by putting all the blue blocks in a box).

Language Tactic 15b

There are a number of games that use attributes and provide a structured interaction with other children. Blink (Out of the Box Publishers) has players sort by color, shape, or number and can be played with children with relatively little language. Other games, such as Secret Square (University Games) or Guess Who? (Hasbro), use attributes and verbal descriptions.

Guess Who? is an excellent game to work on attributes. Many children learn the standard questions (Does your person wear a hat? Is your person a girl?). The real test is near the end of the game, when children have to discern the critical difference between the remaining characters. Once a child can do that, I know he truly understands attributes.

Use barrier activities, such as telling another person what to draw or where to place objects, to practice using attributes to describe. Teach and practice using appropriate adjectives and adverbs to identify objects and actions.

Language Tactic 15c

Attributes and descriptors come into play in the language of higher-level academics. The student is required to learn an entirely new vocabulary of descriptive words in each discipline. In science units, teach the student with ASD to identify characteristics of plants, rocks, or animals. In literature, have the student describe a scene in a movie or play. Use a template to create a fictional character, and assign attributes and traits to that character. For example, list the characteristics of gender, age, hair and eye color, body type, family constellation, place of origin, profession, and likes and dislikes. Then write a paragraph describing the character.

LANGUAGE TACTIC 16: TEACH EXPLAINING AND DESCRIBING

Explaining and describing require skills in sequencing, organizing, and understanding what the other person needs to know. Very often people with ASD have an explanation from their perspective or a description from their experience, but theory-of-mind issues arise as they try to communicate their thoughts to others.

Language Tactic 16a
Look for indications that the child remembers a past event or past procedure. For example, have the child show the way to the therapy room, show where he put his shoes, or take a cell phone photo or video as he is participating in an activity, and show it to him.

Language Tactic 16b
Teach the verbal child to tell about a past event. Use picture cues, photos, or videos to stimulate language related to the event.

Language Tactic 16c
Help the individual with ASD accurately describe an incident and explain why it happened. This task involves understanding what is "true" and which details the listener needs to understand what happened.

> Austin was reprimanded in his transition-to-work program. He was required to stay after dismissal time to deal with his behavior, which made him late for an appointment. When he got to the appointment, he explained that he was late because "they told me I was rude." He said that he was upset mainly because "they" had made him late. The staff thought he was upset because of the reprimand. Austin hadn't explained that he was going to be late for an appointment. A cycle of misunderstanding occurred not only because Austin couldn't explain what had happened, but also because he misjudged the people in the situation.

LANGUAGE TACTIC 17: TEACH HOW TO CREATE NARRATIVES AND DIALOGUES
Understanding and creating narratives and dialogues is a many-layered task. It is a skill necessary for succeeding academically, but it is also a skill that frames and gives order to our daily lives and relationships with others. People with ASD can learn to create their personal stories as well as understand the stories of others. Some of these tactics are described in the social skills section of this chapter.

Language Tactic 17a
Help the child follow the plot of a simple, patterned-language picture book. *The Gingerbread Man* or *Are You My Mother?* are good beginning books. Use toys or puppets to create a play narrative, which can be a nonverbal sequence such as a bedtime drama with a doll (giving it a bottle, putting it to bed, giving it a kiss goodnight).

Language Tactic 17b
Teach the child to narrate play schemes, such as, "The car is going fast. Oh, no. It crashed. Here comes the police car." Help the child retell a familiar story or part of a video, game, or book. Some of the retelling may be scripted, but then help the child paraphrase, using his own words. Tactics for making associations, understanding cause and effect, and sequencing also come into play at this level.

Language Tactic 17c
If you listen to teenage conversation, you will hear a litany of "he said/she said" or "he goes _____/she goes _____." A tactic for the individual with ASD is to understand and recount dialogue in a conversation. A further tactic would be to put what was said into a context.

> Darryl and I have been reviewing videos for a number of years in the hope that he will observe the conversations of others, notice nonverbal cues, and understand the plot of a short dramatic show. Once we have chosen an appropriate video, we first try to

determine the plot. I find that Darryl often misses the dialogue or only retains the last thing that was said. We pause and replay it until he understands. We analyze why the character reacted in a particular way and predict what will happen next. Darryl often needs help, but he usually catches details like references to twentieth-century popular culture. At our next session, Darryl summarizes the plot up to the point we left off, and we go on from there. Interestingly, old episodes of *Bonanza* and *Star Trek* have been the easiest for Darryl to understand because the scenes are longer and the plot is generally presented in sequential order. There is often a problem that gets resolved in a single episode. Modern family shows have shorter scenes and often shift from place to place, following several characters simultaneously. These are more confusing to Darryl.

LANGUAGE TACTIC 18: TEACH GRAMMAR RULES

Typical children absorb grammar rules as they learn language, though most 4- and 5-year-olds need to be taught rules for irregular grammatical forms. Students with ASD need tactics for constructing grammatical sentences and for understanding precisely what a sentence means. They need help listening for plural and tense markers.

Language Tactic 18a

Ask the child to give a singular object or several objects (Give me your shoe. Give me shoes). Have the child listen to models of grammatical structures paired with actions to emphasize tense markers (You are eating the pretzel. You ate the pretzel. You are drinking your milk. You drank your milk).

Language Tactic 18b

Direct teaching and practice are the most common tactics for helping a student with ASD develop grammar skills. Numerous picture cards are available to practice structures such as *is (verb)ing*, *is/are*, and *was/were*. State the grammar rules explicitly and simply. Give many examples and help the student generate his own sentences.

> Ali began expressing herself verbally at age 4. By the time she was 10, she could make her wants and needs understood, comment, question, and describe. She rarely used the articles *the* and a, however. She would say, "Little boy wants ball." After much direct practice, Ali began to put in those little words, and her communications sounded more age appropriate.

Language Tactic 18c

Help students learn higher level grammar. Some grammatical sentences are ambiguous and may have multiple meanings depending upon the context. Teach the individual with ASD to give two alternate meanings to ambiguous sentences. Teach how dependent clauses modify the meaning of a sentence. Use grammar books to learn rules and exceptions.

> Some adults with ASD become sticklers for proper grammar. Their attention to detail is amazing. We asked an English teacher to review Kate's poetry in preparation for publishing a book. He thought that Kate might enjoy looking at the manuscript that he was preparing for publication himself. She did such a thorough job of finding minute errors in grammar and punctuation that he mentioned her in his acknowledgments.

There is a wide range of topics and tactics related to language goals for children with ASD. The above list is not exhaustive, by any means, but it provides a base from which to start thinking about the importance of each aspect of language and how to begin to design interventions. The expressive and receptive language tactics cannot truly be separated from tactics for academics, but the next sections cover tactics as they apply to work in the classroom.

Classroom Tactics

Although individual academic goals are generated through the IEP process, the overarching goal for children with ASD is to facilitate accommodation to school structure and group learning. The tactics outlined in this section relate to all types of educational strategies and apply to self-contained, mainstreamed, inclusive, and fully inclusive settings. Teachers of children with ASD will create activities that will allow as much access to the curriculum as possible. In selecting tactics, remember to incorporate basic tactics as well to take the child's learning style into consideration.

No matter what the setting, children with ASD do better in classrooms with the following characteristics:

- Small class size
- Strong emphasis on language learning
- Structured but not rigid class routines
- Variety of behavioral interventions
- Use of visuals and manipulatives
- Flexible teaching methods
- Opportunities for peer interaction
- Adequate support services and teacher assistants
- Opportunities to shine

CLASSROOM TACTIC 1: IDENTIFY CLASSROOM AND INDIVIDUAL RULES

As children with ASD enter the school setting, they must learn school rules, class rules, and special rules about classroom assignments. School personnel must understand that unstated rules that "everyone" knows may not be apparent to children with ASD. State rules as concretely as possible, and tell the students what *to* do, not merely what *not to* do. Post classroom rules where the children can see them and the teacher can refer to them. Post individual rules on the child's desk or table. Use positive behavior techniques and/or rewards to help students follow the rules.

Classroom Tactic 1a

There are several advantages to visual rules. First, the rule is tangible and it doesn't go away. Second, the adult can point to the rule or show the child the picture as a cue rather than trying to get the child's attention via verbal directions or interrupting the class presentation. Some children respond to a gesture or a physical prompt.

Post general classroom rules. For example, a basic rule is, "Stay inside the classroom." Others might be "Hang your coat in your cubby," "Sit on your carpet square," or "Hands to yourself." Individual rules, such as "Keep your pants on" or "Use a tissue," can be posted on the child's table or desk. Write the rule below a graphic or picture since some children respond to written words better than pictures.

> Some students with ASD follow rules rigidly. They may become anxious in a circumstance when a rule is changed. They may become the "rule police" and loudly announce when other students are not following the rules. Although this behavior does not make them very popular with their classmates, the students with ASD feel justified because the other students are breaking the rules. One teacher handled this situation by making herself the chief of the rule police. The student with ASD was her deputy. If he saw an infraction, he could quietly hand the teacher a "yellow card." It was then the teacher's decision as to whether to enforce the rule.

Classroom Tactic 1b

Classroom rules do not only refer to classroom behaviors. There are also rules for classroom assignments or for taking exams. Some examples are "Put your homework in the blue in-basket at the beginning of class" or "Keep your eyes on your own paper when taking a test." Write a reason for each rule. For example, "Put your homework in the blue in-basket at the beginning of class so the teacher can check it and see if you understand the work" or "Keep your eyes on your own paper when taking a test because on tests, you must do your own work without help."

Classroom Tactic 1c

Practice following the rules for completing an assignment, such as, "For your science project, you must ask a measurable question, state your hypothesis, describe your experimental method, and show your results." Make sure that the student understands the vocabulary and language of the rule (*measurable, hypothesis, experimental*).

CLASSROOM TACTIC 2: USE VISUAL SCHEDULES

Visual schedules using pictures and/or written words are extremely useful in helping children with ASD, particularly in the school setting. Many classrooms have schedule items backed with Velcro so teachers can fasten the items to the schedule board and rearrange them when necessary. Some children do well with general schedules, but some need more specific schedules.

> Aaron was very excited to be in first grade because he knew that the first grade class went to the art room on Thursday afternoons. Aaron knew a lot about art because he had watched PBS specials about Leonardo da Vinci and the Impressionists. All week he talked incessantly about going to the art room. When he got there, he looked around and began to cry. There were no big easels with oil paints and canvasses, no massive blocks of marble or chisels. There was nothing that he had conceptualized as "art." For several weeks after that, Aaron refused to go to art, even though it was on his schedule. Finally his teacher figured out what to do. Instead of putting "art" on his schedule, she wrote what the class was doing that day. They were not doing "art," they were "making masks."

Classroom Tactic 2a

Use the schedule as a cue to help the student transition between activities. It is difficult for a student to move from a favored activity or from one that she hasn't finished. The TEACCH Program uses a schedule with a basket for each task. When the child finishes a task, she takes the basket to the "all done" area and checks what is next on the schedule. Some classes use both macro-schedules for the general themes (center time, circle time, reading time) and micro-schedules for specific tasks (math cubes, cutting squares).

Classroom Tactic 2b

The student can learn flexibility through schedules. Flag changes in the daily routine on the schedule board. If something unplanned happens, insert it into the schedule in a different color or with a special symbol. Sometimes it helps to frame an unplanned event with a particular word, such as *unexpected*. Add a special column for unexpected schedule changes so the child can see the change graphically. It is usually a good idea to warn the child ahead of time about a change in schedule, though some children with ASD become so anxious about the change that they cannot think of anything else. In the latter case, just a few minutes' warning would be sufficient.

Classroom Tactic 2c

Help the older student keep her own schedule. She could learn to write down when assignments are due, when there will be a test, or when there will be a field trip. Some students like the autonomy of choosing the order of items on the schedule. The key tactic is to make sure that the student actually looks at the schedule.

Mike and his classroom aide made sure that his homework schedule was filled out, but Mike could never remember to take the books home that he needed for the assignments. This frustration was alleviated when Mike's mother asked for an extra set of textbooks to keep at home.

CLASSROOM TACTIC 3: CLARIFY EXPECTATIONS AND ACCOMMODATIONS

While many students with ASD need an adapted curriculum, some are able to master nearly all aspects of a school curriculum with accommodations. Some may need accommodations for the length of an assignment. For example, if they process slowly but have good math skills, they may be expected to do half the number of problems. Units can be designed around an "all-most-some" planning pyramid, as shown in Figure 4.2. Teachers should be sure that their assessments match expectations at all the levels.

> Margaret could not master all of the curriculum on the solar system, but the team felt that she should be exposed to as much as she could handle. They looked at the text and chose key concepts that she needed to know: the idea that the planets revolved around the sun, the names of the planets, and whether or not the planets had moons or rings. Margaret could make a model and tell about it. The typical students got into much more detail about gravitational forces, distances, and atmospheres, but Margaret memorized and retained her modified unit.

Classroom Tactic 3a

Take the student's capabilities into consideration when teaching specific information and skills, and make accommodations accordingly. Take care not to underestimate the student as children with ASD frequently surprise us. On the other hand, take care to be realistic about what can be accomplished in each area of the curriculum. Remember, too, that the individual is a developing child as well as a child with ASD. She may not be developmentally ready for certain academic concepts at a typical age, but if those concepts are presented later, she may learn them easily. Tailor accommodations to her interests, attention abilities, method of response, and sensory issues to increase the chances of success.

The need for accommodations may also vary with the time of day. In the morning, the student may be able to handle the workload and the requirements of the class. At the end of the day, she may be tired and her frustration tolerance may decrease. Remember that the school environment

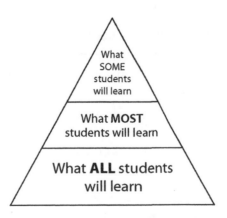

Figure 4.2. *Note.* Adapted from "Planning Pyramid: A Framework for Planning for Diversive Student Needs During Content Area Instruction," by J. S. Schumm, S. Vaughn, and A. G. Leavell, 1994, *The Reading Teacher, 47*(8), p. 610. [1994] International Reading Association. Adapted with permission.

is not easy for a child with ASD, and the child may be doing all she can to hold it together. It often helps to add more frequent breaks in the afternoon and to let minor infractions go. Choose your battles wisely.

> At the end of one school day, Carolyn's teacher handed out new work folders of various colors. Carolyn wanted a blue folder, but the teacher had announced that the children had to take whatever color they got. Carolyn, who had had a pretty good day up to that point, had a meltdown when she was handed a green folder. On one hand, the teacher didn't feel that he should single out the girl with ASD for special treatment, but the meltdown could have been avoided if the teacher "randomly" gave Carolyn a blue folder. Earlier in the day, Carolyn would probably have handled her frustration, but at that time she needed the accommodation.

Classroom Tactic 3b
The student with ASD may get overwhelmed by the number of questions she needs to answer or the confusing layout of a worksheet page. Accommodate the child by giving her a modified worksheet or by spreading the questions out so that there are fewer on each page. The child with ASD may need a longer time to do an assignment or a shorter assignment. She may need a quiet space to work. All these are accommodations that many school districts routinely make for students with ASD.

Classroom Tactic 3c
Middle school and high school teachers may need more information on ASD. Teachers who are not familiar with ASD may not realize what affects a child's performance in class. For example, randomly assigning a student with ASD to a cooperative learning group may not work because the child may lack the social skills to interact with unfamiliar peers. The peers may marginalize the student in the group because they don't understand her strengths and weaknesses. A very bright student with ASD may not get the help she needs because she seems to be doing "all right." Each child deserves to have the expectation that she will be able to develop to her full potential.

In the past, high school programs for midlevel students with ASD shifted from academics to life skills and prevocational training. More high school programs today are aware that students with ASD can continue to develop better reading, writing, and problem-solving skills throughout their lifetimes. Students are now included in a variety of classes and often earn enough credits to graduate with their peers. Three young men I know who struggled academically took drivers' education in high school and are good drivers. Their success is reflected in the expectations set out for them by their family and their school team.

CLASSROOM TACTIC 4: ACCOMMODATE CONCRETE LEARNING
Since students with ASD tend to interpret language in a very concrete way, teach them with tangible examples and show them explicitly how to generalize the concepts.

Classroom Tactic 4a
Whenever possible, provide hands-on experiences and make connections to other curriculum areas. For example, provide red, yellow, and blue paint and show how the colors mix together to make green, purple, orange, and brown. Next, add words to the concept: "Red and yellow make orange." Then ask the question "How can I make the color orange?"

> Be careful to use unambiguous language. When one young boy was asked, "What number comes after 11?" he answered, "18, 22, and 40." When the teacher rephrased the question, "What number comes next after 11?" the boy answered, "12, of course."

Classroom Tactic 4b
Use a variety of graphic organizers to show how one concept relates to another. Keep the organizers as simple as possible. Use organizers to show part/whole relationships, cause and effect, sequence, or main idea versus details. Use the same organizer for a variety of topics until the child gets the pattern.

Classroom Tactic 4c
The student with ASD may need a cookbook approach to solving problems in math or applying equations in chemistry or physics. Analyze tasks step by step, and clearly demonstrate the steps. While this approach limits the child's understanding to some basic concepts, it can help her pass a course that may otherwise be beyond her scope. Learning assessments and tests should use the same language as in the initial presentation of the material.

Backward chaining is a tactic that can be applied to academics. In a four-step task, the teacher does the first three steps and the student completes the fourth step. After several successful trials, the teacher does the first two steps and the student completes the third and fourth steps. This procedure continues until the student can do all four steps independently.

CLASSROOM TACTIC 5: FACILITATE GROUP LEARNING AND PARTICIPATION
Students with ASD may not realize that when a teacher is addressing the class, she is talking to them too. They may have trouble knowing whom to listen to if there are several cooperative learning groups going on at once. They may not process quickly enough to ask or answer a question, and the class may have moved to another topic before they can participate. They may have trouble sitting close to another student or staying still in their seats.

Classroom Tactic 5a
Make circle time easier with a special seat to sit in and a special job for each day. It helps to have a set routine of activities that alternate between verbal and motor tasks. A special signal, word, or gesture can help cue the student to attend.

Classroom Tactic 5b
Prepare the student ahead of time with a scripted question and/or answer so she will be ready when the teacher calls on her. *Pre-teaching* goes a long way to orient the student to curriculum information. Be alert to the student's strengths or special knowledge and help her respond in front of her classmates.

> Carolyn had a wonderful second-grade teacher who truly understood each of the 32 students in his classroom. He looked for opportunities for Carolyn to look smart in front of her classmates, and he called on her when he was sure she knew the answer. Because the students saw her capabilities, they were able to overlook her humming and her occasional outbursts.

Classroom Tactic 5c
In a cooperative learning group, coach the student to ask a question and listen to the answer. If she does not understand the answer, she can use phrases such as, "Do you mean _____?" or "Could you explain it again?" Structure the group so each student has a special assignment to bring back to the next group meeting.

CLASSROOM TACTIC 6: TARGET CLASSROOM BEHAVIOR
Managing particular behaviors in the classroom is a major concern of most teachers. While most children with ASD have strengths that can be accessed in the school curriculum, some exhibit unpredictable, problematic behavior. A basic tactic is educating the teachers, staff, and children about

the child with ASD in their class. Even very young children can understand that all students are treated according to their own needs and their own abilities. Some teachers try to be "fair" and have the same requirements for the children with ASD who are included or mainstreamed into their classes as they have for typical children. This approach is likely to result in behavior problems and frustration for everyone in the classroom. *Fair* is giving each child what she needs, not treating each child the same.

Classroom Tactic 6a

Choose one behavior and develop a behavioral plan to modify it. The intervention need not solely use a discrete trials approach. Changing the environment; redirecting; or using sensory breaks, calming activities, or schedule changes may also be effective. Collect data to track the behavior. Note any factors that might be affecting the child, such as illness, interrupted sleep, anxiety, or excitement.

> When one boy disrupted morning meetings by making noises, climbing over the other children, and pulling things off the shelves, the staff got him a cube chair and gave him a handheld video game. It was made clear to him that he could only play the game if he was sitting in the chair, and after he tested the rules a few times, he settled down rather quickly. This tactic was controversial. Was he being rewarded for negative behavior? He was sitting, but he was not listening to the morning meeting. Would his classmates want to play the game too? For this child, it was a judgment call. He had trouble tuning in to what other children were saying in the morning meeting. The alternative was to excuse him from the meeting altogether and have him do something else. The teachers felt that there was value in his being in the room with the other children. As it turned out, once the routine was established, the boy frequently looked up from his game to see what was going on. It became his job to announce that morning meeting was over.

> Brianna was frequently frustrated and had trouble regulating her emotions. Rather than trying to reduce the frustration behaviorally, her mother drew her in and told her she needed a hug. This gave her some deep pressure and some comfort from her mom. Gradually, her frustration was reduced, and she began to seek comfort from others as a way to regulate herself.

Classroom Tactic 6b

Modify general classroom behavioral tactics to meet the needs of the student with ASD. Some teachers write children's names on the board for classroom infractions. Many children with ASD get very anxious when their name is on the board and cannot concentrate on their schoolwork. One teacher modified the tactic by writing a note to the child about what the child should do (Dear Jon, Please keep all four legs of your chair on the floor so you won't fall over. Yours truly, Ms. M).

Understand that what may seem like noncompliance may be slow processing, lack of comprehension, or performance anxiety. Pushing for quick responses may exacerbate the situation.

> Aiden took so long to get his math workbook out that the rest of the class was nearly finished with their work as he was just starting. He wanted to finish his math, but the class was already moving on to the next subject. He yelled at the teacher when she tried to help him and tore up his paper. The behavioral intervention was to change the environment. His teacher set up a Math Station and a Reading Station, complete with railroad signs since Aiden loved trains. At math time, the Aiden train (as he called himself) pulled into the Math Station that was already set up with the work of the day. That way, he

could stay on schedule with the class and move on to the Reading Station at the proper time. The other children joined the train theme and helped the Aiden train move to the next station.

Classroom Tactic 6c

At a higher level, rules with rewards and social stories help mediate rigid and egocentric behavior. Give reasons for why the student needs to comply. Write scripts for the student to use when she is upset. Remember that the student with ASD has difficulty taking the perspective of others and usually doesn't understand that her words or actions affect other people. The student may also model her behavior on movies or cartoons, and she is surprised that real people don't react as she expects.

> George watched a television show in which the character got mad and swept a dish of spaghetti off the table onto his friend's lap. A burst of laughter echoed from the laugh track, and George thought it was very funny. Although he knew it was "inappropriate behavior," he kept talking about it. When spaghetti was served in the school cafeteria and George reenacted the scene, he kept asking, "Where's the laugh?" He had no thoughts at all about the boy who had a lap full of spaghetti.

Reading Tactics

Differences in learning styles affect reading decoding and reading comprehension in students with ASD. While some children with ASD are unable to acquire reading skills, others are precocious readers. Some students read quite well, but others struggle with reading throughout their lives. The tactics in this section refer to the National Reading Panel (NRP) report (2000) on the efficacy of various teaching strategies based on a review of the research.

READING TACTIC 1: DEVELOP DECODING

NRP (2000) reported that instruction in phonemic awareness and phonics improved reading decoding skills for typical students. Students with ASD can also benefit from this instruction, with some adaptations (Calhoon, 2004; Gillon, 2000; Heimann, Nelson, Tjus, & Gillberg, 1995; Nation, Clarke, Wright, & Williams, 2006).

Reading Tactic 1a

Use patterned activities to promote phonemic awareness. Use rhymes with cloze formats (The cat sat on the ⎯⎯⎯⎯.), word family patterns (*cake, bake, lake*), and sound/symbol relationships (*b*, /b/, *ball*) supported by pictures, computer programs, apps, and music.

Develop print awareness by pointing to words while reading, using written words in picture identification activities, using product logos, and using computer programs, apps, and videos related to letters and words.

Many children with ASD are attracted to letters, whether or not they develop reading skills. Letters are ever-present in the environment, and alphabetical order is always the same. Eric, an adult severely affected with ASD, has loved alphabet puzzles since he was 2 years old. Although he doesn't read, he loves to page through books. The tactic is to use this interest as much as possible.

Reading Tactic 1b

Use sight words. Match words to words, words to words plus pictures, and then words to pictures. Use first-sound cues and have the student guess from context or pictured scenes. For example, show a picture of a dinner scene. Hold up the word *milk* and say, "The girl is drinking m⎯⎯⎯⎯."

Use patterned reading books. Here are some suggestions:

- *Cat Traps* by Molly Coxe
- *Sweet Potato Pie* by Anne Rockwell
- *Are You My Mother?* by P. D. Eastman
- *Peanut Butter and Jelly* by Nadine Bernard Westcott
- *I Know an Old Lady Who Swallowed a Fly* by Mary Ann Hoberman and Nadine Bernard Westcott

Reading Tactic 1c

Teach sound blending. Do oral exercises first (/b/ – /i/ – /n/ = *bean*). Transfer the skill to regular words in print. Use a combination of sight-reading techniques for nonphonetic words and phonics techniques. For example, practice *-ight* words: *right, night, sight, tight*.

> Some students with ASD are very rule-bound. Mikey went through a period where he would only decode phonetically. We knew he could recognize many words by sight, but he would slowly and laboriously say each sound before saying the word.

Use high-interest materials. Students are motivated to decode words about their favorite topics. They also like to decode stories they have dictated.

READING TACTIC 2: IMPROVE READING FLUENCY

Reading fluency is oral reading with speed, accuracy, and expression. NRP (2000) found that fluency is a necessary factor in reading comprehension. My clinical observations of the oral reading of students with ASD have revealed word omissions, skipped lines, missed punctuation cues, and stereotyped intonation patterns, resulting in decreased fluency. This is true for precocious readers as well as struggling readers. Tactics specifically targeting fluency are necessary for these children. The NRP did not find enough data to support the idea that increased silent reading improved reading fluency.

Reading Tactic 2a

Use the tactic of guided oral reading. Have the student read aloud, and support his decoding of unfamiliar words. Monitor his reading rate, and encourage the student to read every word. Reading the same passage three times improves fluency and fits well with the patterned learning style of students with ASD. Have students read in unison with a teacher to improve phrasing, expression, and prosody.

Reading Tactic 2b

Highlight punctuation markers. The student with ASD may read to the end of a line and stop. Take turns reading dialogue. Alternate reading aloud, paragraph by paragraph, or page by page. Use line guides for the student if he loses his place or skips lines.

Reading Tactic 2c

Although oral reading is common in the lower grades, it is not used as much in middle school or high school. For the student with ASD, continue to use oral reading, especially as material becomes more difficult. Listen to the student read, and note decoding errors, omissions, and transpositions. Have the student practice reading in front of the class. Use a variety of materials—fact, fiction, directions, explanations, magazine and newspaper items, and poetry. Chart progress in fluency by having the student periodically read a standard passage. Count the number of errors, and mark the time it took to read the passage.

Be aware that some students with ASD are very fluent readers but still have difficulty with comprehension. Although poor fluency decreases reading comprehension, good fluency does not guarantee that the student understands.

> Andy could read at a very early age, and he read with great expression. He wanted to be president of the United States, and he read like an orator giving the State of the Union address. However, he missed the meaning of much of what he read. He understood the basic vocabulary and could recount some details, but usually he could not retell main ideas.

READING TACTIC 3: TEACH VOCABULARY

NRP (2000) found evidence that vocabulary instruction (oral or print) is critical for reading comprehension. The report emphasized using a variety of methods: using direct and indirect teaching, offering repetition and multiple exposures, embedding words in rich contexts, using digital learning, and actively engaging the students. Some students with ASD are able to acquire new vocabulary quickly if they are specifically taught. The methods with proven efficacy for typical populations may be effective with students with ASD as well.

Reading Tactic 3a

Introduce new vocabulary words before a lesson or before reading a book. Write them out, draw a picture, or give a demonstration. Have the student say the words and use them in a sentence. Then read the lesson or story, highlighting the words in the text.

> A story about dandelions described the seeds floating down on little parachutes. The teacher was surprised when many children did not know what a parachute was. They had played with a parachute in gym class, but they didn't know what it was used for otherwise. She had the children make parachutes using tissues, tape, and bits of chalk. They dropped the chalk with and without a parachute and found out how the parachute slowed the fall. They blew the parachute as it was falling. Only then did they go back to the story and read about dandelion seeds on little parachutes. The teacher followed this activity with a video of parachute jumpers. It was a wonderful lesson. Our boy Gary, however, went home and told his mom that he had learned about "pair-a-shoes."

Reading Tactic 3b

Use a standard vocabulary sheet to introduce new words.

Word:	delighted
Synonym:	happy
Opposite:	sad
Sentence:	The girl was delighted when she got an A on her test.

Post a list of vocabulary words on the wall. Review them often.

Reading Tactic 3c

Scan a reading selection onto the computer and use double line spacing. Highlight new or difficult vocabulary, and write synonyms above those words. Read the text with the synonyms and then with the original vocabulary.

READING TACTIC 4: USE ROTE LEARNING

While many teachers dismiss rote learning as memorization without understanding, many students with ASD learn new material in a rote way before integrating or comprehending what they have learned. Students with ASD also have difficulty using what they have learned in a flexible way. They can answer questions about what they have read, but only if the questions use the exact same language as in the text (Mishkin & Appenzeller, 1987; Rumsey, Vitiello, Cooper, & Hirtz, 2000).

Reading Tactic 4a

Use rote learning as a first step. Remember that the student with ASD often learns from the outside-in. He first needs to acquire the information and later can apply what he has learned. Rote learning is good for learning lists of facts (names of dinosaurs, states and capitals, presidents of the United States, countries in Africa). Recognize rote learning for the advantage it can give the student with ASD, but then help him integrate or use the information in a productive way.

Reading Tactic 4b

Broaden the scope of what the student can memorize. The skill that allows him to memorize scripts and dialogues can be used in drama club or a school play. Teach the student the Preamble to the U.S. Constitution or the Gettysburg Address.

> Finn was given the biggest speaking part in the 5- and 6-year-old drama club production because he could read well and could memorize his lines better than the typical children in the group. He could not always pay attention or participate in the rehearsals, but he could shine on stage.

Reading Tactic 4c

Teach the higher-level student how to break rote material into smaller chunks. Directly show the student how to apply what he has learned. Take the rote material and reverse it or change it to show the student how to use the material more flexibly. Associate new information to what has already been learned. For example, a student who was interested in states could trace Lewis and Clark's journey on a map or could plan a route for a cross-country road trip.

READING TACTIC 5: PROMOTE JOINT ATTENTION

Books have many things on a page besides text. There are illustrations, photographs, graphics, charts, page numbers, and sidebars. Students with ASD sometimes have great difficulty focusing on a story because they find the rest of the page interesting or distracting. In picture books, the illustrations provide information that is not in the text. Children need to pay attention to both pictures and text in order to understand the story. To accomplish this task, children need to understand the whole illustration rather than focus on an irrelevant detail (a behavior common to those with ASD).

Reading Tactic 5a

Look at the pictures first. Talk about what the pictures tell a reader. Cover the pictures or retype the text and read aloud in unison. Redirect and refocus if necessary.

Reading Tactic 5b

Have the student listen to the text and draw or write what he heard. Be aware of difficulties in shifting attention among parts of a task. While typical students can multitask (listen and takes notes at the same time), students with ASD usually need to focus on one task at a time. In the upper grades, enlist other students as note takers or provide notes ahead of time.

Reading Tactic 5c

Teach the student to look at the charts and graphs in informational texts. Point out the paragraphs in the text that relate to the charts and graphs. Show the student how to stop at the end of a paragraph and then look at the illustrative material before reading to the bottom of the page.

As you promote joint attention during reading tasks, keep in mind the student's need for completion and closure. Leaving one task in the middle to start another frequently causes anxiety in a student with ASD. He may have a hard time putting the first task out of his mind. For example, try to read to the end of a chapter. If there isn't time, write the specific time that the student can come back to complete the assignment.

> In middle school, Erin was assigned to go to the resource room after each of her major classes: math, science, and social studies. She learned that she could finish her work there with the guidance of the resource teacher. Erin's English class was scheduled at the end of the day, and she could bring her work home with her. This schedule meant some creative management on the part of the school personnel, since it cut into her time in music, art, P.E., and lunch. All agreed, however, that Erin was less anxious, attended better in class, and had fewer outbursts with this support in place.

READING TACTIC 6: TEACH THE CONCEPT OF MAIN IDEA VERSUS DETAILS

It is classic for students with ASD to be detail oriented and miss the big picture. They have difficulty synthesizing the details to form a bigger picture. They also have difficulty analyzing or breaking the big picture into its component parts. These learning differences affect reading comprehension, but tactics for direct teaching of *main idea versus details* can make this concept clear to students.

Reading Tactic 6a

Prepare the student for reading by talking about the main idea. For example, when reading the book *Henry and Mudge*, by Cynthia Rylant, tell the student that this book is about a boy and his big dog. Then explain the main idea of the first chapter (Henry had no one to play with and he was lonely). Write the main ideas on a chart or graphic organizer. Then read the chapter and fill in the details on the chart. Make sure the language is simple (Henry wanted a brother or sister. Mom and Dad said no. Henry wanted to move. They said no. Henry wanted a dog. They said yes).

Henry and Mudge, Chapter 1

Main Idea	Details
Henry had no one to play with, and he was lonely.	
	Henry wanted a brother or sister, but his parents said no.
	Henry wanted to move, but his parents said no.
	Henry wanted a dog, and his parents said yes.
Henry was happy that he could get a dog to play with.	

Practice retelling the story using the chart.

Reading Tactic 6b

Teach the student how to highlight and refer to text. Point out that the main idea is often in the first sentence of a paragraph. Highlight the main idea in one color and the details in another color. Use the highlighted texts to study for tests.

Reading Tactic 6c

Use the *main idea versus details* tactic in written reports. Teach the student to start with the main idea. Use the cloze sentence, "The main idea of this chapter is _____."

> Austin enjoys telling me about movies he sees. Although he usually understands the basic plot, the details he shares are ones that he found particularly funny and not necessarily the ones important to the story. It is enlightening to go online and read the plot summary together to help him see how the details relate to the movie's main idea. Often, though, I will catch him chuckling to himself. When I ask him why he is laughing, he tells me he is thinking of that funny part.

READING TACTIC 7: DEVELOP SCHEMAS

The term *schema* refers to information placed into a context in order to be understood. The process of organizing and associating new information depends on previous knowledge or schemas. Koppenhaver and Erickson (1998) wrote, "To plan background knowledge instruction, teachers must first ask what purpose is to be set for the student reading the text. . . . The nature of the purpose, the difficulty of the text relative to the student's abilities, and the experiential background of the student then determine which concepts and vocabulary should be taught prior to student reading."

> Marla loved giraffes. She had giraffe toys, giraffe pictures, and books about giraffes. She became very excited when she saw a giraffe on TV. Her parents thought it would be a big treat to take her to the zoo to see a real giraffe. When they got there, they followed the signs to the giraffe house, with Marla happily pointing out each giraffe icon as they went. When Marla finally saw a real giraffe, she began screaming and running away in fright. When her parents finally calmed her down, she sobbed, "Big, too big." Her schema for giraffes was a small, cuddly thing, not the towering creature in the zoo.

Reading Tactic 7a

Direct experience is the best way to build schemas or background knowledge for a student with ASD. Help him remember the experience by taking photographs or videotaping. Then read a story or text that relates to that experience and state the relationship of the story to the experience. Be aware that the student may relate to a detail of the experience rather than the whole.

> Carolyn was reading *Angelina Ballerina*. The characters were preparing to do the Butterfly Ballet, a dance that Carolyn had performed in her own ballet class. When I drew the analogy of her experience to the story, Carolyn informed me that it was not the same. "I wore a pink tutu and Angelina wore a white tutu. And anyway, Angelina is a mouse and I'm not," she told me.

Reading Tactic 7b

Watch a video, movie, or television special about the new topic or story. Find information on the Internet. Organize the information and show how it is similar to what the student already knows. Gather books and encyclopedia entries to build on the knowledge. Explicitly draw parallels and make associations for the student.

Reading Tactic 7c

Have the student explain how new information relates to his own experience. For example, if a character in a story is nervous or scared, have the student tell of a time when he was nervous or scared. Watch for misapprehensions or inaccurate background information. Help the student distinguish reality from fantasy.

> When studying a unit on astronomy, Cody was insistent that people live on other planets. After all, he had just seen the movie *Lost in Space*.

READING TACTIC 8: PROMOTE GENERALIZATION AND INTEGRATION

Why do we want students to understand what they read? One reason is so they can apply the information to new situations. Because of learning-style differences, students with ASD have particular challenges in this area. In one of the few studies on reading comprehension in students with ASD, O'Connor and Klein (2004) compared three tactics for facilitating reading comprehension.

The three tactics were as follows:

- priming: asking questions before reading so the student can look for the answers while reading

- anaphoric cueing: writing the referent above the pronoun or other phrase

- cloze task: asking for information in a fill-in-the-blank format

O'Connor and Klein found that although all tactics improved comprehension abilities somewhat, anaphoric cueing was the most beneficial, particularly for students with lower grammatical ability.

Reading Tactic 8a

Pronoun use is often a problem as the student with ASD is first learning language. For some, pronoun confusion persists for many years. Write the referent above the pronoun in stories and texts even for the very young student. Rephrase after oral reading so the meaning is perfectly clear. Use priming questions frequently *during* reading. For the student with ASD, priming *before* reading is usually not sufficient.

Reading Tactic 8b

Have the student write a two-sentence summary of what he has read. As he reads chapter books, writing a two-sentence summary for each chapter will remind him of what he has already read so he can integrate each new chapter with earlier chapters. You can also have the student draw a comic book summary of chapters. The drawings will help him visualize what he has read.

> One middle school boy and I were slogging through the book *Eragon*. He drew quick sketches of the action in each chapter, and it helped him recall the story from week to week. We ended up with a 32-page comic book before we gave up on this very long book. A year later, he became interested in The World of Warcraft, an online game that had similar types of characters, and he wanted to try reading *Eragon* again. We were able to pick up where we left off because his comic book summary reminded him of the part of the story we had already read.

Reading Tactic 8c

Have the student with ASD immediately retell a story or share new information with a classmate or an adult to promote short-term storage (memory). Have the student write a note or letter incorporating the new information. An hour, a day, and a week later, paraphrase and review the information to aid in long-term storage. Help the student use his own words to explain, describe, and generalize the story or information.

READING TACTIC 9: DISTINGUISH FICTION FROM NONFICTION

Because of their tendencies to think in concrete terms, students with ASD learn, remember, and comprehend facts better than fiction. They like to learn lists of specialized vocabulary, and they think that once they have learned a fact, it is always the same. Fiction makes some students with ASD uncomfortable. In fiction, anything goes and it may not match their reality. Some students and adults with ASD, however, love fiction books and movies. They learn to understand the characters, and when they reread the book or see the movie again, the characters always behave in the same way. These individuals with ASD have much more trouble with characters they meet in real life. Real-life characters are never predictable.

> Adam was a very bright student with ASD. When he read *Flowers for Algernon* in middle school, I was totally blown away by his insights into the mentally handicapped character who briefly became smart and could better understand the people around him, which was not always a good thing. When I tried to draw parallels to Adam's own situation, he could not understand what I was talking about. To him, internalizing fictional material was a completely foreign and nonsensical concept. What did a fictional story have to do with him?

Reading Tactic 9a

For nonfiction, pre-teach vocabulary. Use pictures, videos, and the Internet. Use hands-on, experiential activities. For fiction, teach the concepts of real, pretend, fantasy, and could-be-true. For example, the Henry and Mudge stories could be true. There could be a boy who has a big English mastiff dog. On the other hand, *Clifford the Big Red Dog*, by Norman Bridwell, is fantasy, because there is no such thing as a red dog that big.

Reading Tactic 9b

For nonfiction, use tactics for facilitating comprehension (priming, anaphoric cueing, cloze formats). For fiction, look for the author's unstated assumptions, and outline those clearly. For example, with respect to the folktale "The Gingerbread Man," children with ASD may not know that fictional foxes are often devious and should not be trusted. Watch for hard-to-understand flashbacks or parallel constructions in fiction, and outline the book in sequential and logical order using a chart or graphic organizer.

Reading Tactic 9c

For nonfiction, have the student tell and show what he has learned. Have the student make dioramas, posters, and models to reinforce learning. For fiction, ask the student to predict the plot outcomes. Specifically state feelings, and talk about the motivations of the characters. State the unstated. Do not assume that the student with ASD automatically knows how people would act or feel in certain situations in the story.

> I asked one student about the "Three Little Pigs" story. "Why did the first pig use straw to build his house?" He couldn't answer. He could tell me the story in great detail, and he liked it a lot. He particularly liked the huffing and puffing and blowing the houses down; but the moral of the story eluded him.

READING TACTIC 10: TEACH VISUALIZING FROM THE VERBAL

In the book *Thinking in Pictures*, Temple Grandin explained how she and many other individuals with ASD think primarily in pictures. Academics are presented primarily through words, though the words may be supported by visuals. Students with ASD often have difficulty creating mental pictures from verbal descriptions.

Reading Tactic 10a

Link the verbal to the visual first. Compare and contrast characters. The child with ASD may not see the critical differences. For example, when reading the Frog and Toad books, make sure to teach the difference between a frog and a toad. Who is short and who is tall? Who is brown and who is green? Make frog and toad puppets, and hold them up as you read the dialogue. Act out the story, or create a play based on the story.

Reading Tactic 10b

Draw a picture from a description in a book. For example, in the book *Junie B. Jones Smells Something Fishy*, what color hair does Junie B. have? Draw her carrying her pet fish stick to school. Draw her holding up the fish stick. Draw the other children looking at her fish stick.

Reading Tactic 10c

Have the student with ASD see the video, movie, documentary, or demonstration *before* reading the book. It is much easier for the student to understand the plot if he already knows what the setting, the characters, and the props look like.

> Michael's high school English class was reading Dickens's *Great Expectations*. There was no way Michael could access this material if he hadn't seen the movie several times to help him understand the plot. The movie was slightly different from the book, and Michael delighted in pointing out the differences.

Sometimes this tactic can backfire.

> Sima was very upset that the illustration of Winnie the Pooh in the version her teacher was reading to the class didn't look like the Disney version she had seen on television. Her quick-thinking teacher used the labels "Pooh 1" and "Pooh 2" for the different versions, understanding that it would be difficult to convince Sima that the two Poohs were the same since they didn't look the same.

Writing Tactics

Although writing tactics are presented separately in this section, integrate reading and writing as much as possible. Reading and writing are analogous to receptive and expressive language, but written language conventions are different from spoken language (Parisse, 2002; Ravid & Tolchinsky, 2002). Even picture books for very young children use different language than what is heard in daily life. For example, in the story "The Little Red Hen," the predominant pattern is "'Not I,' said the duck. 'Not I,' said the cat. 'Then I will,' said the little red hen, and she did." Children with ASD often do not realize that they have to attribute dialogue to a speaker when they are writing.

Many students with ASD also have fine-motor, motor-planning, and/or grapho-motor problems that make the act of writing a chore. They may have perfectionist tendencies and want to erase too much. On the other hand, some may not care enough about how their writing looks and whether it is legible. Despite these difficulties, some students with ASD find writing to be one of their strengths. They may write on and on without editing themselves, much in the same way that they talk.

WRITING TACTIC 1: DECREASE BLANK-PAGE ANXIETY

Students with ASD very often have difficulty starting a writing assignment. They can't think of what to write even though the teacher may provide a topic or a starter sentence. Students with ASD have difficulty formulating the language and organizing the writing task at the same time. The blank page causes anxiety and makes it even harder to do the assignment. The tactics here are aimed at getting the writing process started without worrying too much about the content of the writing.

Writing Tactic 1a

For daily journal writing, have the student write the same few sentences every day. Gradually help the student add a sentence or change a few words in the paragraph to make it new. Use patterned entries, and have the student fill in a few words at the end. In this exercise, the process of writing is more important than the product.

Writing Tactic 1b

Have the student write a simple story that she already knows. Use a script from a video, a passage from a book, or words to a song. Let the student write about her favorite topic. Modify the length of the assignment as needed. Allow the student to keep writing without checking for spelling, capitalization, or punctuation. Later, go back and help the student edit. You might also have the student dictate a story to a "scribe" and have her watch the scribe write the words.

Writing Tactic 1c

Help the student combine two scripts or stories to make a new one. Place characters from one story into the setting of another.

> Throughout elementary school, most of Michael's writing assignments were based on memorized scripts. When he got to high school, we wanted him to develop more flexible

writing skills. Michael and his family loved watching *Lord of the Rings* movies. Michael even found a website that had the written movie scripts. He also had a longtime love of the Disney characters Mickey, Donald, and Goofy. We decided to write a "chapter book" entitled Mickey, Donald, and Goofy in Middle Earth. Michael envisioned what would happen if the cartoon characters were battling the orcs and what conversations they could have with Frodo, Gandalf, and the other characters.

WRITING TACTIC 2: USE AUGMENTATIVE AND ALTERNATIVE COMMUNICATION (AAC) TECHNIQUES

Take advantage of low-tech and high-tech AAC techniques and devices to stimulate writing. Some students with ASD have severe verbal apraxia but can learn to communicate through the use of these systems. Those with severe motor difficulties need AAC devices to do written assignments. Even if they do not need specialized equipment, the vast majority of students with ASD find using the computer a flexible, enjoyable way to write.

Writing Tactic 2a

Use letter tiles to create words. Use word tiles to create sentences. At first narrow the field to those letters or words needed. Later, widen the choices. Write the word or sentence that the student created with the tiles. The words and sentences can match pictures or they can give directions for an action. Use sentence strips to create a story. The student can fill in the blank at the end of a sentence with a word or picture.

Writing Tactic 2b

Investigate the wide variety of digital AAC devices on the market. Some have arrays of commonly used words that can be accessed with one keystroke. Some are simple devices that can be preprogrammed with possible sentences the student can choose from. Others are like the sophisticated flexible devices used by the physicist Stephen Hawking and the movie critic Roger Ebert. Although these devices are primarily used to give voice to those who cannot talk, they are adaptable to written language as well.

Writing Tactic 2c

Introduce digital devices to students with ASD at a very young age. Text-to-speech and speech-to-text programs are very motivating. Word processing programs allow a student to correct, edit, or change her writing easily. The student can access her work at school or at home, giving continuity to homework assignments. Many schools have online access and online courses or may post supplementary materials on their website. Most students with ASD quickly learn the keyboard and can often type with two fingers or two thumbs very rapidly. Although English teachers may still malign text messaging, it is now completely integrated into our culture. Siri will even type your text message for you. Students with ASD find that they can often communicate with people via email or text messaging more easily than they can talk to them.

> One 4-year-old with ASD was disturbed that the keyboard was not arranged in alphabetical order. Each time he approached the computer, he complained that the letters were all mixed up. Finally we thought to show him that all computer keyboards and keypads are arranged in exactly the same way. "Oh," he said. "It's keyboard order." That solved the dilemma for him and his two-finger typing got much faster as he learned the new letter placements.

WRITING TACTIC 3: USE GUIDED WRITING

The tactic of guided writing has been very helpful in developing writing skills in students with ASD. Usually it begins with dictation, and then, as the students progress, they become the scribes. The ideas for a story should come from the child as much as possible, but the adult can structure the sentences and paragraphs, ask leading questions, and clarify. Gradually, as the student becomes more able, the student takes on more of the responsibility. No matter how much help is given, the student should be made to feel that she is the author of the work. In this process, the product is important. The advantage of guided writing is that the adult can give immediate feedback to the student to aid in generalization and integration. It is a dynamic process as compared with having the student write a paper, turn it in, and a week later, get back her work with comments. Guided writing lends itself to both fiction and nonfiction.

Writing Tactic 3a

Use guided writing techniques even before the student can read or write. Sit next to the student while she is playing, and write what she says and does. Most often, the student begins to understand that you are writing a story and gets engaged with the process. At first, stories can be quite simple. For example, "Pam is rolling the balls down the ramp. She says, 'Ready, set, go.' The balls go fast. Pam claps." Then reenact the story with the child and encourage her to say "Ready, set, go" at the appropriate time. Take a digital picture of Pam and the ball ramp and Pam clapping, type the story below it, and make a big show of how Pam wrote a wonderful book of her own.

Writing Tactic 3b

Use pretend play as the basis of stories. Many preteen girls like dressing fashion dolls and creating scenarios where girls and boys go skating, swimming, or riding in cars. Many boys like to create stories about firefighters, superheroes, or video game characters. The students dictate dialogue. The adult scribe can help keep a consistent theme and can discuss the social aspects of the dialogue. Help the students expand the stories into a chapter book that they dictate or type on the computer.

> One 9-year-old boy with ASD wrote a story about a family who kept secrets from one another. As we wrote together, we discussed how each character would react and how we could come up with a plausible resolution to their problems. The story took weeks to complete, but in the end, we had good, believable characters and a realistic story. I was constantly amazed by his ability to show each character's perspective because in real life he had trouble understanding relationships and motivations. Some of his ideas came from movies or television shows. For example, he used his fascination with the business concepts on the TV show *The Apprentice* to write a story about students having a contest to create and market a mascot for their school. Throughout the writing, I guided him to keep the story organized, to write background information, and to understand how one character's words might affect another.

Writing Tactic 3c

Show the student how expository writing differs from fiction. Introduce the concept of fact versus opinion. Introduce the concept of truth versus fiction. Begin with writing about facts supported by direct observations. Science concepts lend themselves well to this type of writing. For example, the student could state that the earliest sunset does not coincide with the shortest day of the year. Then the student can supply almanac data and explain why this statement is true. Later help the student state an opinion and support that opinion with reasons. Use starter phrases such as "I think . . ." or "I believe . . ." For example, the student might write, "I think that Abraham Lincoln was a great president" and tell why. Her reasons should support the statement. Help the student understand that others may have different opinions.

WRITING TACTIC 4: DEMONSTRATE STORY ORGANIZATION

In guided writing, suggest ways to organize sentences and paragraphs and to sequence a story in a logical way. As students with ASD become better at independent writing, templates, outlines, graphic organizers, and computer software are helpful.

Writing Tactic 4a

Because students with ASD have different language-learning styles than typical language learners, they often have trouble constructing sentences. They may write run-on sentences, leaving out punctuation and capitals. Their stories tend to be a series of events consisting of sentences that begin with *then*. Provide a structure to follow by introducing a template for a five-sentence paragraph:

- Main idea

- Three details

- Closing sentence

Usually the student with ASD needs direct instruction about what a main idea is. Use terms like *big umbrella, big thought, the who or what,* and *the action* to make the concept of the main idea clearer. Use a graphic illustration to show the relationship of the main idea to the details. You might also look at paragraphs in books. Highlight main-idea sentences in one color and details in another. Show how closing sentences relate to both. The five-sentence paragraph can be used for factual, fictional, and informational writing.

> Felix resisted all writing assignments. He had good ideas, but he didn't like the process of writing them. For him, the five-sentence paragraph worked because it was short and concrete, and it had a beginning and an end. At first he wrote as little as he could. "I went to the park. I went on the swings. I went down the slide. I saw a dog. It was fun." After a while, he became more comfortable with writing, and the sentences became more elaborate. "I saw the *Star Wars* exhibit at the museum. There was a model of the Millennium Falcon space ship. They showed how it looked like it was flying. I saw the Darth Vader costume. It is hard to make a movie."

Writing Tactic 4b

Show the student how to plan her story ahead of time by using graphic organizers and outlines. Be sure to choose a clear, concrete graphic.

Try the train-yard organizer: Give the train yard a title. Each paragraph is a train. The engine contains the main idea. Different kinds of cars contain the details, and the caboose contains the closing sentence. Build a story by adding trains to the train yard. Students with ASD love this one because many are fascinated by trains.

Teach the older student about outlines. Start by looking at simple outlines. Construct a story from an outline, showing the student how to make complete sentences from the words or phrases. After the student can see how the main ideas and details are related, she will be better able to construct her own outlines.

Writing Tactic 4c

As the student begins to read chapter books, she may become interested in writing them. Guided writing tactics can be used at first, but as the student becomes a more independent writer, she needs to analyze what makes a chapter and how chapters are organized into a whole story. Chapters can be short or long. Share the following rules on when to start a new chapter:

- There is a new scene or topic.

- The event is over.

- Time goes by.

- Something happens to a different character.

Look at simple chapter books and discuss the topics of each. Henry and Mudge books and Junie B. Jones books are good examples for beginning readers.

Go through the editing process with the student and make adjustments. Bind the manuscript into book form, starting each chapter on a different page. Have the student make a title page and a front and back cover, complete with illustrations. Look at the back cover of many books and see how it gets the reader interested in reading the book. Have the student write back-cover summaries and marketing teasers.

WRITING TACTIC 5: USE STUDENT WRITING AS TEXT

Apply reading comprehension tactics to the student's own writing. Have a book discussion about the story. Relate the fictional story to examples in the student's real-life experiences. Show the student how the factual information in her essay applies to her daily life and/or adds to the development of schemas.

Writing Tactic 5a

Show the student how to edit her work. Always use word processing programs when editing student writing. Show the student how to cut and paste to rearrange paragraphs or sentences. The computer underlining for spelling and grammar is helpful, but the student with ASD may get nervous or distracted when she sees those colored lines. Show the student that the computer isn't always right. Use guided editing until the student can spot her own errors.

Writing Tactic 5b

Because the student has created the text, she may be better able to answer inferential questions. It is always interesting to probe what the student with ASD thinks about her own characters. Many times she may give explanations that were in her mind but not in the story. Analyze the feelings and motivations of the characters, even when they are not stated.

> Carmen, a 9-year-old with ASD, wrote a story about a family with a father, a mother, a girl, and her younger brother. The girl was taking care of her younger brother while her mother went shopping when he fell down and got hurt. The girl tried to call the mother's cell phone, but she couldn't get through. She didn't know what to do. When I asked why the girl didn't call her father, Carmen looked at me as though I were crazy. "The father?" she said, "The father was away in Africa on a safari. You know that." Of course I didn't because it was not in the story. When I asked how the girl felt when she could not get through to her mother, Carmen said, "Scared and mad." This was a good analysis, but it was not directly stated in the story.

Writing Tactic 5d

Enlist other students to take part in a book club discussion about a story written by the student with ASD. Book club discussions are not based on comprehension questions, and they often use the story as a jumping-off point for conversations. As the moderator, you might start with discussing why the students liked the story. Phrase your question in a positive way ("What did you like about the story?" or "Why did you enjoy the story?") to avoid negative reactions. Encourage students to relate the story to their own experiences or to tell how they would have reacted in a similar situation.

> The book club discussion for Carmen's story raised questions about how old a babysitter should be, the frailties of cell phones, and a myriad of falling-down experiences. Carmen could not always follow the discussion, but the other students discovered that Carmen could write a good story.

Math Tactics

Math is a language unto itself. Words are used in ways that are different from conversation and literature. New vocabulary is used to describe abstract concepts, and directions are given using this vocabulary. Word problems are written so students have to figure out which math processes to use. Many school districts have adopted math programs that are highly verbal and conceptual. These programs are based on developing math reasoning skills. The curriculum spirals and touches on various concepts, coming back to them later. School districts hold training programs for parents to introduce them to the math programs so they can help their children with homework. Some students with ASD are talented mathematicians, but they have difficulty with the language of math. Here are some general math tactics that help students with ASD navigate math in school.

MATH TACTIC 1: INTRODUCE NUMBERS AT AN EARLY AGE

Many students with ASD are interested in numbers. Show how to count with one-to-one correspondence and teach them the words *more* and *less*. Use manipulatives and show how to give a specified number of items. Use dice and spinners to play games in which they need to move a marker the specified number of spaces.

MATH TACTIC 2: TEACH MATH FACTS FIRST

At various levels, teach addition and subtraction facts. Have students memorize the multiplication tables, and show them how to do division. Later add words to concrete examples. Put these facts into the context of daily activities or games (There are 5 children at the snack table. Jackie brought 3 cups. How many more cups do we need?).

MATH TACTIC 3: INTRODUCE WORD PROBLEMS IN PATTERNS

Spend a long time on a particular type of word problem before introducing a new one. In the snack table example above, first practice one way to solve the problem ($3 + 2 = 5$). After this method is mastered, show that the same problem can be solved by subtraction ($5 - 3 = 2$). Show how the words change, but the problem is the same (How many children still need a cup?). Identify key math words in word problems, such as *in all* and *left*.

> Eve loved to play Mancala, and we played it for weeks at the end of our sessions. She always knew who won (usually her) and had no trouble with the concepts of more and less. Soon I began asking, "How many more marbles do you have?" First we lined up the marbles so she could count how many more she had. Since she was learning subtraction, I showed her how to subtract mine from hers. Later, I had her calculate how many marbles I had after she counted hers. For this problem she needed to subtract her marbles from 48 (the number of marbles in the game). She became quite good at these calculations and was very proud that she knew what to do. My proudest moment came when we switched games to Scrambled States of America. At the end of the game, I asked her to count her state cards and figure out how many I had. Her first question showed that she truly understood. "How many states are there in this game?" When I told her there were 50, she did the calculation easily. We used the Mancala game as she got older to introduce multiplication and the idea of fractions as well.

MATH TACTIC 4: TEACH THE VOCABULARY

Explain and demonstrate terms such as *number sentence, equation,* and *factors.* Make a glossary with clear examples for students to refer to. Practice doing problems that use those words. Teach variations in vocabulary. For example, when teaching how to tell time, explain that 8:40 is the same as 20 minutes to 9, and that a quarter after 6 is the same as 6:15. Similarly, when teaching about money, explain that a dime is 10 cents, a nickel is 5 cents, and so on.

> Faraz is a numbers guy. He carried a calculator around for a long time, just to have the numbers near him at all times. At age 6, he discovered military time and informed me that our session was going to be over at 1700 hours. I had to think about it. He was right. Our session was over at 5:00 p.m.

MATH TACTIC 5: BEWARE OF THE WORD *ESTIMATE*

Students with ASD do not like to guess. They want to know precisely. Why should you guess if you can know? They often balk at rounding numbers up or down to the nearest tens or hundreds. Why round 78 up to 80 when you know it is 78? Accept this precision as a strength rather than press the issue.

> One student handled her discomfort with estimation by saying, "YOU could guess that the length of the rope is about 1 foot, but I KNOW that it is exactly 12 inches long."

MATH TACTIC 6: USE NUMBER LINES, CHARTS, AND GRAPHS

Although some worry that students with ASD will become too dependent on number lines and visuals, they are very useful aides for many children. Show students how to use charts and graphs to illustrate numerical values.

> During the presidential primary season, CNN showed pie charts of election results every day. Carolyn loved the pie charts and reproduced them for me the next day. She learned a lot about percentages during those months.

MATH TACTIC 7: USE COMPUTER PROGRAMS AND APPS
TO DEVELOP MATH CALCULATION AND CONCEPTS

There are many math programs and apps at various levels that teach and/or reinforce math concepts, calculating skills, and word problems. Students with ASD will practice digital math games more readily than paper-and-pencil tasks. They are attractive, have funny animated reinforcers, are predictable, and can be repeated over and over again.

MATH TACTIC 8: BEWARE OF VISUAL PROCESSING PROBLEMS

Some students with ASD have difficulty lining up the problems in columns. It makes it hard to add or subtract if the numbers are not in line. Have students write their number problems on graph paper so they can more easily line up the numbers. Some students with ASD have trouble with visual tracking and in following a line of math problems across a page. Draw heavy lines under each row of problems, or outline sets of problems in a box. Reduce the number of problems on a given page to minimize visual distractibility. If there is more than one set of directions, make sure that it's clear which directions go with which problems. Reduce distracting information on the page—such as fancy borders or cute illustrations—that doesn't help solve the problems.

MATH TACTIC 9: WORK HARD ON MONEY SKILLS

We are moving toward a cashless society. Students can use a debit or credit card to pay for most things in person or online. If they earn money, it is often directly deposited into their bank accounts. The only contact that many of them have with actual money is the $20 bills that they get from the ATM. Often they have no clear idea where that money comes from. In addition, many adults with ASD don't understand about the relative cost of items and why they need money at all.

From an early age, students with ASD need to have a set allowance and opportunities to earn money for specific chores. They need to shop and compare prices in their favorite stores and restaurants. Some families provide refillable gift cards for a set amount for their children to use for purchases because these cards are safer and more controllable than providing credit or debit cards. The student can see that the cash she earned is recorded on the gift card. She can look at the gift receipt to see how much is left and determine whether she has enough money to purchase a desired item. Older students need practice recording purchases or withdrawals in their checking account ledger and checking their balance online.

> Austin is working on life and employment skills in a post–high school transition program. He truly does not understand why "they" want him to work. We've had numerous circular conversations that go like this:
>
> Why do you need to work? To get money.
>
> Why do you need money? To buy things.
>
> What things? *Simpsons* videos.
>
> What about gas for the car? I use my card.
>
> Where does the money for the card come from? The bank.
>
> Where does the bank get it? Mom and Dad.
>
> How do Mom and Dad get money? Dad's salary.
>
> What does Dad do for his salary? He works.
>
> Oh, so Dad works to get money? Yes.
>
> So you can work to get money too? No. I volunteer.
>
> The problem is that he doesn't earn a salary for his job training. We're working on fixing that, because without pay, he has very little motivation to do the repetitive job he is training for. Without any effort on his part, money magically gets into the bank (his parents deposit it), and he gets it from the ATM. He feels that his parents will always provide for him, and as an adult, he does not see why he needs to be able to provide for himself. Without a salary, he has little idea of the value of his work.

MATH TACTIC 10: TEACH CALCULATOR SKILLS

Some students with ASD will not be able to process quickly enough in real life to use their hard-earned math skills. Most adults use the calculator app on their phones, and students with ASD should learn to use these tools as well.

Thinking and Problem-Solving Tactics

A variety of tactics can be used to solve problems. Students with ASD need to learn and practice these tactics as they apply to academic subjects and life skills. Thinking and problem solving have linguistic components as well as nonverbal elements. Both can be problematic for students with ASD.

THINKING TACTIC 1: PRACTICE TRIAL AND ERROR

This is the simplest and most widely used tactic for problem solving, but many students with ASD don't like to make mistakes. They want to know what is right before they try. First convince them that it is okay to make mistakes. Help them realize that mistakes are good because you can learn from making mistakes. Teach the students how to make "educated guesses," and teach them how to evaluate when they guess correctly. Play games that depend strictly on luck, such as flipping a coin and calling heads or tails. Make a graph to see how many times they guessed correctly.

THINKING TACTIC 2: INTRODUCE THE CONCEPT OF THINKING VS. KNOWING

Children with ASD sometimes have a hard time understanding the difference between what might be true and what you know is true. If you put a ball in a box and ask the child, "What do you think is in the box?," some children get confused because they *know* that a ball is in the box. If you show them another box and ask the same question, they often have a hard time saying, "I don't know." Rather they will tell you that there is a ball in that box also. Theory-of-mind experiments show that children with ASD have a hard time perceiving what other people think or know. Use simple magic tricks or optical illusions to demonstrate that what you see and "know" from your senses may not be true.

THINKING TACTIC 3: MAKE PREDICTIONS

Make sure that the children understand the language of predicting. They must recognize future-tense markers and be willing to guess what might happen. Outline, draw, or summarize the present situation, and clearly state the variables. Demonstrate the possible outcome of each prediction and the varying probabilities of what might happen. For example, when building with blocks, try to predict how many blocks can be stacked before the tower falls down. A tower of 5 blocks will probably stand, but a tower of 10 blocks will probably fall. Test the prediction by building with real blocks.

> Carolyn wanted lottery tickets for her birthday. She was sure the numbers she picked would win big money. Her parents tried to explain that the probability of winning was very slight, but Carolyn continued to believe she would win. Her prediction was firm. She was extremely disappointed when she checked the numbers in the newspaper and learned she did not win.

THINKING TACTIC 4: PRACTICE SEQUENCING

Logical reasoning depends on organizing what is known into a sequence. Teach children with ASD words such as *first, then, later, after, before,* and *next.* Use sequence patterns, lists, recipes, and sequenced directions for crafts. Cut up a written story, mix up the sentences, and then reassemble the story. Outline steps for solving a math problem or completing a science experiment. Show the consequences if you don't follow the proper sequence for these activities.

THINKING TACTIC 5: DISCERN ATTRIBUTES

In order to organize information, children need to identify particular attributes. Teach words such as *all, some, belong, go together, same,* and *different.* Teach what does and does not belong in a category and why. Teach the concept of *part/whole.* Identify multiple attribute classes (all those with red hair and glasses). Discern the common attribute in a group (They all have brown eyes). Play games that depend on attributes, such as Blink (Mattel Games), Set (Set Enterprises, Inc.), Guess Who? (Hasbro), and Scattergories (Milton Bradley-Hasbro).

THINKING TACTIC 6: TEACH THE PROCESS OF ELIMINATION

Make sure the child understands *yes/no.* Use a multiple-choice format for possible answers. Use graphic or tangible examples and cross out or discard those that are eliminated. Guess Who? is a classic game using process of elimination as a tactic. Play Twenty Questions, but provide a list of possible guesses. For example, if there is a long list of animals, the child can ask, "Does it have four legs?" If the answer is *no,* the child can eliminate dog, cow, horse, tiger, and elephant by crossing them out on the list.

THINKING TACTIC 7: TEACH CAUSE AND EFFECT

Teach the vocabulary *if/then, when/then,* and *why/because.* Demonstrate physical cause-and-effect experiments. Make sure to explain in clear language. For example, "If you flip the switch, the light will go off and it will be dark in the room." Flipping the switch has two effects. Some effects are not as clearly related, but the concept can be used for understanding consequences. For example, "If you put on your shoes, we can go out to the swing. No shoes, no swing." Putting on shoes did not cause the swinging, but it did cause the adult to take the child outside.

THINKING TACTIC 8: USE INFORMATION TO DRAW CONCLUSIONS (SYNTHESIZING)

Individuals with ASD may gather many bits of information, but they may have trouble putting things together to form a conclusion and/or they may draw the wrong conclusion.

> Russell knew that his grandmother was coming to stay for a week, and he was very excited. He saw his parents packing their suitcases, and he knew that they were going on a trip. It wasn't until they were saying good-bye that he realized he was going to stay alone with his grandmother. He began to wail. His parents thought they had been quite explicit, but Russell hadn't put two and two together.

Write down important information, and help the child draw conclusions. Play detective and follow the clues. Read *Nate the Great* books and point out important clues. Teach the scientific method: how to make a guess (hypothesis), how to set up an experiment, how to gather data, and how to draw a conclusion based on the data. For example, the child can guess which liquids mix with water. Set up the experiment with 6 separate cups of colored water. Add 2 tablespoons of the following to each cup: milk, olive oil, soda pop, vegetable oil, juice, or WD-40 oil. Observe what happens, and chart the data. Help the child draw the conclusion that oil and water don't mix.

THINKING TACTIC 9: USE STORED INFORMATION (REMEMBERING)

Many individuals with ASD have uncanny memories for details, but they have difficulty using this information for thinking and reasoning. Ben remembers what airline he flew on in 1997, but he can't tell you much about the trip itself. Students with ASD can memorize specific information for a test but have difficulty organizing the information into a concept. Try to use the strength in memory to develop the weakness in conceptualization. You might use the student's ability to memorize states on the U.S. map to develop the concepts of north-south-east-west directions. You might have the child study a picture for 1 minute and then recall the details of the picture. Next have the child use those details to construct a story about what is happening in the picture.

THINKING TACTIC 10: TEACH PLANNING TACTICS

In order to plan, students need to decide what to do and then sequence the steps to accomplish the plan, gather materials, and enlist help if needed. Practice simple plans at first. For example, make a plan for snack time. List items needed, describe how to set the table, and list who is in charge of the juice and apple slices. Talk about who needs to cut the apples. As students progress, make more elaborate plans. Keep in mind that children with ASD tend to think plans are set in stone and are upset if their plans do not work out.

> Two boys with ASD were in a social group together. After an adjustment period, they began to look forward to their sessions and thought about it all week. When the boys came in, each had a plan for something he wanted to do. Sometimes things did not go as planned. Sometimes the other child did not want to cooperate or sometimes we ran out of time. Negotiation of the plan became a major tactic. Both boys had difficulty being flexible, and one or the other usually ended up crying. The parents worked with the boys to help them see that plans could be changed. Imagine our surprise when, at the next session, the boys spontaneously compromised their plans and made a new plan together.

Teach basic games that require planning strategy. Although all of these games can be played without much planning, more sophisticated players will plan their moves ahead of time (i.e., strategize). Play Connect Four (Hasbro), checkers, chess, Othello (Mattel), connect the dots, and tic-tac-toe.

THINKING TACTIC 11: TEACH THE CONCEPT OF TRUE/FALSE

This reasoning tactic is used in assessment, and because of the language construction, it often poses difficulties for children with ASD. It is especially troublesome when a positive statement must be judged as being wrong. For example, a test item might state *Dogs have wings. True or false?* To make matters more complicated, there are statements that may be true sometimes and false other times. Children with ASD often focus on the exception to the rule.

> Toby was given the statement "People eat breakfast in the morning. True or false?" Toby answered "false." They had had pancakes for dinner the night before, and pancakes meant breakfast to Toby.

THINKING TACTIC 12: COMPARE AND CONTRAST

Teach the concepts of same/different and alike. Demonstrate how to answer "How are these items the same?" and "How are these items different?" Children with ASD have trouble picking out critical similarities and differences and are apt to focus on a detail.

> When asked, "How are a watch and a clock different?" Marty answered that the numbers on the clock were bigger. When asked how they were the same, he replied, "They both have numbers." He did not concern himself with the purpose of the timepieces or their location.

THINKING TACTIC 13: DISCERN INCONGRUITIES AND ABSURDITIES

"What's wrong?" or "What's silly?" pictures are commonly available. Puzzle pages often have "what's wrong" pictures. It is an important thinking and linguistic concept for children with ASD to be able to find incongruities and to express how things should be. For a higher-level task, they could explain why it would be a problem. For example, here are three levels of responses for a "What's wrong?" task.

> The bed is in the soccer net. (low level)
>
> It should be in the bedroom. (medium)
>
> The soccer ball could hit the bed. (high level)

THINKING TACTIC 14: USE ANALOGIES, SIMILES, METAPHORS, AND REPRESENTATIONS

Higher-level thinking requires understanding that one thing can relate to another in a similar way. It requires understanding how figurative language can illuminate an idea. With students with ASD, begin with simplified language and a cloze sentence format.

> Birds have feathers. Bears have _____.
>
> Analogy: Bird is to feathers as bear is to _____.

Some children with ASD love this exercise because they are able to figure out the pattern. Alex often chooses the set of analogy cards as a reward for good work even though he is unable to use analogies to solve problems.

Use similes before teaching metaphors and representations.

> Simile: He looks like a potato sitting on the couch.
>
> Explanation: A potato is buried in the ground and doesn't move.

> Metaphor: He's a couch potato.
>
> Meaning: He sits on the couch watching TV and doesn't do anything active. You might say he is "vegging out" (acting like a vegetable).

A *representation* is the mental image you construct when you hear a figure of speech. Images conjured up by poetry are good examples. Representation is related to semantic–pragmatic understanding of language. Individuals with ASD often make concrete representations in response to figures of speech.

> Representation: What does the person think of when she hears, "He's a couch potato"? Does the person visualize a potato on a couch, or does she visualize a person lying on a couch?

Tactics for Social Skill Development

Differences in social communication and social interaction are core symptoms of autism spectrum disorders. The problem in developing tactics for social skill development lies in the ever-changing social environment. True social competence requires flexibility and constant vigilance to the reactions of other people. It requires rapid processing of verbal and nonverbal signals and interpretation of the underlying meaning of the communication. Protocols for even the most superficial social interactions change with age and environment. Unlike other skills, social signals cannot be turned off. Body language, eye-gaze, and posture all communicate even when people are sitting perfectly still. Also, social competence is rarely noticed when it is right, but it is easily noticed when it is even a little bit off the mark.

Although some would argue that we need to try to work on social skill development from the inside-out (developmental approaches), the tactics in this section deal with social behavior taught from the outside-in (behavioral approaches). The National Research Council publication *Educating Children with Autism* (National Research Council, 2001) presented a thorough discussion of the research available for various approaches in developing social abilities in those with ASD (pp. 75–81). We can teach individuals with ASD how to behave, what to notice, what to say, and how to listen to others. We can teach the concepts of perspective taking and empathy that are necessary for social competence, but it is much more difficult to develop the simultaneous processing and associative thinking that are core deficits in autism spectrum disorders. A variety of activities is included for each tactic in this section. The tactics and activities are arranged in a general hierarchy as in previous sections.

SOCIAL SKILL TACTIC 1: IDENTIFY THE TARGET BEHAVIOR
Although it is hard to break social behavior into its component parts because so much goes on simultaneously, begin by teaching a behavior that is the most noticeable. Choosing the behavior is like peeling an onion, however. There is always another layer underneath.

> Years ago, when we were first learning about social behavior, we held a picnic for families with children with ASD. We prepared the children to greet each other and introduce themselves, but we were shocked to see that even the most verbal children had no idea how to continue the conversation or how to engage another child in play.

Social Skill Tactic 1a
Teach the child to respond to his name when called. The response may be turning toward the speaker or saying, "What?" Develop "socialization interchanges" like greeting people or leave-taking by using words or gestures. Develop patterned responses to greet others, such as high fives.

Social Skill Tactic 1b

Give the child specific social rules. For example, "If someone speaks to you, you must answer," "Raise your hand in class and wait until the teacher says your name," or "Ask before you borrow a pencil." Rules that state what to do are more helpful than those that state what not to do.

> Zachary's sister created a rulebook with explanations when her brother was to be a junior groomsman in her wedding. She wrote and illustrated the sequence of the preparations and the wedding in great detail. Here is an excerpt:
>
> *[Zachary will be measured] so they can get him a special outfit called a tuxedo. Sometimes, a tuxedo is also called a tux. Zachary will get his own special tux for the wedding, one that will be just his size. . . . A tuxedo has black pants, a white shirt, and a black jacket. The rules for wearing a tux are:*
>
> > *1. Stand up straight.*
> >
> > *2. Keep your tie on.*
> >
> > *3. Don't scratch.*
> >
> > *4. Don't eat messy foods.*
> >
> > *5. Keep your shirt tucked in.*

Social Skill Tactic 1c

Make a general rule for behavior, such as "No talking during the movie," "Stand an arm's length away from the next person in line," or "Use a quiet voice in a restaurant." Although those with ASD like to point out the exceptions to these very general rules, providing rules is helpful because even high-functioning adults with ASD have difficulty with the nuances of social judgments.

> When Darryl began working in the community, we realized that he needed some rules to cover new experiences. One was "Do not mention race or ethnicity or ethnic foods in the workplace." Because he lacked the social nuances to judge what was appropriate, we thought it would be best to avoid the topic completely. As far as I knew, he followed the rule at work, but that didn't keep him from telling me or his parents about how Mr. Mendez eats burritos all the time.

SOCIAL SKILL TACTIC 2: PROVIDE PARALLELS AND MODELS TO OBSERVE

Typical young children begin developing play skills first through parallel play. Older children try to fit in with their peers in various ways. Provide opportunities for children with ASD to play and learn alongside typical peers. Teach them to observe the behavior of others, since they may not do it naturally themselves.

Social Skill Tactic 2a

Encourage the child with ASD to play near a peer or a group of peers. Be aware that some children are sensitive to loud noises and may do better with one peer in a quiet place. Others may like to be in the mix of a group of children. Facilitate the child staying in the same spot for increasingly longer periods of time, and help the peers stay engaged as well.

> Olson was in a typical preschool class with an assistant. He liked the water table and would play there for a long time, but when I went to observe, he was often playing alone. Typical peers would come for a while, but when Olson didn't respond to them, they would move off. We talked to the children about how it helps Olson to play alongside other children, and a number of them began to stay at the water table with him.

Social Skill Tactic 2b

Introduce the older child to activities that interest his peers. This tactic is important even if he doesn't directly participate.

> Many of the boys in Drew's class liked to play kickball during recess. Drew never could have kept up with them, but he became the "ball boy." He carried the bag of balls out to the playground and retrieved balls when they went out of bounds. This way he was tangentially part of the action and had a role to play. It also kept him from walking the perimeter of the playground over and over as he had been doing before.

Make sure the student wears clothing like his typical peers. Middle school students spend a lot of time thinking about what to wear (boys as well as girls) because they know that clothing and hairstyles (technically known as *objectics*) can communicate a lot to peers. Adults have to decide which clothes are appropriate for a variety of occasions.

> Nate was most comfortable wearing sweatpants to school. In middle school, most boys saved their sweats for sports and wore jeans or khakis. Nate's mom realized that the sweats immediately signaled that something was different about him, so she found some soft jeans and washed them until they were acceptable to Nate. She made a big deal about how he looked more like a middle school student with his nice jeans. Although it didn't have a real effect on Nate's social skills, his brothers liked that he fit into the scene better.

Social Skill Tactic 2c

Go on a people-watching expedition with the older student with ASD. Point out how people act in various environments. Show how it is okay to yell at a basketball game, but not at a concert. Show how people hold a door open for mothers with strollers in a shopping mall. Observe body language when people are engaged in conversation. Point out how people follow posted rules at a pool. You can also watch videos or movies, pausing the action to observe and talk about facial expressions or posture.

SOCIAL SKILL TACTIC 3: PROMOTE JOINT ATTENTION

Typical children engage in joint attention at a very early age. They follow eye-gaze and pointing. Children with ASD often lack this social skill. When playing with a toy together, the child may look at a small detail rather than enjoy the action. When listening to someone talking, the child may be paying attention to a few words rather than the main message. An adult with ASD may start out with joint attention to a topic of conversation, but a random word might send him off on a different path. Look at eye-gaze, and check in frequently to ensure that the individual is on the same page as you are.

Social Skill Tactic 3a

While it is common to direct the child with ASD to "look at me," merely looking does not guarantee joint attention. Try to draw the child's attention with an object or an action that will get him to look. For example, when swinging a child in a sheet, wait until the child looks up before starting the swinging again. Be aware that lack of eye contact does not always mean the child was not paying attention. Some children cannot look and listen at the same time. Although their body language may not reflect listening behavior, if you ask them what you said, or if you give them a direction, they may respond appropriately.

Social Skill Tactic 3b

Engage the child in a structured card or board game, preferably with another child. With children with ASD, we often start teaching social interactions using structured games because they promote joint attention, have patterned interactions, and have a definite beginning and end. Children with

ASD often have trouble keeping up with the shifts in focus in free–play activities. By the time they have figured out what the play scheme is, their typical peers have moved on to something else.

Social Skill Tactic 3c
Use physical activities to promote joint attention. Play catch or do a soccer drill, and prompt the child to pay attention for a set number of turns. Balloon tennis is a good indoor game for promoting joint attention. The balloon moves slowly enough for the child with ASD to keep track of it. Though some children lack the eye–hand coordination to hit the balloon with the racquet, the play partner can aim the balloon at the child's racquet while the child stands in position. The child can keep score, adding to the attraction of the game for those who love numbers.

SOCIAL SKILL TACTIC 4: DEVELOP LIFE STORIES AND THEORY OF MIND
A basis for developing theory of mind is to understand oneself as a person separate and different from other people. We develop our sense of self through our interactions with others and through telling stories about ourselves. We learn about others by watching them and listening to their stories. Individuals with ASD have problems with both sides of this equation.

Social Skill Tactic 4a
Play the Favorites Game. Ask about favorite foods, colors, books, and so on. Use a graphic to illustrate the favorites. Put a drawing or photo of the person in the middle, and arrange the favorites around the person like spokes of a wheel, as shown in Figure 4.3. Compare and contrast each person's favorites.

> A variation of this game was popular with a group of 6- and 7-year-old girls with ASD. Each would draw a picture of a girl and give her a name. The others would then ask about that character's favorites. The favorites attributed to the character were often quite different from those of her creator.

Social Skill Tactic 4b
Develop the child's life story. With the nonverbal or preverbal individual with ASD, look at a photo album or videos and point out that person at each stage of his life.

> Austin began talking quite late. When he was 8 years old, he was watching family videos of himself when he was 4. His father was trying to get him to respond to the camera, but Austin could not. Austin looked at his mother and asked, "Why I didn't talk to Dad?" It was the beginning of a lifelong discussion.

Have the child draw a self-portrait and then dictate a story about it.

> One 6-year-old boy drew a picture of himself as a baby in a diaper.

> He dictated the following story:

> *When I was a baby, I wore a bib. Now I don't need a bib.*

> *When I was a baby, I hit my mom. Now I don't do that.*

> *When I was a baby, I only said, "Mie, mie." Now I can talk.*

> *When I was a baby, I wore a baby coat. Now I wear a jacket.*

> Another boy, who is diagnosed with ASD and hyperlexia, drew his life story, past and future. With amazing detail, 8-year-old Nate started the panel with a picture of himself reading a book in his old house on the red dining room rug. He labeled the picture "ages 0 to 3 and 1 to 4." Each of the next 10 panels showed him at a different age and grade in school and depicted the activity he did or wanted to do. He ate pizza in the cafeteria in third grade. He wanted to be in the school play (Peter and the Wolf) in fourth grade. The

last panel was labeled "Adult (13–16)" and showed him working as a plumber and fixing a leaking pipe. Nate did not have the facility with language to describe his past and his hopes for the future, but this drawing provided a window into his sense of self.

Write stories about the past. Type them on the computer. Make them into a life storybook.

Michael wrote: "When I was little, I liked Thomas the Tank Engine. I had a Thomas the Tank Engine collection. My family had a Thomas the Tank Engine postcard from Sir Topham Hatt. When I was 9 years old, I got a *Rusty to the Rescue* video in the mail. I still like Thomas the Tank Engine today."

Social Skill Tactic 4c

To develop a sense of self versus other people, it is good to know your own strengths and weaknesses. Show the individual with ASD what he can do well and what his challenges are. Introduce the term *autism spectrum disorders* as soon as you think the child can understand it. Introduce the term to classmates or co-workers and explain the individual's strengths and weaknesses as they relate to the diagnosis. The more we openly educate, the easier it will be for the individual to accept himself and to be valued in society. On many college campuses, "Aspie" groups are forming. Some children with ASD wear T-shirts that say, "I'm autistic. What's your excuse?" Their parents may get critical looks when their child wears the T-shirt in public, but being open about the diagnosis is helping to inform and educate.

One hot day, when Adam's brother was supposed to be watching him, Adam took off on his bicycle. When his brother looked up from his video game, Adam was gone. Adam's brother called their parents and the police. Meanwhile, Adam had crossed several busy intersections and was several miles from home. He got tired and flopped down on someone's lawn to rest. The concerned home owner came out and offered the young boy

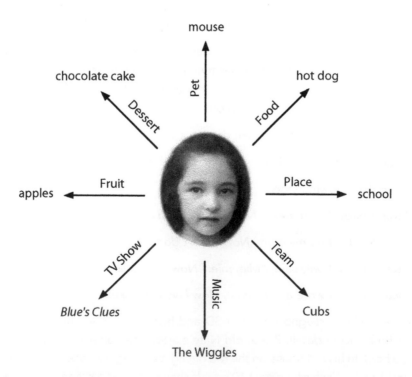

Figure 4.3. Example graphic for the Favorites Game.

a drink. When he quickly drank three glasses of water, the woman asked, "My goodness. Are you diabetic? Should I call the paramedics?" "No, no," said Adam. "I'm not diabetic. I'm something, but that's not it." All ended well when the woman called the police to help. Now that Adam is older, he knows he has ASD, and he often gives presentations with his mother to groups of teachers and college classes about his life experiences.

I received a call from a woman who was just realizing she might have ASD. She was a PhD candidate, but she could not make good social judgments. She couldn't keep a roommate, and she got taken for several thousand dollars that she had "lent" to someone who "promised" to pay her back. When I asked her about her family support, she said she'd gotten along with her father, but he had died several years ago. "He was just like me and he understood me," she said. Her mother and she, however, had always had a thorny relationship. "She had expectations for me, but I never knew what they were," she told me. Her mother would say, "Why didn't you know? Everyone knows that." The young woman would reply, "How can I know if you didn't tell me?" Like most people with ASD, she needed the social rules explicitly spelled out. It was a great comfort to her to have a name to explain her difficulties and to know there are many others just like her.

SOCIAL SKILL TACTIC 5: SCRIPT AND REHEARSE

We all use social scripts at times to initiate conversations, to manage tricky social interactions, to make conversational transitions, and to signal conversation. For example, if a person wants to end a phone conversation, he may say, "I'll let you go now," to soften the end of the conversation. Scripts like "It was nice meeting you" or "I'm pleased to be here" grease the social wheels. While social scripts do not encompass all that individuals need to know about social conversations, they are good starting points for those with ASD.

Social Skill Tactic 5a

Give the child the exact words to say and help him say it. Write the script on cards or use picture cues. Act as a coach to prompt the child to use the script. Make sure the child is close enough to the listener and that the listener is engaged in the conversation. Help the child match body language to the script. Some children with ASD learn to say the right things, but they say it with their backs turned or while they are looking down, making their communications ineffective. Practice with an adult until the child can use the script. Then practice with a peer, and coach both of them so that the communication attempt is rewarded with the appropriate response. For example, teach the script "Do you want to play with _____?" Then give the child an attractive toy, and coach a peer to accept his invitation to play.

> Observe how typical children approach each other. Years ago we made the mistake of teaching young boys to greet each other by saying, "Hi, my name is Joey. What's your name?" First, the boys did not know what to say after that. Second, typical children do not usually say that (unless prompted by an adult). Typical children either watch the action and join in, ask "whatchya doing?," or ask to play. Learning names is not a priority.

Social Skill Tactic 5b

Take age, gender, and developmental level into account when choosing scripts to teach. For young boys, the social script usually results in action. For example, "Let's play *Star Wars*. You be Darth Vader." For many young girls, the social script results in more conversation. For example, "Let's play Pollies. I have a purple dress. What do you have?"

> I learned long ago the pitfalls of relying only on women to teach boys with ASD to socialize. When running social language groups with young boys, we tend to organize

and negotiate too much. In one session, I brought in a basketball hoop and organized a game of H-O-R-S-E, in which the boys took turns shooting baskets. Soon the game deteriorated into a free-for-all with the boys diving for the ball and grabbing it from each other. I was just about to call it to a halt when I heard the dads behind the one-way mirror cheering. They later told me that it was the first time they had seen their boys roughhouse without crying. They were learning to play like boys.

Social Skill Tactic 5c
Provide social predictability. Prepare the individual as much as possible about new situations, what he can say, and what he can expect. Birthday parties generally have a predictable pattern, and the child with ASD can be prompted to go through the social ritual. Birthday parties also have unexpected traps, and parents must be prepared to deal with meltdowns. Perhaps the child did not get the piece of cake with the yellow flower. Perhaps the child did not like what was in the goody bag. Learn the triggers for the particular child and prepare him with a script. For example, "If you don't get the yellow flower say, 'No big deal'" or "If you don't like your goody bag, say 'No thanks.'"

SOCIAL SKILL TACTIC 6: WRITE OR ACT OUT NARRATIVES ABOUT SOCIAL INTERACTIONS
If a particular interaction was a problem, then write or act out a better way to handle it. The narratives or scenarios should be both descriptive and prescriptive, including dialogues about what was said and what could have been said. Do not dwell on the negative. Build up and reinforce the positive.

Social Skill Tactic 6a
Help the student act the appropriate social role. He may not have an understanding of why he must behave that way, but he still might be able to do the right thing.

> Sam was building with his favorite blocks in his preschool class. Another child accidentally bumped Sam's arm, knocking over a few blocks. Sam immediately hit the child. The teacher moved in and had Sam apologize for hitting. Later, we acted out the scenario but had it end differently. In our scene, Sam stood up and said, "Hey!" loudly, and we had the other child apologize. Nobody got into trouble. We then wrote a story about Sam and the blocks. In that story, the other child apologized immediately and Sam said, "That's okay. I can fix it." Sam's first impulse was to hit if someone interfered with him, but now the teacher steps in and reenacts the scene with two children whenever she can. Sam is starting to get the idea of how to act.

Social Skill Tactic 6b
Play the "What if . . ." game. Since no real social interaction plays out exactly as written in a prescriptive narrative, think of many possible alternatives that may occur in a social interaction. Use fill-in-the-blank rules such as "What if _____ happens? I'll say _____ or I'll _____ (action)." Always have a backup plan of "I'll tell (or ask) Mom (or the teacher or an adult)."

> Adam and his sister were drawing on the board while his mother and I were talking. They began to bicker, so we drew a line down the middle of the board and told them to each draw on their own side. Adam's sister began to tease him by encroaching on his space. We heard Adam use the scripts we had taught him. "Stop!" "I don't like that!" "Don't bother me!" Nothing deterred his little sister, and Adam began to have a meltdown. We realized that the script we hadn't taught him was to say, "I'm telling Mom."

> Once in a while the "What if . . ." game backfires. One mild-mannered, generally polite young man with ASD found it funny to imagine doing rude things. I asked him, "What

if your friend came over to play video games with you?" He answered, with a sly smile, "I'd slam the door and tell him to go away." To my knowledge, he never did anything like that, but maybe he was telling us that he'd like to break the rules once in a while.

Social Skill Tactic 6c

Use writing narratives, reading chapter books, and watching movies to explore social interactions at a higher level. Discuss motivations and reactions. Analyze and predict outcomes.

> Michael and his family watched *Air Bud* together. The movie is about a dog that plays basketball. The bad guys want to steal him from the boy who is his owner. At one point in the movie, the boy wants to hide the dog on an island. The dog does not want to leave the boy, so the boy throws a ball onto the island. When the dog runs to fetch it, the boy speeds away on his boat. Michael's mother and sister were teary eyed. Michael looked at them and asked, "Why are you sad?" "Why do you think?" asked his mother. "Because he lost his ball," said Michael. They stopped the video and helped Michael understand why the boy sent the dog away and why they were so sad that the dog could not stay with the boy he loved.

SOCIAL SKILL TACTIC 7: DEVELOP TACTICS TO DEAL WITH TEASING, BULLYING, SOCIAL VULNERABILITY, AND ISOLATION

Individuals with ASD are easily victimized. There are many reasons. They may not process quickly enough to assess the situation. They may not recognize the tone of voice that indicates whether someone is being mean or funny. They may not understand the facial expression that signals whether roughhousing is playful or hurtful. They may not read a person's body language and may persist when the other person wants them to stop. In general, they may not understand the requirements of the environment and may not adjust their behavior accordingly. They interpret language literally and may not comprehend the intent behind the words. Add this difficulty to the need to follow rigid patterns and rules and the tendency to become upset, and you have a person who is easily provoked. Individuals with ASD lack "street smarts" and have difficulty judging friend or foe. Living in a social minefield they cannot fully understand, it is no wonder they want to spend time alone. When they are alone, however, they are even more vulnerable since they have no one to turn to if they need help.

Social Skill Tactic 7a

Understand that most children with ASD cannot process fast enough to come back with a verbal retort if someone is teasing them. Teach the child to say, "Whatever," and walk away.

> There was one school bully who constantly bothered O. on the playground. We taught O. to say "Whatever" and walk away, but when we practiced it, O. slunk away like a victim. His mother, knowing that O. loved old movies said, "Walk away like John Wayne in *True Grit*." O. knew just what she meant and strode away straight and tall. To our amazement, O. started doing this and the bully began to lose interest in him.

Social Skill Tactic 7b

Educate students and co-workers in general about autism spectrum disorders, and promote tolerance, kindness, understanding, and inclusion in school, at work, and in life. Sometimes it works to enlist some "cool" students to "protect" the student with ASD, like in the old movie *My Bodyguard*, in which a small bookish teenager hires another student to be his bodyguard in high school.

> In middle school, O. was on the swim team and in the band, and those students looked out for him. Once, however, O. took fate into his own hands. A bully was bothering O.'s

one true friend, another boy who had some learning difficulties. O. went up to the bully and punched him in the nose and drew blood. The other students on the playground cheered. They all had wanted to do that to the bully, but they never dared. O. was immediately filled with remorse. He went to the principal's office and told him that he was very sorry that he had broken the rule of "No violence." The principal inwardly cheered. A boy with ASD who protected another student was progress indeed. O., however, was expecting punishment, so the principal said in his sternest voice, "O., go call your mother and tell her what you have done." O. tearfully called his mother, told her that he had committed "violence," and she had to come and get him. When he got into the car, he told her, "Mom, I need to go to confession. I committed a sin of violence." He was thinking of classic movies in which Bing Crosby and Barry Fitzgerald played priests. "But O.," said his mother. "We don't go to confession. We're Methodists."

Social Skill Tactic 7c

Teens with ASD, because of their egocentricity and their difficulties in perspective taking or theory of mind, often interpret other students' behavior in terms of themselves. Teach older students with ASD to use a big word to frame the behavior of others. The word catalogs the behavior with emotionally neutral labels. These words are for the students' own use, since other students may pick up on the words and tease them. The words are used to quickly identify the behavior and respond according to a rule. For example, if someone tells a lie, the student can note that it was a *prevarication*. Prevarication is duly noted and ignored. It is the prevaricator's problem, not the problem of the student with ASD. If someone was acting silly, the student can note the *frivolity*. Frivolity is the behavior of other students and does not need intervention by the student with ASD.

Most teens with ASD continue to improve socially and academically during high school. Some have difficulty with the physiological changes and emotional volatility associated with puberty. Watch for signs of depression, particularly in teens with ASD. Sometimes it is related to brain chemistry, and sometimes it is exacerbated by social isolation. Some teens enjoy their isolation, and some wish to be part of the social scene. Some are not at all interested in the opposite sex, and some cannot think of anything else. Teach appropriate behavior in regard to touching other people. Figure 4.4 and the following description of Alex show one method that can be used to teach appropriate touching.

> Alex wanted to hug everyone. His family used a circle graphic to help Alex understand who was appropriate to hug. The green zone was his family, and he could hug family members. The yellow zone was friends, fellow students, teachers, camp counselors, acquaintances, or people to whom he was introduced. With these people, he could shake hands or give high fives. The red zone consisted of strangers, store clerks, people in an audience, and museum guards. No physical contact was allowed with these people. If Alex was going to a family wedding, they added more people to the green zone. If he was going to a school party, everyone was in the yellow zone. If Alex crossed the line with a particular person, that person was added to the red zone. Once Alex learned the system, his parents could cue him with the color, and he would behave accordingly.

SOCIAL SKILL TACTIC 8: IDENTIFY SOCIAL BEHAVIORS AND OPPORTUNITIES IN VARIOUS ENVIRONMENTS

Help individuals with ASD identify the social behaviors required in different environments. Also identify any inappropriate behaviors for these settings. Generate a set of specific, concrete rules. Clearly identify the time and place for behaviors, and always provide an alternative if the individual cannot comply.

Social Skill Tactic 8a

Many young children with ASD need to learn to keep their hands out of their pants in public. Merely making a rule to keep hands out of pants rarely works. Rather, identify a more appropriate place, like when alone in the bathroom or bedroom. Rules are also necessary to remind children to pull up their pants before leaving the bathroom.

Social Skill Tactic 8b

Since many rules are unstated, carefully observe the student in the environment and give explicit instructions where needed. Social rules about talking are particularly difficult for those with ASD to identify since each environment has different requirements. Children may be encouraged to talk to one another in kindergarten, but in first grade, they must work quietly and raise their hands. In middle school, they must not interrupt the teacher every time they have a question. Identify what adults may do and what children may do. More than one child with ASD has been found in the teachers' lounge eating the teachers' treats. At work, outline a protocol to follow if a person has a grievance. For example, it is not appropriate to write to the CEO to report that the bathroom needs more supplies, as one employee with ASD did.

Social Skill Tactic 8c

Some social behavior requirements are subtle. Continually refine expectations for the individual with ASD to help him avoid social embarrassment. The adult with ASD often must try very hard to learn to "act" in a way that comes naturally for everyone else. Fortunately, over time, most individuals realize their actions affect how others react to them.

> One young man was working on his restaurant skills. He mastered ordering from the menu. He learned not to divulge personal information to the server. He learned to politely ask directions to the men's room. On the way back from the men's room, however, he walked slowly, looking at the food on the plates of the other diners. He thought he was not being noticed, but it was clear the other diners were becoming uncomfortable. In his view, he was following the rules. "I didn't touch anything and I kept on moving," he said.

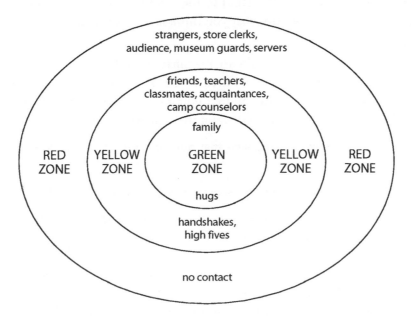

Figure 4.4. Example of a circle graphic used to teach appropriate touching.

We hadn't made a rule about not looking.

J.J. had been told somewhere along the way that it was nice to smile at people to signal friendliness. J.J. was certainly friendly to everyone, but his smile came across as fake and too big. His mentor tried to get him to modulate it, but this nonverbal behavior had become a habit. It was difficult for J.J. to monitor since he couldn't see himself. J.J. is working on putting his hand up to his mouth as he smiles, so he looks bemused rather than clownish.

SOCIAL SKILL TACTIC 9: EMPOWER PARENTS AND FAMILY TO DEVELOP TACTICS

Although there are certain kinds of social opportunities in school and at work, much of the social life of individuals with ASD revolves around family. Families set the tone for developing relationships with others. They model caring and love, and they demonstrate how to value each person. They provide opportunities to help as well as receive help, to give as well as take. Everyone is included in family gatherings and outings.

Social Skill Tactic 9a

Educate your family and extended family. Be open about your child's goals, strategies, and tactics. Spell out behaviors you are working on and accommodations you are making for the child. Explain to siblings and cousins that each of them receives help they need. The child with ASD sometimes needs special help, and that is what is fair in your family.

> One boy had very limited food preferences. He'd been doing so well in other areas that the family decided to accommodate to his diet rather than fight him. The family Thanksgiving dinner was definitely not the time to insist he try the delicious food, even though that was the expectation for the other children at the table. A matter-of-fact explanation defused a cousin's questions as to why he got to eat what he wanted and they didn't.

Accept help from family, but be clear about the help you need. For example, if you need a break, ask a family member to take the child to the swing set. Be tolerant of well-meaning but unsolicited advice. Don't argue, but do what you think is right for your child.

Social Skill Tactic 9b

Get your child involved. Set up playdates with a compatible child. At first, the playdate should be short and consist of a specific activity the children engage in together with some adult supervision. Open-ended playdates usually result in children going off on their own rather than interacting. Make sure the other child has fun so he will want to come back.

> Jules's family invested in a trampoline that attracted neighborhood kids to come and jump with Jules.

> One girl's mother invited a friend to decorate gingerbread cookies with her daughter.

Provide experiences in a variety of settings. Go to siblings' sports events or concerts. Go to the water park. Big family amusement parks will often make special accommodations for families of children with ASD.

Provide incentives, rewards, and bribes to assist in the development of social behaviors. Sometimes the incentives are the activities themselves. For example, going to the water park can be an incentive that has social learning benefits built in to the experience. Sometimes the activity is contingent on appropriate behavior in another activity. For example, good behavior at the concert will result in a treat afterward.

Social Skill Tactic 9c

Encourage involvement in typical activities. Provide access to "kid culture." Look at what other children are playing with and buy toys, action figures, books, and videos for your child. Exposure to these items builds schemas for understanding the world of peers. If another child talks about Elsa or *Kung Fu Panda*, the child with ASD will have some clue.

> In a social language group of 9- and 10-year-old boys, the conversation usually reverts to video games at some point. The boys animatedly discuss scenarios that make no sense to the adults who are listening, but the boys know exactly what is going on.

Help the child develop a skill or talent that encourages group activity and/or enhances the child's status with other children. Choose a sport that develops an individual skill as well as team participation. Soccer and basketball beyond the basic skill level are too fast moving and rely on reading other players' body language. Some children with ASD have found success at swimming, golf, bowling, and track. Enroll your child in music lessons or art classes. He can use those talents to join band or orchestra, or to make posters for school activities. Join the model train or model airplane club and enlist your child as a helper. Along the way, encourage and support your child's interests and use these interests to expand his world.

> Darryl enjoys collecting *Peanuts* memorabilia. He discovered there are Snoopy Swap Meets held annually in different parts of the country, where collectors can buy and sell *Peanuts* items. Darryl has gone to many of these swap meets, and he spends time looking, buying, and selling. Last year, the meet was held at a hotel. Darryl stayed there by himself and negotiated his meals and his deals completely independently.

> Learning to drive can make a great deal of difference in the lives of young people with ASD. Our best drivers are not necessarily those with the best academic skills, but learning to drive can function as a powerful motivator for the development of other skills. Learning to drive gives individuals a sense of responsibility and independence. They learn to exercise good judgment and to handle unexpected circumstances. In a very tangible way, they become a part of mainstream society.

SOCIAL SKILL TACTIC 10: USE HUMOR

Sharing humor is a distinctly human trait. Although it develops quite early in typical development, it is the culmination of many tactics discussed in this section. It requires joint attention and shared enjoyment. It assumes the rudiments of theory of mind. It involves understanding schemas and making predictions based on what you know. Verbal humor involves high-level linguistic skills. In spite of all the prerequisites, many children with ASD develop a sense of humor.

Social Skill Tactic 10a

Basic humor is based on the incongruity of expectation versus surprise. Infants laugh when you play peek-a-boo. Use humor to draw the child into joint attention. Build anticipation by doing the same thing over and over, and then change it by doing something funny. Another form of humor is based on exaggeration. Use a tiny action to get a big reaction. When trying to engage a young or severely impaired child, I often fall over backwards at the slightest touch or act silly the moment he looks at me. Verbal children with ASD seem to understand the humor of the song "I know an old lady who swallowed a fly" because of the exaggeration.

Social Skill Tactic 10b

Typical children develop a sense that impropriety is funny. Talk to any 4-year-old and you will soon get around to potty humor. Captain Underpants books tickle the funny bones of young school-age children. Many children with ASD like this humor too, but they tend to get stuck in this phase for a long time. It was a year before we could mention Winnie the Pooh to Angelo without his dissolving into uncontrollable giggles. Physical humor has roots in impropriety, and care must be taken so the child with ASD understands that although the girl in the commercial squirted her mother with soda pop, he should not try the same thing at home.

Social Skill Tactic 10c

Understanding puns, riddles, and knock-knock jokes depends on knowledge of multiple meanings of words as well as understanding background information. Just as typical children tell knock-knock jokes before they can really understand them, students with ASD can learn to deliver knock-knock jokes without knowing why they are funny.

When I was in Louisiana, someone told me the following riddle:

> *Why did the chicken cross the road?*
>
> *To show the armadillo that it could be done.*

Being from Chicago, I didn't get it until they explained that armadillos are the most common road kill in Louisiana. I didn't have that background information.

> Allison's big word for framing problem situations was *predicament.* It was more emotionally neutral than talking about a problem or troubles. One day she came in and said with a grin, "I have a predicament." She handed me a box of peppermints with a picture of Lucille Ball and the word "Predic-a-Mints" on the label. We enjoyed our Predic-a-Mints together.

Social Skill Tactic 10d

Humor relieves tension and helps us survive the day. Many of the stories in this book are good-humored tales that help us see those with ASD in a positive light. In most of the stories, the humor was inadvertent and related to the learning style of those with ASD. When someone with ASD makes a joke on purpose, it is truly a glorious day.

> O. was a percussionist in the middle school band. Here his precision came in handy because if the percussionist makes a mistake, everyone hears it. At one concert, he even played a drum solo. When the piece was over, everyone cheered, and O. raised both his hands in V-for-victory fashion. He looked so proud of himself. After the concert, his family congratulated him and he said, "Yes, and did you like my Richard Nixon imitation?"

Chapter 4 Appendix

Related Tactics

When choosing a tactic in the left-hand column, also consider related tactics in the right-hand column.

Basic Tactics		Related Tactics
Basic Tactic 1	Use visual patterns.	Math Tactics 3 and 6
Basic Tactic 2	Teach vocabulary.	Language Tactics 2 and 3, Reading Tactic 3, Math Tactic 4
Basic Tactic 3	Use simple grammar.	Language Tactics 4b, 6b, and 18
Basic Tactic 4	Use examples and demonstrations.	Social Skill Tactic 2
Basic Tactic 5	Repeat, repeat, repeat.	Basic Tactic 9, S5
Basic Tactic 6	Follow the child.	Writing Tactic 1b
Basic Tactic 7	Use cloze sentence formats.	Language Tactics 2b, 4b, 6b, and 12b
Basic Tactic 8	Go from concrete to abstract.	Classroom Tactic 4
Basic Tactic 9	Use rote learning.	Reading Tactic 4, Basic Tactic 5, Math Tactic 2
Basic Tactic 10	Use lists and schedules.	Classroom Tactic 2
Basic Tactic 11	Develop behavior systems.	Social Skill Tactic 1, Classroom Tactic 6
Basic Tactic 12	Develop teamwork.	Social Skill Tactic 9, Basic Tactic 13
Basic Tactic 13	Develop communication systems.	Social Skill Tactic 9, Basic Tactic 12
Basic Tactic 14	Expand the context.	Social Skill Tactic 8
Basic Tactic 15	Have fun.	Social Skill Tactic 10
Language Tactics		**Related Tactics**
Language Tactic 1	Teach referencing and indicating.	Reading Tactic 5, Social Skill Tactic 3
Language Tactic 2	Teach labeling.	Basic Tactic 2, Reading Tactic 3, Math Tactic 4, Language Tactic 3
Language Tactic 3	Expand vocabulary.	Basic Tactic 2, Language Tactic 2, Reading Tactic 3, Math Tactic 4
Language Tactic 4	Teach how to communicate wants and needs.	Writing Tactic 2
Language Tactic 5	Teach requesting.	Social Skill Tactic 1, Classroom Tactic 6
Language Tactic 6	Practice protesting.	Social Skill Tactic 1, Classroom Tactic 6
Language Tactic 7	Offer choices.	Thinking Tactics 6 and 1
Language Tactic 8	Teach how to follow directions.	Classroom Tactics 1 and 3, Thinking Tactic 4
Language Tactic 9	Teach cause and effect.	Thinking Tactic 7, Reading Tactic 8, Social Skill Tactic 5
Language Tactic 10	Teach language concepts.	Thinking Tactics 12 and 13
Language Tactic 11	Make associations.	Thinking Tactics 12 and 14
Language Tactic 12	Teach how to answer questions.	Thinking Tactic 11

Language Tactic 13	Teach how to ask questions.	Social Skill Tactic 8
Language Tactic 14	Teach sequencing.	Thinking Tactic 4
Language Tactic 15	Teach about attributes and descriptors.	Thinking Tactic 5
Language Tactic 16	Teach explaining and describing.	Writing Tactic 3, Reading Tactic 10
Language Tactic 17	Teach how to create narratives and dialogues.	Writing Tactics 3 and 4
Language Tactic 18	Teach grammar rules.	Writing Tactics 3 and 5a
Classroom Tactics		**Related Tactics**
Classroom Tactic 1	Identify classroom and individual rules.	Language Tactic 8
Classroom Tactic 2	Use visual schedules.	Basic Tactic 10
Classroom Tactic 3	Clarify expectations and accommodations.	Language Tactic 8
Classroom Tactic 4	Accommodate concrete learning.	Basic Tactic 8
Classroom Tactic 5	Facilitate group learning and participation.	Writing Tactic 5c
Classroom Tactic 6	Target classroom behavior.	Social Skill Tactic 1, Basic Tactic 11, Language Tactics 5 and 6
Reading Tactics		**Related Tactics**
Reading Tactic 1	Develop decoding.	—
Reading Tactic 2	Improve reading fluency.	Math Tactic 8
Reading Tactic 3	Teach vocabulary.	Language Tactics 2 and 3, Math Tactic 4, Basic Tactic 2
Reading Tactic 4	Use rote learning.	Basic Tactic 9
Reading Tactic 5	Promote joint attention.	Language Tactic 1, Social Skill Tactic 3
Reading Tactic 6	Teach the concept of main idea vs. details.	Writing Tactic 4
Reading Tactic 7	Develop schemas.	Social Skill Tactic 5
Reading Tactic 8	Promote generalization and integration.	Thinking Tactics 8 and 9, Language Tactic 9c, Social Skill Tactic 6
Reading Tactic 9	Distinguish fiction from nonfiction.	Thinking Tactic 3
Reading Tactic 10	Teach visualizing from the verbal.	Language Tactic 16
Writing Tactics		**Related Tactics**
Writing Tactic 1	Decrease blank-page anxiety.	—
Writing Tactic 2	Use augmentative and alternative communication (AAC) techniques.	Writing Tactic 5a
Writing Tactic 3	Use guided writing.	Language Tactics 16, 17, and 18; Social Skill Tactic 6
Writing Tactic 4	Demonstrate story organization.	Language Tactic 17, Reading Tactic 6, Thinking Tactic 10
Writing Tactic 5	Use student writing as text.	Language Tactic 18, Classroom Tactic 5
Math Tactics		**Related Tactics**
Math Tactic 1	Introduce numbers at an early age.	Language Tactic 14a, Basic Tactic 9
Math Tactic 2	Teach math facts first.	Basic Tactic 9
Math Tactic 3	Introduce word problems in patterns.	Basic Tactic 1
Math Tactic 4	Teach the vocabulary.	Language Tactics 2 and 3, Basic Tactic 2, Reading Tactic 3

Math Tactic 5	Beware of the word *estimate*.	Basic Tactic 8, Thinking Tactic 2
Math Tactic 6	Use number lines, charts, and graphs.	Basic Tactic 1
Math Tactic 7	Use computer programs and apps to develop math calculation and concepts.	Writing Tactic 2
Math Tactic 8	Beware of visual processing problems.	Reading Tactic 2
Math Tactic 9	Work hard on money skills.	Social Skill Tactic 8
Math Tactic 10	Teach calculator skills.	Writing Tactic 2
Thinking and Problem-Solving Tactics		**Related Tactics**
Thinking Tactic 1	Practice trial and error.	Language Tactic 7
Thinking Tactic 2	Introduce the concept of thinking vs. knowing.	Math Tactic 5, Basic Tactic 8
Thinking Tactic 3	Make predictions.	Reading Tactic 9c
Thinking Tactic 4	Practice sequencing.	Language Tactic 14
Thinking Tactic 5	Discern attributes.	Language Tactic 15
Thinking Tactic 6	Teach the process of elimination.	Language Tactic 7
Thinking Tactic 7	Teach cause and effect.	Language Tactic 9
Thinking Tactic 8	Use information to draw conclusions (synthesizing).	Reading Tactic 8
Thinking Tactic 9	Use stored information (remembering).	Reading Tactic 8
Thinking Tactic 10	Teach planning tactics.	Writing Tactic 4
Thinking Tactic 11	Teach the concept of true/false.	Language Tactic 12
Thinking Tactic 12	Compare and contrast.	Language Tactics 10 and 11
Thinking Tactic 13	Discern incongruities and absurdities.	Language Tactic 10
Thinking Tactic 14	Use analogies, similes, metaphors, and representations.	Language Tactic 11
Tactics for Social Skill Development		**Related Tactics**
Social Skill Tactic 1	Identify the target behavior.	Basic Tactic 11, Classroom Tactic 6, Language Tactics 5 and 6 Basic Tactic 4
Social Skill Tactic 2	Provide parallels and models to observe.	
Social Skill Tactic 3	Promote joint attention.	Language Tactic 1, Reading Tactic 5
Social Skill Tactic 4	Develop life stories and theory of mind.	Reading Tactic 7
Social Skill Tactic 5	Script and rehearse.	Basic Tactic 5
Social Skill Tactic 6	Write or act out narratives about social interactions.	Writing Tactic 3, Reading Tactic 8
Social Skill Tactic 7	Develop tactics to deal with teasing, bullying, social vulnerability, and isolation.	—

Social Skill Tactic 8	Identify social behaviors and opportunities in various environments.	Language Tactic 13c, Basic Tactic 14, Math Tactic 9
Social Skill Tactic 9	Empower parents and family to develop tactics.	Basic Tactics 12 and 13
Social Skill Tactic 10	Use humor.	Basic Tactic 15

Chapter 5

ASD Through the Lifespan

The birth of a child evokes myriad emotions: joy and elation, hope and fear, and overwhelming responsibility and awe. Parents can never be fully prepared for what is to come as they watch their child grow and develop, fuss and cry, and wake and sleep. Parents slowly learn about this new little person. Does the baby like to be cuddled and rocked? Does he like music? What makes him smile? Each child is unique, and parents search for ways to integrate their son or daughter into their family life. When families begin to realize that there is something different about their child's development, the search begins to take them down a different path. As the path twists and turns, they come to a place they'd never imagined they would be.

This chapter covers how clinicians can interact with families at various places along the path of life. It describes life stages and typical reactions at each one, as well as family priorities and concerns. For each stage, the priorities and concerns are listed in order of importance for that time. Many priorities and concerns are the same, but the order of their importance changes through the lifespan. It is important that as clinicians, we respect the families' priorities as we manage treatment for them and their children.

> I have been very lucky in my professional life. Since I have stayed in one place for more than 35 years, I have been privileged to stay in contact with many families who brought in their toddlers before they could talk. I worked with them as they entered school and stayed with them as they became adults. These families have enriched my life in unexpected ways, and they have taught me how to help them. As a speech–language pathologist, I learned that my work was not limited to the child. I learned that as the child grows, the family develops different priorities. I learned to listen to the concerns of the entire family and to provide the kind of support and intervention that was needed at each stage of life.

Coping

All parents who raise children experience stress, and they develop strategies to cope with that stress. Parents of children with ASD encounter stressful challenges far more frequently. There is the stress of coming to terms with their child's condition and limitations, finding and funding providers of services, finding community resources, and planning for the future (Glidden, Billings, & Jobe, 2006). In addition, their lives may be complicated by financial or medical worries, job-related stresses, and the myriad societal problems associated with living in the modern world.

Mackintosh, Myers, and Goin-Kochel (2005) found that lower-income parents used fewer information sources and reported fewer supports than middle- or upper-income parents. In particular, lower-income parents were less likely to attend group gatherings around autism issues.

Coping is defined as the process of response to threats of stress. Coping strategies are often grouped into two general clusters. *Emotion-focused coping* includes strategies that aim to reduce or manage the feelings of distress. *Problem-focused coping* includes strategies that aim to solve the problem or take some action to change the source of stress (Smith, Seltzer, Tager-Flusberg, Greenberg, & Carter, 2008). Parents of children with ASD may cope in different ways. Coping strategies may depend on the family situation, the severity of the child's symptoms, the parents' personalities, and the availability of supports. Coping strategies may shift through the child's lifespan.

Some parents may not be ready to accept that there is a problem. They may wish to listen to those who advise watching and waiting. They may eagerly embrace stories about other children who spoke late but who are doing fine in college. They may rationalize reasons for the troublesome behaviors, and they may adjust their expectations to match their child's abilities. This is an emotional coping mechanism known as Escape-Avoidance. If you encounter a family trying to cope in this way, tread gently. Offer help in a way that allows the family to begin treating the child, and also gradually help them realize the nature of the disorder. Little by little, offer information and resources so the family can begin to search for and accept a diagnosis.

Some parents may react to a diagnosis of ASD with sadness and/or anger. It isn't fair. It was not the expectation. It was not in the plan. They may distance themselves from the problem in an effort to cope with the pain. Studies have shown that these emotional coping mechanisms are related to a reduced sense of well-being and to depression (Benson, 2010; Pottie & Ingram, 2008; Smith, Seltzer, Tager-Flusberg, Greenberg, & Carter, 2008). Empathize with the family's position and try to understand what they are going through. While you may refer the parents to a counselor or psychotherapist so they can express their feelings, it is usually not helpful to try to cheer them up. This is a time to listen. It is *not* a time to tell parents what they *should* do. Remember that the most common response to *you should* is *yes, but. . . .* This is not a time for action or big changes. It is a time for reflection and sorrow. Work with the child, and limit any demands on the parents.

Some parents cope by going into action. Planful Problem Solving is a coping strategy that is associated with a greater sense of parental feelings of well-being (Glidden, Billings, & Jobe, 2006). Some parents use Confrontative coping. They say, "This is what I want and I'm going to fight to get it." Extroverted parents will begin seeking social supports from their extended families, online, and/or in the community. These Problem-Focused coping strategies may have a downside as well, however. Sometimes the family is looking for the "cure" or the perfect treatment to fix their child. They go "shopping" for the best treatment or the one professional who "knows." They may feel there is an answer out there and if they just can find it, their child will be okay. While the family may begin some good treatments and see some progress, the expectation of a cure is not realistic. Support the family in their search, but also provide resources to help them make informed choices. Keep the lines of communication open so parents can have a sounding board for their ideas.

Another Problem-Focused coping strategy is Positive Reappraisal. Parents begin to see the positives as well as the negatives of the child's situation. A smile or a sloppy kiss goes a long way in helping a parent cope with a sleepless night or a temper tantrum. The parents may adjust their child's programs, seek an in-depth evaluation, and find ways to integrate their child into family life for the benefit of all family members. For these parents, we provide information and support to aid them in developing strategies and tactics. In addressing the needs of the family, it is important to also recognize the needs of siblings, grandparents, and the extended family. We often invite them to join us in treatment sessions. We help them find a role in the child's life and find ways to interact in positive ways.

Parents' moods may change from day to day as they try to cope with the stress of rearing a child with ASD. Pottie and Ingram (2008) studied the daily moods and feelings of well-being of parents of children with ASD. They found that higher levels of daily positive mood were associated with the Problem-Focused, Social Support, Positive Reframing, Emotional Regulation, and Compromise coping strategies. They also found that decreases in positive mood were associated with the Escape, Blaming Withdrawal, and Helplessness coping strategies. Interestingly, Distraction coping (i.e., engaging in alternative, distracting, or pleasurable activities) in response to parental stresses reduced daily negative mood. They also found that Problem-Focused coping strategies were related to increases in both positive and negative daily mood reports. The authors suggested that perhaps because some of the daily stressors, such as the difficult behaviors associated with ASD, are problems that cannot easily be solved, a flexible repertoire of coping strategies may be most effective.

As we look at concerns and priorities through the lifespan, we also need to look at how families cope as their children age. Smith et al. (2008) compared the coping strategies of mothers of toddlers to those of mothers of adolescents with ASD. Although there were similarities in the strategies used by both groups, they found that for the mothers of adolescents, coping often acted as a buffer when autism symptoms were high. The mothers of adolescents were more likely to report higher levels of anger and behavioral disengagement than the mothers of toddlers, perhaps reflecting "wear and tear" over time. They suggested that parents of adolescents with severe autism symptoms may need intervention focusing both on reducing the severity of the adolescent's symptoms and on improving coping strategies. This study supports the idea that families need support continuously from the early years following diagnosis through the transitional years of adolescence and beyond.

As we have joined the journey of families with children with ASD, we have watched them cope with their unexpected situation. In the best scenarios, they begin to look at their child with clearer eyes. They recognize their child's strengths and weaknesses and begin to find ways to take pleasure in their child's accomplishments. As they develop a sense of perspective, many families find satisfaction in helping others in similar situations. Clinicians can help provide opportunities for leadership in parent support groups, parent-to-parent mentorships, or special interest groups. Some parents find that writing about their experiences helps them put their worries into perspective. Publish their work in newsletters. Have them give presentations to school and professional groups. Even though their lives are far from perfect, it is inspiring to know families who are able to adjust their hopes and dreams, find joy, and continue to lead useful, productive lives.

Early Development and Preschool Years

Research finds that the time from parents' suspicions of developmental delays or disability to a professional diagnosis of ASD is at least 6 months or greater (Twoy, Connolly, & Novak, 2007). As clinicians, we must listen carefully as the family tells their child's story. Before offering our opinions, ask the parents what they think is going on with their child. Use the interview to get an idea of how the family is coping with this crisis, and be sensitive to their particular situation.

In general, during a child's early years, parents' major concerns are in obtaining a diagnosis and treatment. They may enroll their child in a birth-to-three early intervention program and may be guided in obtaining a diagnosis through that system. They may also seek evaluations by a variety of specialists. They read books, surf the Internet, and choose treatments and therapists. They seek school programs that fit their child's needs. They also learn that insurance coverage for services for their children is often lacking. They learn to be case managers.

At this stage, parents want their child to learn to talk and understand. They want him to behave appropriately. They want to be able to manage their child at home. They want to be comfortable taking him out in public and to family gatherings. They want him to fit in with other children at the playground and at school.

Priorities for Early Development and Preschool Years	Concerns
• Obtaining a diagnosis and evaluations	• Speech and language
• Finding treatment programs	• Behavior management
• Assembling a team	• Social interactions
• Choosing school programs	
• Advocating for insurance coverage	

Early School Years

By the time a child reaches kindergarten age, most parents have been dealing with the child's issues for several years. Nonetheless, the transition from preschool to kindergarten causes anxiety. Often the child is reevaluated by the school district, and parents worry about whether their child can meet new expectations. These evaluations often trigger a new cycle of old emotions, even when the child has made good progress. It is graphic evidence of the disability, and it is very hard for parents to listen to the reports objectively.

As the child progresses to first grade, new questions arise:

- Will she be able to learn to read or write?

- Will she be included in a regular classroom?

- Can supports and accommodations be put in place?

- Will she be able to handle a full day of school?

- Can they find time to schedule outside therapy?

- Can the child participate in other activities?

- Will she develop the necessary social skills?

- Will the new teacher understand their child's special needs and value her strengths and build up her weaknesses?

> Josh was exceeding his teachers' expectations in kindergarten. While he exhibited the rigidity and single-mindedness that characterized his autism spectrum disorder, he was able to read and write better than all of his classmates. His teachers were able to prepare him for transitions and accommodate his needs in the classroom. Their reports were glowing. When his mother went to help at school one day, her view was not as rosy. She saw that Josh did not always understand the directions. He did not complete his tasks, even when they were well within his abilities. Josh never disrupted the class, but he was often not fully engaged. He was "so close and yet so far" from his typical classmates. She wanted the staff to work on developing his weaknesses and not be overawed by his strengths. She wanted the bar set as high as possible for her son.

Priorities for Early School Years	Concerns

• Developing a school program
• Providing outside supports and therapy
• Developing social skills
	• Developing academic skills
	  ‣ reading
	  ‣ writing
	  ‣ math
	• Adjusting to greater demands
	  ‣ longer school day
	  ‣ more on-task time
	  ‣ transitions
	• Developing higher level language
	• Managing school behavior

Middle School Years

Middle school years are difficult for every child. The school curriculum demands higher-level thinking and reasoning. The content of classes is more difficult. Students need to navigate between classes, stay organized, and set priorities for homework and long-term projects. The social atmosphere is hard enough for typical students to understand, let alone students with ASD. It is a time when all children are developing a sense of who they are, and they want desperately to fit in. Very few typical youngsters truly feel good about themselves in middle school, but most manage somehow to get through it.

> When O. was about to enter middle school, I met with his teachers. Many of them had seen the movie *Rain Man*, and when they saw the diagnosis of autism, they expected O. to be like the Dustin Hoffman character. I explained that O.'s difficulties were quite different and much more subtle. One teacher wished that O. would have come to the new student open house so that they could have met him in person. I was sure that he was there, but none of the teachers had noticed him. I was elated that O. did not stand out in a crowd, but when I reported this to his mother, she was not so happy. She told me that O. was at the open house, but he was the only student who greeted every teacher. "Hi, my name is O.," he'd say, shaking their hands. "I am so happy that I will be in your class next year. I am really looking forward to it." The teachers had seen a polite young man. His mother had seen how different he was from the other preteens.

Academics become more of an issue in middle school. There is more emphasis on taking quizzes and tests. Students are expected to learn independently. Teachers are more interested in conveying content than on developing learning strategies. Some lessons are presented in a lecture format, and note-taking is expected. Long-term projects are more common, and cooperative learning and group projects are often required. Each of these areas taxes skills that are problems for most students with ASD.

Girls with ASD have a particularly difficult time in middle school. While the curricular demands can be accommodated and the difficulties in maintaining organization can be supported, the social scene is often brutal. Girls who had been nice to them in fifth grade are now too self-conscious to be seen with girls who are "different." The subtleties of the dress code at this age are hard to discern. The social mores with respect to boys are complex and difficult to model. A number of parents opt to homeschool at this point because their daughters become so unhappy.

During the middle school years, parents often look for a group to help develop a skill or talent in a social setting that their child can understand. Teams that depend on individual skills, such as bowling, skiing, swimming, golf, or track, are good choices. Students can also learn to play an instrument or write an article for the school newspaper. The Special Olympics program has provided a wonderful opportunity for students with ASD to develop physical skills. Special recreation programs in local park districts provide opportunities for participation in group activities. At this stage, parents begin to realize that their child needs some independence from their family, and supervised activities are a way to start.

Priorities for Middle School Years	Concerns
Navigating social interactions	Developing abstract language and thinking skills
Developing organizational skills (executive functioning)	Finding talent/interest and/or participating in extracurricular activities
Learning strategies for academic content	Balancing need for independence vs. need for support

High School Years

Although social issues remain a high priority in high school, in some ways the social scene becomes a bit more understandable. Students socialize with others in their interest group, and there are often discernible cliques (for better or for worse). Students are often more confident and mature, and it again becomes cool to befriend students with special needs. In some schools, Best Buddies programs have become quite popular, benefiting both typical and special students.

Students with ASD need direct instruction and practice in talking to both boys and girls and in understanding the social customs of the school. They need instruction about what it means to be a friend. They are encouraged to participate in school life, but they need help understanding how to behave at various school functions. Students with ASD are not street smart, and they become easy prey to those who ask them for money, offer them drugs, or sexually harass them. Supervision is still needed, but high school students with ASD may not want to be so closely supervised.

Puberty affects those with ASD in much the same ways it does typical teens. There will be greater volatility, increased sexual interest, and other physical changes. The small, manageable boy grows into a towering young man. The cute girl becomes a fully developed young lady. In contrast, there is an increased risk for depression and seizures in students with ASD when compared to typical peers. Hygiene issues also need to be addressed more directly with these students.

Many students with ASD are included in the regular high school curriculum to some degree. Issues of accommodation and expectations arise in completing assignments, testing, organizing homework, and completing long-term projects. Both students and teachers often need help in making adjustments. On the other hand, students can specialize in their studies more in high school than they could in previous years. There are opportunities to take classes in areas of interest. While some students can complete the requirements for a high school diploma, others take advantage of only those classes/skills that they can master.

> Michael's school allowed him to enroll in the wood shop class as many times as he wanted. The teacher took a special interest in him, and Michael was quite proud of the projects he completed. It made the rest of the high school day bearable for him.

High schools offer opportunities for life-skills training. Some students have had special accommodations for drivers' education and have earned their drivers' licenses in high school. In most states, students are eligible for additional years in a high school transition program that prepares them for independent living and jobs. In Illinois, for example, high schools must provide programs until students are 21 years old.

As students reach the age of 18, parents need to consider the issue of legal guardianship. Many parents of high-functioning students with ASD want to at least maintain supervision of financial and legal transactions because of their child's continued social vulnerability. Parents also seek legal advice and information about eligibility for social security disability benefits at this time.

Priorities for High School Years	Concerns
Developing social skills	Increased desire for independence
Reaching academic goals	Social vulnerability
Developing a talent or interest	Social behavior and friendship
Developing prevocational skills and/or driving	Issues related to puberty and adolescence
	Appropriate response to authorities or police
	Risk of depression/seizures
	Guardianship issues

Young Adulthood

Most parents assume that once their child finishes high school, he can move smoothly into a program for adults. Unfortunately, good services, employment opportunities, and housing for adults with disabilities are hard to find. There is a shortage of good residential facilities that can handle severely affected adults. Staff turnover in these facilities is high, and the quality of care is uneven. Day programs and workshops can serve some people with ASD, but since these programs usually serve adults with a variety of disabilities, finding an appropriate day program can be tricky. There are few programs for adults at all levels of the autism disorder spectrum. As parents age, this becomes a huge problem.

Of the mid- to high-functioning adults with ASD that I know, most live at home with varying degrees of independence. A few attend a special college living skill academy, some are enrolled in a few community college courses, some are pursuing college degrees with some assistance, and some have jobs in the community. They are largely supported by their parents. Of those employed, most have jobs that do not take advantage of their abilities. A few have found jobs through friends or connections, and these are the most gainfully employed. There are, of course, college professors, artists, researchers, writers, and doctors who have accommodated to their disabilities and have led successful lives. These are exceptions to the rule.

> A few families have used their creativity to start businesses that employ their sons and daughters. Harry's Buttons (www.harrysbuttons.com) is one such success story. Harry's father created a button-manufacturing business to employ his son. Harry makes buttons for fund-raisers and other events, and now the company employs others who need jobs. Harry is a celebrity at autism walks and has improved his social skills as a result. Another family created a booth to take to art fairs to sell their son's paintings. He, too, has learned to talk to customers about his work.

Young adults with ASD need to learn a whole new set of social skills so they can converse on an adult level. They need to learn the social rules of the workplace or college programs. They need to develop leisure time activities that they can engage in independently.

> Every few months, J.J. meets another young man with ASD for dinner and a movie. They are more acquaintances than friends, and while they both like to talk, neither listens very well. They both seem to like the idea of going out together, but neither has much to say about it afterward.

Individuals with ASD also need to move toward independence and learn to care for themselves. They need to know how to react to emergencies and how to communicate with first responders. They need to pursue education and/or training to obtain marketable skills in order to find a satisfying job. Because young adults with ASD may no longer be enrolled in structured programs and may not be able to organize social contacts on their own, they are also at risk for depression.

Priorities for Young Adulthood	Concerns
Pursuing work/higher education/training	Living arrangements
Achieving independence vs. needing support	Independent living skills
Developing adult-level social skills for college or the workplace	Response to emergencies
	Leisure activities
	Risk of depression

In this chapter we have looked at some issues, priorities, and concerns that families and professionals have about those with ASD from early childhood through young adulthood. Most of those with ASD improve as they get older, though the effects of their neurological differences continue to be apparent to some degree in all aspects of their lives. As a society, we need to value those differences and provide support and opportunities for the growing number of people diagnosed with ASD. We need to support families, create programs, train teachers and staffs, provide meaningful employment, and promote public awareness so those with ASD can be welcomed as contributing members of our communities. We need to support research to find scientifically sound causes and treatments. We need to give accurate information to the public so each one of us can make a difference in the lives of those with ASD.

Austin's dad was vice president of a large national company. Having a son with ASD made Austin's father aware of the need for employment opportunities for people with disabilities. Under his leadership, the company built a new distribution center specifically designed to employ 200 people with disabilities to work alongside neurotypical colleagues. All employees receive equal pay for equal work. Local and state agencies work hand in hand with the company to help people take advantage of this wonderful opportunity. Because of the success of this operation, the company built another distribution center following the same model. Austin's dad is careful to point out that this is a good business model and that the company is hiring good workers who can do the job. His book, *No Greatness Without Goodness: How a Father's Love Changed a Company and Sparked a Movement* (Lewis, 2014), should be required reading for all CEOs and business school students. If we follow his lead, we will become a more inclusive society because some of those who can do the job are people with ASD.

References

American Academy of Pediatrics (AAP). (2012). *Policy Statement: Sensory Integration Therapies for Children With Developmental and Behavioral Disorders.* Retrieved from www.pediatrics.org/cgi/doi:10.1542/peds.2012-0876

American Psychiatric Association. (2000). Pervasive developmental disorders. In *Diagnostic and statistical manual of mental disorders* (Fourth edition–text revision) (DSM-IV-TR) (pp. 69–70). Washington, DC: Author.

American Psychiatric Association. (2013). Autism spectrum disorder. In *Diagnostic and statistical manual of mental disorders* (5th ed., pp. 50–59). Washington, DC: Author.

American Psychiatric Association. (2013). Social (pragmatic) communication disorder. In *Diagnostic and statistical manual of mental disorders* (5th ed., pp. 47–49). Washington, DC: Author.

American Speech-Language-Hearing Association (n.d.). *Autism (Practice Portal).* www.asha.org/Practice-Portal/Clinical-Topics/Autism/

Awdry, W. V. (1991). *Toby the tram engine.* New York, NY: Random House.

Barbera, M. L., & Rasmussen, T. (2007). *The verbal behavior approach: How to teach children with autism and related disorders.* London, UK and Philadelphia, PA: Jessica Kingsley.

Baron-Cohen, S. (2002). The extreme male brain theory of autism. *Trends in Cognitive Sciences. 6*(6), 248–254.

Baron-Cohen, S. (2009, November 9). The short life of a diagnosis. *New York Times.*

Baron-Cohen, S., Ring, H. A., Wheelwright, S., Bullmore, E. T., Brammer, M. J., Simmons, A., et al. (1999). Social intelligence in the normal and autistic brain: An fMRI study. *European Journal of Neuroscience, 11*(6), 1891–1898.

Baron-Cohen, S., Tager-Flusberg, H., & Cohen, D. (Eds.). (1993). *Understanding other minds: Perspectives from autism.* New York, NY: Oxford University Press.

Benson, P. R. (2010). Coping, distress, and well-being in mothers of children with autism. *Research in Autism Spectrum Disorders 4,* 217–228.

Beversdorf, D. Q., Smith, B. W., Cruciand, G. P., Anderson, J. M., Keillorf, J. M., Barrett, A. M., and Williams, S. C. (2000). Increased discrimination of "false memories" in autism spectrum disorder. *Proceedings of the National Academy of Sciences, 97*(15), 8734–8737.

Bishop, D. (2003). *Children's communication checklist–2.* San Antonio, TX: Harcourt Assessment.

Bogin, J., Sullivan, L., Rogers, S., & Stabel. A. (2010). *Steps for implementation: Discrete trial training.* Sacramento, CA: The National Professional Development Center on Autism Spectrum Disorders, The M.I.N.D. Institute, The University of California at Davis School of Medicine.

Bowers, L., Huisingh, R., LoGiudice, C., & Orman, J. (2002). *Test of semantic skills–Primary.* East Moline, IL: LinguiSystems, Inc.

Calhoon, J. A. (2004). Factors affecting the reading of rimes in words and nonwords in beginning readers with cognitive disabilities and typically developing readers: Explorations in similarity and difference in word recognition cue use. *Journal of Autism and Developmental Disorders, 31*(5), 491–504.

Carlson, G. A., Jensen, P. S., & Nottelmann, E. D. (Eds.). (1998). Special issue: Current issues in childhood bipolarity. *Journal of Affective Disorders, 51.*

Carver, L. J., & Cornew, L. (2009). Development of social information gathering in infancy: A model of neural substrates and developmental mechanisms. In M. de Haan & M. Gunnar (Eds.), *Handbook of developmental social neuroscience* (122–141). New York, NY: Guilford.

CCBICMU. (2011, March 16). *CMU Researchers Scan Temple Grandin's Brain to Study Autism* [Video file]. Retrieved from https://www.youtube.com/watch?v=-j5bIYuVGDw

Centers for Disease Control and Prevention. (2014). *Prevalence of Autism Spectrum Disorder among Children Aged 8 Years–Autism and Developmental Disabilities Monitoring Network, 11 Sites, United States, 2010.* Retrieved from https://www.cdc.gov/mmwr/preview/mmwrhtml/ss6302a1.htm

Cheng, Y., Chou, K-H., Chen, I-Y., Fan, Y-T., Decety, J., & Lin, C-P. (2010). Atypical development of white matter microstructure in adolescents with autism spectrum disorders. *Neuroimage, 50*(3), 873–882.

Children with autism have extra synapses in brain (2014, August 21). [Blog post]. Retrieved from http://newsroom.cumc.columbia.edu/blog/2014/08/21/children-autism-extra-synapses-brain/

Constantino, J. N. (2012). *Social responsiveness scale* (2nd ed.). Los Angeles, CA: Western Psychological Services.

Cooper, J. O., Heron, T. A., & Heward, W. L. (1987). *Applied behavioral analysis.* Upper Saddle River, NJ: Prentice Hall.

Coulter, L. (1998). Semantic pragmatic disorder with application of selected pragmatic concepts. *International Journal of Language and Communication Disorders, 33,* 434–438.

Courchesne, E., Carper, R., & Akshoomoff, N. (2003). Evidence of brain overgrowth in the first year of life in autism. *Journal of the American Medical Association, 290*(3), 337–344.

Dapretto, M., Davies, M. S., Pfeifer, J. H., Scott, A. A., Sigman, M., Bookheimer, S. Y., et al. (2006). Understanding emotions in others: Mirror neuron dysfunction in children with autism spectrum disorders. *Nature Neuroscience 9*(1), 28–30.

Dawson, G., Ashman, S. B., & Carver, L. J. (2000). The role of early experience in shaping behavioral and brain development and its implications for social policy. *Developmental Psychopathology, 12*(4), 695–712.

De Fossé, L., Hodge, S., Makris, N., Kennedy, D., Caviness, V. S., McGrath, L., et al. (2004). Language-association cortex asymmetry in autism and specific language impairment. *Annals of Neurology, 56*(6), 757–766.

Duke, M., Nowicki, S., & Martin, E. (1996). *Teaching your child the language of social success.* Atlanta, GA: Peachtree.

Duvall, K. (2004). *That's all: Selected poems.* Elmhurst, IL: Center for Speech and Language Disorders.

Edelson, M. G. (2006). Are the majority of children with autism mentally retarded? A systematic evaluation of the data. *Focus on Autism and Other Developmental Disabilities, 21,* 66–83.

Feinberg, J. I., Bakulski, K. M., Jaffe, A. E., Tryggvadottir, R., Brown, S. C., Goldman, L. R., et al. (2015). Paternal sperm DNA methylation associated with early signs of autism risk in an autism-enriched cohort. *International Journal of Epidemiology,* 1199–1210. doi:10.1093/ije/dyv028

Frith, U. (Ed.) (1991). *Autism and Asperger syndrome.* Cambridge, UK: Cambridge University Press.

Frith, U., & Snowling, M. (1983). Reading for meaning and reading for sound in autistic and dyslexic children. *British Journal of Developmental Psychology, 1,* 329–342.

Frye, R. E., Rossignol, D., Casanova, M. F., Brown, G. L., Martin, V., Edelson, S., et al. (2013). A review of traditional and novel treatments for seizures in autism spectrum disorder: Findings from a systematic review and expert panel. *Frontiers in Public Health, 1*(31). doi:10.3389/fpubh.2013.00031

Frye, R. E., Sreenivasula, S., & Adams, J. B. (2011). Traditional and non-traditional treatments for autism spectrum disorder with seizures: An on-line survey. *BMC Pediatrics, 11*(37). doi:10.1186/1471-2431-11-37

Fulghum, R. (1986, 2004). *All I really need to know I learned in kindergarten.* New York, NY: Ballantine Books.

Geller, B., & Luby, J. (1997). Child and adolescent bipolar disorder: A review of the past 10 years. *Journal of the American Academy of Child and Adolescent Psychiatry, 36,* 1168–1176.

Gepner, B., & Féron, F. (2009). Autism: A world changing too fast for a mis-wired brain? *Neuroscience and Biobehavioral Reviews, 33,* 1227–1242.

Ghaziuddin, M., Ghaziuddin, N., & Greden, J. (2002). Depression in persons with autism: Implications for research and clinical care. *Journal of Autism and Developmental Disorders, 32*(4), 299–306.

Ghaziuddin, M., & Greden, J. (1998). Depression in children with autism/pervasive developmental disorders: A case-control family history study. *Journal of Autism and Developmental Disorders, 28,* 111–115.

Gilberg, C., & Coleman, M. (2000). *The biology of the autistic syndromes* (3rd ed.). London, UK: Cambridge University Press.

Gilliam, J. E. (2014). *Gilliam autism rating scale, examiner's manual* (3rd ed.). Austin, TX: PRO-ED.

Gillon, G. T. (2000). The efficacy of phonological awareness intervention for children with spoken language impairment. *Language, Speech, and Hearing Services in Schools, 31,* 126–141.

Glidden, L. M., Billings, F. J., & Jobe, B. M. (2006). Personality, coping style and well-being of parents rearing children with developmental disabilities. *Journal of Intellectual Disability Research, 50*(12), 949–962. doi:10.1111/j.1365=2788.2006.00929.x

Gogtay, N., Giedd, J. N., Lusk, L., Hayashi, K. M., Greenstein, D., Vaituzis, A. C., et al. (2004). Dynamic mapping of human cortical development during childhood through early adulthood. *Proceedings of the National Academy of Sciences, 101*(21), 8174–8179.

Goldstein, S., & Naglieri, J. A. (2009) *Autism spectrum rating scales.* Cheektowaga, NY: Multi-Health Systems.

Gopnik, A., Meltzoff, A., & Kuhl, P. (1999). *The scientist in the crib: What early learning tells us about the mind.* New York, NY: Harper Collins.

Grandin, T. (1995). *Thinking in pictures: And other reports from my life with autism.* New York, NY: Doubleday.

Green, V. A., Pituch, K. A., Itchon, J., Choi, A., O'Reilly, M., & Sigafoos, J. (2006). Internet survey of treatments used by parents of children with autism. *Research in Developmental Disabilities, 27*(1), 70–84.

Greenspan, S. I., & Wieder, S. (1997a). An integrated developmental approach to interventions for young children with severe difficulties in relating and communicating. *Zero to Three, 17*(5), 5–18.

Greenspan, S. I., & Wieder, S. (1997b). Developmental patterns and outcomes in infants and children with disorders in relating and communicating. *Journal of Developmental Learning Disorders, 1,* 28–37.

Greenspan, S. I., & Wieder, S. (2006). *Engaging autism: The Floortime approach to helping children relate, communicate and think.* Cambridge, MA: DaCapo Press.

Happé, F. G. E. (1995). The role of age and verbal ability in the theory of mind task performance of subjects with autism. *Child Development, 66*(3), 843–855.

Happé, F. (2011). Criteria, categories, and continua: Autism and related disorders in DSM-5. *Journal of the American Academy of Child & Adolescent Psychiatry, 50*(6), 540–542.

Harris, S. L., & Handleman, J. S. (2000). Age and IQ intake as predictors of placement for young children with autism: A four- and six-year follow-up. *Journal of Autism and Developmental Disorders, 30*, 137–149.

Hassink, S. G. (2015). AAP Statement on U.S. Preventive Services Task Force Draft Recommendation Statement on Autism Screening. *American Academy of Pediatrics,* Retrieved from https://www.aap.org/en-us/about-the-aap/aap-press-room/Pages/AAP-Statement-on-U-S-Preventive-Services-Task-Force-Draft-Recommendation-Statement-on-Autism-Screening.aspx#sthash.60nTdyD1.dpuf

Hazel, P. (2002). Depression in children. *British Medical Journal, 325,* 229–231.

Healy, J. (1982). The enigma of hyperlexia. *Reading Research Quarterly, 17*(3), 319–338.

Hedley, D., & Young, R. (2006). Social comparison processes and depressive symptoms in children and adolescents with Asperger syndrome. *Autism, 10*(2), 139–153. doi:10.1177/1362361306062020

Hedvall, Å., Fernell, E., Holm, A., Johnels, J. Å., Gillberg, C., & Billstedt, E. (2013). Autism, processing speed, and adaptive functioning in preschool children. *The Scientific World Journal,* Volume 2013, Article ID 158263, 7 pages. Retrieved from http://dx.doi.org/10.1155/2013/158263

Heimann, M., Nelson, K. E., Tjus, T., & Gillberg, C. (1995). Increasing reading and communication skills in children with autism through an interactive multimedia computer program. *Journal of Autism and Developmental Disorders, 25*(5), 459–480.

Herbert, M. R., Harris, G. J., Adrien, K. T., Ziegler, B. S., Makris, N., Kennedy, D., et al. (2002). Abnormal asymmetry in language association cortex in autism. *Annals of Neurology, 52*(5), 588–596.

Herbert, M. R., Ziegler, D. A., Makris, N., Filipek, P. A., Kemper, T. L., Normandin, J. J., et al. (2004). Localization of white matter volume increase in autism and developmental language disorder. *Annals of Neurology, 55,* 530–540.

Heward, W. L. (2003). Ten faulty notions about teaching and learning that hinder the effectiveness of special education. *The Journal of Special Education, 36*(4), 186–205.

Hobson, P. (1989). On sharing experiences. *Development and Psychopathology, 1,* 197–203.

Human Connectome Project, www.humanconnectomeproject.org/gallery/

Huttenlocher, P. R. (2002). *Neural plasticity: The effects of environment on the development of the cerebral cortex.* Cambridge, MA: Harvard University Press.

Individuals With Disabilities Education Improvement Act of 2004, 20 U.S.C. § 1400 *et seq.* (2004) (reauthorization of IDEA 1990). Retrieved from idea.ed.gov

International Molecular Genetic Study of Autism Consortium. (1998–2008). Retrieved from www.well.ox.ac.uk/monaco/autism/IMGSAC/IMGSAC_publications.shtml

Jacobson, J. W., Mulick, J. A., & Green, G. (1998). Cost-benefit estimates for early intensive behavioral interventions for young children with autism. *Behavioral Interventions, 13,* 201–226.

Jain, A., Marshall, J., Buikema, A., Bancroft, T., Kelly, J. P., & Newschaffer, C. J. (2015). Autism occurrence by MMR vaccine status among US children with older siblings with and without autism. *Journal of the American Medical Association. 313*(15), 1534–1540. doi:10.1001/jama.2015.3077

Jiang, Y., Yuen, R. K. C., Jin, X., Wang, M., Chen, N., Wu, X., et al. (2013). Detection of clinically relevant genetic variants in autism spectrum disorder by whole-genome sequencing. *American Journal of Human Genetics, 93*(2), 249–263. doi:10.1016/j.ajhg.2013.06.012

Joseph, R. M. Fricker, Z., Fenoglio, A., Lindgren, K. A., Knaus, T. A., & Tager-Flusberg, H. (2014). Structural asymmetries of language-related gray and white matter and their relationship to language function in young children with ASD. *Brain Imaging and Behavior 8*(1):60–72. doi:10.1007/s11682-013-9245-0

Just, M. A., Cherkassky, V. L., Keller. T. A., & Minshew, N. J. (2004). Cortical activation and synchronization during sentence comprehension in high-functioning autism: Evidence of underconnectivity. *Brain, 127,* 1811–1821.

Kanner, L. (1943). Autistic disturbances of affective contact. *Nervous Child, 2,* 217–250.

Karmiloff-Smith, A. (2007). Atypical epigenesis. *Developmental Science, 10*(1), 84–88.

Kasari, C., Gulsrud, A., Freeman, S., Paparella, T., & Hellemann, G. (2012). Longitudinal follow-up of children with autism receiving targeted interventions on joint attention and play. *Journal of the American Academy of Child & Adolescent Psychiatry, 51,* 487–495.

Kim, K. H., Hirsch, J., Relkin, N., DeLa Paz, R., & Lee, K. M. (1996). Localization of cortical areas activated by native and second languages with functional magnetic resonance imaging (fMRI). *Proceedings of the International Society for Magnetic Resonance Imaging, 1.*

Kim, K. H., Relkin, N. R., Lee, K. M., & Hirsch, J. (1997). Distinct cortical areas associated with native and second languages. *Nature, 388,* 171–174.

Kim, Y. S., Frombonne, E., Koh, Y-J., Kim, S-J., Cheon, K-A., & Leventhal, B. (2014). A comparison of DSM-IV PDD and DSM-5 ASD prevalence in an epidemiologic sample. *Journal of the American Academy of Child & Adolescent Psychiatry, 53*(5), 500–508. doi:10.1016/j.jaac.2013.12.021

Kim, Y. S., Leventhal B. L, Koh Y. J., Fombonne, E., Laska, E., Lim, E. C., et al. (2011). Prevalence of autism spectrum disorders in a total population sample. *American Journal of Psychiatry, 168*(9), 904–912. doi:10.1176/appi.ajp.2011.10101532

King, L. J. (1987). A sensory-integrative approach to the education of the autistic child. *Occupational Therapy in Health Care, 4*(2), 77.

Koegel, L. K., Koegel, R., Shoshan, Y., & McNerney, E. (1999). Pivotal response intervention II: Preliminary long-term outcome data. *Journal of the Association of Persons with Severe Handicaps, 24,* 186–198.

Koegel, L. K., Koegel, R., & Smith, A. (1997). Variables related to differences in standardized test outcomes for children with autism. *Journal of Autism and Developmental Disorders, 27*(3), 233–243.

Koppenhaver, D., & Erickson, K. (1998). *Technologies to support reading comprehension in children with disabilities.* Paper presented at the 1998 California State University Northridge Conference. Retrieved from www.dinf.ne.jp/doc/english/Us_Eu/conf/csun_98/csun98_026.htm

Koshino, H., Carpenter, P., Minshew, N., Cherkassky, V. L., Keller, T. A., & Just, M. A. (2005). Functional connectivity in an fMRI working memory task in high-functioning autism. *NeuroImage, 24,* 810–821.

Krashen, S., & Scarcella, R. (1978). On routines and patterns in language acquisition and performance. *Language Learning, 28,* 283–300.

Landa, R. (2007). Early communication development and intervention for children with autism. *Mental Retardation and Developmental Disabilities Research Reviews, 13*(1), 16–25.

Lauritsen, M., Pedersen, C., & Mortensen, P. (2004). The incidence and prevalence of pervasive developmental disorders: A Danish population-based study. *Psychological Medicine, 34,* 1339–1346.

Lewis, R. (2014). *No greatness without goodness: How a father's love changed a company and sparked a movement.* Carol Stream, IL: Tyndale House.

Lord, C., & Jones, R. M. (2012). Re-thinking the classification of autism spectrum disorders. *Journal of Child Psychology and Psychiatry, 53*(5), 490–509. doi:10.1111/j.1469-7610.2012.02547.x

Lord, C., Petkova, E., Hus, V., Gan, W., Lu, F., Martin, D. M., et al.(2012). A multisite study of the clinical diagnosis of different autism spectrum disorders. *Archives of General Psychiatry, 69*(3), 306–313. doi:10.1001/archgenpsychiatry.2011.148

Lord, C., Risi, S., Lambrecht, L., Cook, E. H., Leventhal, B. I., DiLavore, P. C., et al. (2000). The autism diagnostic observation schedule–generic: A standard measure of social and communication deficits associated with the spectrum of autism. *Journal of Autism and Developmental Disorders, 30*(3), 205–233.

Lord, C., Rutter, M., DiLavore, P. C., Risi, S., Gotham, K., Bishop, S. L., Luyster, R. J., & Guthrie, W. (2012). *Autism diagnostic observation schedule* (2nd ed.). Torrance, CA: Western Psychological Services.

Mackintosh, V. H., Myers, B. J., & Goin-Kochel, R. P. (2005). Sources of information and support used by parents of children with autism spectrum disorders. *Journal on Developmental Disabilities, 12*(1), 41–51.

Mahoney, G., & Perales, F. (2005). Relationship-focused early intervention with children with pervasive developmental disorders and other disabilities: A comparative study. *Journal of Developmental and Behavioral Pediatrics, 26*(2), 77–85.

Making Action Plans. Retrieved from http://www.inclusion.com/maps.html

Matson, J. L., & Nebel-Schwalm, M. S. (2007). Comorbid psychopathology with autism spectrum disorder in children: An overview. *Research in Developmental Disabilities, 28,* 341–352.

Mauer, D. M. (1999). Clinical forum: Sensory integration therapy: Issues and applications of sensory integration theory and treatment with children with language disorders. *Language, Speech, and Hearing Services In Schools, 30,* 383–392.

Mayes, S. D. (2012). *Checklist for autism spectrum disorder* (CASD). Torrance, CA: Western Psychological Services.

McDougle, C. J., & Posey, D. (2002). Genetics of childhood disorders: XLIV. Autism, part 3: Psychopharmacology of autism. *Journal of the American Academy of Child and Adolescent Psychiatry, 41*(11), 1380–1383.

McGee, G., Morrier, M., & Daly, T. (1999). An incidental teaching approach to early intervention for toddlers with autism. *Journal of the Association for Persons with Severe Handicaps, 24,* 133–146.

McNeill, D. (1987). *Psycholinguistics: A new approach.* New York, NY: Harper & Row.

McPheeters, M. L., Weitlauf, A., Vehorn, A., Taylor, C., Sathe, N. A., Krishnaswami, S., . . . Warren, Z. E. (2015). Screening for autism spectrum disorder in young children: A systematic evidence review for the U.S. Preventive Services Task Force. *Agency for Healthcare Research and Quality, Publication No. 13-05185-EF-1. United States Preventive Services Task Force (USPSTF)* http://www.uspreventiveservicestaskforce.org

Meyer-Lindenberg, A., Hariri, A. R., Munoz, K. E., Mervis, C. B., Mattay, V. S., Morris, C. A., et al. (2005). Neural correlates of genetically abnormal social cognition in Williams syndrome. *Nature Neuroscience, 8*, 991–993.

Miller, G. (2007). Immune molecules prune synapses in developing brain. *Science, 318*(5857), 1710–1711.

Mills, J. L., Hediger, M. L., Molloy, C. A., Chrousos, G. P., Manning-Courtney, P., Yu, K. F., et al. (2007). Elevated levels of growth-related hormones in autism and autism spectrum disorder. *Clinical Endocrinology, 67*(2), 230–237.

Minshew, N. J., Goldstein, G., & Siegel, D. J. (1997). Neuropsychologic functioning in autism: Profile of a complex information processing disorder. *Journal of the International Neuropsychological Society, 3*, 303–316.

Mishkin, M., & Appenzeller, T. (1987). The anatomy of memory. *Scientific American, 256*, 80–89.

Napolitano, A. C., & Sloutsky, V. M. (2004). Is a picture worth a thousand words? The flexible nature of modality dominance in young children. *Child Development, 75*(6), 1850–1870.

Nation, K., Clarke, P., Wright, B., & Williams, C. (2006). Patterns of reading ability in children with autism spectrum disorder. *Journal of Autism and Developmental Disorders, 36*(7), 911–919.

National Reading Panel. (2000). *Teaching children to read: An evidence-based assessment of the scientific research literature on reading and its implications for reading instruction.* Retrieved from https://www.nichd.nih.gov/publications/pubs/nrp/Documents/report.pdf

National Research Council (2001). *Educating children with autism.* Washington, DC: National Academy Press.

New York State Department of Health Early Intervention Program. (1999). *Clinical practice guideline: Report of the recommendations—Autism/pervasive developmental disorders, assessment and intervention of young children (age 0–3 years).* (Publication No. 4215). Albany, NY: Health Education Services.

O'Connor, I., & Klein, P. (2004). Exploration of strategies for facilitating the reading comprehension of high-functioning students with autism spectrum disorders. *Journal of Autism and Developmental Disorders, 34*(2), 115–127.

Olsson, I., Steffenburg, S., & Gillberg, C. (1988). Epilepsy in autism and autistic-like conditions: A population-based study. *Archives of Neurology, 45*, 666–668.

Ozonoff, S., Young, G. S., Carter, A., Messinger, D., Yiemiya, N., Zwaigenbaum, L., . . . Stone, W. L. (2011). Recurrence risk for autism spectrum disorders: A baby siblings research consortium study. *Pediatrics, 128*(3), 488–485. doi:10.1542/peds.2010-2825

Page, T. (2007, August 20). Parallel play: A lifetime of restless isolation explained. *The New Yorker*, 36–41. Retrieved from http://www.newyorker.com/magazine/2007/08/20/parallel-play

Paolicelli, R. C., Bolasco, G., Pagani, F. Maggi, L., Scianni, M., Panzanelli, P., et al. (2011). Synaptic pruning by microglia is necessary for normal brain development. *Science 333*, 1456. doi: 10.1126/science.1202529.

Parisse, C. (2002). Oral language, written language and language awareness. *Journal of Child Language, 29*(2), 449–488.

Pearpoint, J., O'Brien, J., & Forest, M. (1991). *PATH: A workbook for planning possible positive futures.* Toronto, CAN: Inclusion Press.

Pelphrey, K. A., & Carter, E. J. (2008). Charting the typical and atypical development of the social brain. *Development and Psychopathology, 20*, 1081–1102. doi:10.1017/S0954579408000515

Perani, D., Paulesu, E., Galles, N. S., Dupoux, E., Dehaene, S., Bettinardi, V., et al. (1998). The bilingual brain. Proficiency and age of acquisition of the second language. *Brain, 121*, 1841–1852.

Peters, A. (1977). Language learning strategies: Does the whole equal the sum of the parts? *Language, 53*, 560–573.

Pottie, C. G., & Ingram, K. M. (2008). Daily stress, coping and well-being in parents of children with autism: A multilevel modeling approach. *Journal of Family Psychology, 22*(6), 855–864.

Prior, M., & McGillivray, J. (1980). The performance of autistic children on three learning set tasks. *Journal of Child Psychology and Psychiatry, 21*(4), 313–323.

Prizant, B. (1982). Gestalt language and gestalt processing in autism. *Topics in Language Disorders, 3*, 16–23.

Prizant, B. (1983). Language acquisition and communicative behavior in autism: Toward understanding the "whole" of it. *Journal of Speech and Hearing Disorders, 48*, 296–307.

Prizant, B., & Rydell, P. (1984). An analysis of the functions of delayed echolalia in autistic children. *Journal of Speech and Hearing Research, 27*, 183–192.

Rapin, I. (1996). Developmental language disorders: A clinical update. *Journal of Child Psychology and Psychiatry, 37*, 643–656.

Rapin, I., & Allen, D. A. (1983). Developmental language disorders: Nosological considerations. In U. Kirk (Ed.), *Neuropsychology of language, reading and spelling.* New York, NY: Academic Press.

Ravid, D., & Tolchinsky, L. (2002). Developing linguistic literacy: A comprehensive model. *Journal of Child Language, 29*(2), 417–447.

Richard, G. (2000). *The source for treatment methodologies in autism.* East Moline, IL: LinguiSystems, Inc.

Roberts, W., & Hartford, M. (2002). Immunization and children at risk for autism. *Paediatric Child Health, 7*(9), 623–632.

Robins, D., Fein, D., & Barton, M. (2009). *Modified checklist for autism in toddlers* (Rev. ed with follow-up). www.m-chat.org.

Robinson, C., & Sloutsky, V. M. (2004). Auditory dominance and its change in the course of development. *Child Development, 75*(5), 1387–1401.

Rogers, S. J. (1996). Brief report: Early intervention in autism. *Journal of Autism and Developmental Disabilities, 26,* 243–246.

Rogers, S. (2004). Developmental regression in autism spectrum disorders. *Mental Retardation and Developmental Disabilities Research Reviews, 10*(2), 139–143.

Rogers, S. J., & Dawson, G. (2009). *Play and engagement in early autism: The early start Denver model. Volume I: The treatment.* New York, NY: Guilford Press.

Rogers S. J., & Dawson, G. (2009). *Play and engagement in early autism: The early start Denver model. Volume II: The curriculum.* New York, NY: Guilford Press.

Rogers, S. J., Dawson, G., & Vismara, L. (2012). *An early start for your child with autism.* New York, NY: Guilford Press.

Rossetti, L. (2006). *The Rossetti infant-toddler language scale.* East Moline, IL: LinguiSystems, Inc.

Rourke, B. (1989). *Nonverbal learning disabilities: The syndrome and the model.* New York, NY: Guilford Press.

Rumsey, J. M., Vitiello, B., Cooper, J., & Hirtz, D. (2000). Special issue: Treatments for people with autism and other pervasive developmental disorders: Research perspectives–Editorial preface. *Journal of Autism and Developmental Disorders 30*(5), 369–371.

Ruschemeyer, S. A., Fiebach, C. J., Kempe, V., & Friederici, A. D. (2005). Processing lexical semantic and syntactic information in first and second language: fMRI evidence from German and Russian. *Human Brain Mapping, 25,* 266–286.

Schechter, R., & Grether, J. K. (2008). Continuing increases in autism reported in California's developmental services system: Mercury in retrograde. *Archives of General Psychiatry, 65*(1), 19–24.

Scheuerman, W., & Webber, J. (2002). *Autism: Teaching does make a difference.* Belmont, CA: Wadsworth/Thompson Learning.

Schmitz, N., Daly, E., & Murphy, D. (2007). Frontal anatomy and reaction time in autism. *Neuroscience Letters, 412*(1), 12–17. doi:10.1016/j.neulet.2006.07.077

Schumm, J. S., Vaughn, S., & Leavell, A. G. (1994). Planning pyramid: A framework for planning for diverse student needs during content area instruction. *The Reading Teacher, 47,* 608–615.

Sharma, S., Woolfson, L. M., & Hunter, S. C. (2012). Confusion and inconsistency in diagnosis of Asperger syndrome: A review of studies from 1981 to 2010. *Autism, 16*(5), 465–486. doi:10.1177/1362361311411935

Sheinkopf, S. J., & Siegel, B. (1998). Home-based behavioral treatment of young children with autism. *Journal of Autism and Developmental Disorders, 28,* 15–23.

Siu, A. L., & US Preventive Services Task Force (USPSTF). (2016). Screening for autism spectrum disorder in young children: US Preventive Services Task Force Recommendation Statement. *Journal of the American Medical Association, 315*(7), 691–696. doi:10.1001/jama.2016.0018

Sloutsky, V. M., & Napolitano, A. C. (2003). Is a picture worth a thousand words? Preference for auditory modality in young children. *Child Development, 74*(3), 822–833.

Smith, L. E., Seltzer, M. M., Tager-Flusberg, H., Greenberg, J. S., & Carter, A. S. (2008). A comparative analysis of well-being and coping among mothers of toddlers and mothers of adolescents with ASD. *Journal of Autism and Developmental Disorders, 38*(5), 876–889. doi:10.1007/s10803-007-0461-6

Stahl, S. A. (1999). *Vocabulary development.* Brookline, MA: Brookline Books.

Steinberg, L. (April, 2011). Demystifying the adolescent brain. *Educational Leadership,* Association for Supervision & Curriculum Development, www.ascd.org, 41–46.

Steinhauer, K., White, E. J., & Drury, J. E. (2009). Temporal dynamics of late second language acquisition: Evidence from event-related brain potentials. *Second Language Research, 25*(13). doi:10.1177/0267658308098995

Sterling, L., Dawson, G., Estes, A., & Greenson, J. (2008). Characteristics associated with presence of depressive symptoms in adults with autism spectrum disorder. *Journal of Autism and Developmental Disorders, 38*(6), 1011–1018. doi:10.1007/s10803-007-0477-y

Sterponi, L., & Shankey, J. (2014). Rethinking echolalia: Repetition as interactional resource in the communication of a child with autism. *Journal of Child Language, 41*(02), 275–304. doi:http://dx.doi.org/10.1017/S0305000912000682

Stowe, L. A., & Sabourin, L. (2005). Imaging the processing of a second language: Effects of maturation and proficiency on the neural processes involved. *International Review of Applied Linguistics in Language Teaching, 43*(4), 329–353. doi:10.1515/iral.2005.43.4.329

Sundberg, M. L., & Partington, J. W. (1998). *Teaching language to children with autism or other developmental disabilities.* Pleasant Hill, CA: Behavior Analysts.

Tabuchi, K., Blundell, J., Etherton, M. R., Hammer, R. E., Liu, X., Powell, C. M., et al. (2007). A neuroligin-3 mutation implicated in autism increases inhibitory synaptic transmission in mice. *Science, 318*(5847), 71–76.

Tager-Flusberg, H. (1993). What language reveals about the understanding of minds in children with autism. In S. Baron-Cohen, H. Tager-Flusberg, & D. Cohen (Eds.), *Understanding other minds: Perspectives from autism.* New York, NY: Oxford University Press.

Tang, G., Gudsnuk, K., Kuo, S-H., Cotrina, M. L., Rosoklija, G., Sosunov, A., et al. (2014). Loss of mTOR-dependent macroautophagy causes autistic-like synaptic pruning deficits. *Neuron, 83,* 1131–1143.

Tebruegge, M., Nandini, V., & Ritchie, J. (2004). Does routine child health surveillance contribute to the early detection of children with pervasive developmental disorders? An epidemiological study in Kent, UK. *BMC Pediatrics, 4*(4).

Tierney, C., Mayes, S., Lohs, S. R., Black, A., Gisin, E., & Veglia, M. (2015). How valid is the checklist for autism spectrum disorder when a child has apraxia of speech? *Journal of Developmental and Behavioral Pediatrics, 36*(8), 569–574. doi:10.1097/DBP.0000000000000189

Tuchman, R. F., & Rapin, I. (1997). Regression in pervasive developmental disorders: Seizures and epileptiform electroencephalogram correlates. *Pediatrics, 99,* 560–566.

Twoy, R., Connolly, P. M., & Novak, J. M. (2007). Coping strategies used by parents of children with autism. *Journal of the American Academy of Nurse Practitioners, 19*(5), 251–260. doi:10.1111/j.1745-7599.2007.00222.x

Veenstra-VanDerWeele, J., & Cook, E. H. (2003). Genetics of childhood disorders: XLVI. Autism, part 5: Genetics of autism. *Journal of the American Academy of Child and Adolescent Psychiatry, 43*(1), 116–118.

Verly, M., Verhoeven, J., Zink, I., Mantini, D., Peeters, R., Deprez, S., et al. (2014). Altered functional connectivity of the language network in ASD: Role of classical language areas and cerebellum. *NeuroImage: Clinical. 4,* 374–382. doi:10.1016/j.nicl.2014.01.008

Verstynen, T., Jarbo, K., Pathak, S., & Schneider, W. (2011). In vivo mapping of microstructural somatotopies in the human corticospinal pathways. *Journal of Neurophysiology, 105,* 336–346.

Vicker, B., & Naremore, R. (2002). *WH Question Comprehension Test: Exploring the world of WH question comprehension for students with an autism spectrum disorder.* Bloomington, IN: Indiana Resource Center for Autism, Indiana Institute on Disability and Community.

Volkmar, F., Siegel, M., Woodbury-Smith, M., King, B., McCraken, J., State, M., & the American Academy of Child and Adolescent Psychiatry Committee on Quality Issues. (2014). Practice parameter for the assessment and treatment of children and adolescents with autism spectrum disorder. *Journal of the American Academy of Child and Adolescent Psychiatry, 53,* 237–257.

Vouloumanos, A., & Werker, J. F. (2007). Listening to language at birth: Evidence for a bias for speech in neonates. *Developmental Science, 10*(2), 159–171.

Wang, A. T., Lee, S. S., Sigman, M., & Dapretto, M. (2007). Reading affect in the face and voice: Neural correlates of interpreting communicative intent in children and adolescents with autism spectrum disorders. *Archives of General Psychiatry, 64,* 698–708.

Warshaw, S. P. (1992–2006). *Hawaii early learning profile.* Menlo Park, CA: VORT.

Webster's encyclopedic unabridged dictionary of the English language. (1989). New York, NY: Gramercy Books.

Wechsler, D. (2013). *Wechsler intelligence scale for children* (5th ed.). San Antonio, TX: Pearson.

Wellman, H. (1993). Early understanding of the mind: The normal case. In S. Baron-Cohen, H. Tager-Flusberg, & D. Cohen (Eds.), *Understanding other minds: Perspectives from autism.* New York, NY: Oxford University Press.

Westermann, G., Mareschal, D., Johnson, M. H., Sirois, S., Spratling, M. W., & Thomas, M. S. C. (2007). Neuroconstructivism. *Developmental Science, 10*(1), 75–83.

Williams, D. L., Goldstein, G., & Minshew, N. J. (2006). Neuropsychologic functioning in children with autism: Further evidence for disordered complex information-processing. *Child Neuropsychology, 12*(4), 279–298.

Willsey, A. J., Sanders, S. J., Li, M., Dong, S., Tebbenkamp, A. T., Muhle, R. A., et al. (2013). Coexpression networks implicate human midfetal deep cortical projection neurons in the pathogenesis of autism. *Cell, 155*(5), 997–1007. doi:10.1016/j.cell.2013.10.020

Wolery, M. R., & Garfinkle, A. N. (2002). Measures in intervention research with young children who have autism. *Journal of Autism and Developmental Disorders, 32,* 463–478.

Wong, C. C. Y., Meaburn, E. L., Ronald, A., Price, T. S., Jeffries, A. R., Schalkwyk, L. C., et al. (2014). Methylomic analysis of monozygotic twins discordant for autism spectrum disorder and related behavioural traits. *Molecular Psychiatry, 19*(4): 495–503. doi:10.1038/mp.2013.41

Wynn, J. W., & Smith, T. (2003). Generalization between receptive and expressive language in young children with autism. *Behavioral Interventions, 18*(4), 245–266.

Yuen, R. K. C., Thiruvahindrapuram, B., Merico, D., Walker, S., Tammimies, K., Hoang, N., et al. (2015). Whole-genome sequencing of quartet families with autism spectrum disorder. *Nature Medicine, 21,* 185–191. doi:10.1038/nm.3792

Zablotsky, B., Black, L. I., Maenner, M. J., Schieve, L. A., & Blumberg, S. J. (2015). Estimated prevalence of autism and other developmental disabilities following questionnaire changes in the 2014 national health interview survey. *National Health Statistics Reports, 87.*

Zhan, Y., Paolicelli, R. C., Sforazzini, F., Weinhard, L., Bolasco, G., Pagani, F., et al. (2014). Deficient neuron-microglia signaling results in impaired functional brain connectivity and social behavior. *Nature Neuroscience, 17,* 400–406. doi:10.1038/nn.3641